Legal Thought and Philosophy

Legal Thought and Philosophy

What Legal Scholarship is About

Bert van Roermund

Tilburg University, The Netherlands

Edward Elgar

Cheltenham, UK • Northampton, MA, USA

Published by
Edward Elgar Publishing Limited
The Lypiatts
15 Lansdown Road
Cheltenham
Glos GL50 2JA
UK

Edward Elgar Publishing, Inc.
William Pratt House
9 Dewey Court
Northampton
Massachusetts 01060
USA

A catalogue record for this book
is available from the British Library

Library of Congress Control Number: 2013932069

This book is available electronically in the ElgarOnline.com Law Subject Collection, E-ISBN 978 1 78195 551 2

MIX
Paper from responsible sources
FSC www.fsc.org FSC® C013056

ISBN 978 1 78195 549 9 (cased)

Typeset by Columns Design XML Ltd, Reading
Printed and bound in Great Britain by T.J. International Ltd, Padstow

Contents

Preface

Over the years I have had the good fortune of teaching students who pursued a research career in law and related disciplines such as economics, sociology, and political science. This course was announced under various labels: principles of law, foundations of law, fault-lines of legal thinking, and others. Not being a lawyer myself by any standard, least of all by training, I have often invited legal scholars to my class, requesting them to discuss what they regarded as their most incisive, demanding and pertinent work. Moreover, I have always strongly encouraged students to participate in the class from the angle of their individual research projects. Coming from philosophy I have found abundant reason to admire the depth, the wit, and the pertinence of legal thinking as represented by both my students and my colleagues. Distinct as they may remain in many respects, from a certain point onwards law and philosophy start to converge as exercises in systematic, radical thinking, joining long and multifarious traditions. If I am able to tease out these qualities and rephrase them in a vocabulary that would tune in to a more encompassing conceptual framework, thus exceeding the limits of law, it is only because these students and colleagues enabled and allowed me to do so.

In turn, I remember their requests to give them a map of various positions regarding principled issues in law, cleansed from philosophical technicalities. And to mark, by all means, my own position on that map. They had a practical reason for their request, as lawyers usually have; it would save them a lot of time and energy in discussing, sorting out, and defending their options in a coherent way. So this is what this book aims at. Avoiding, though not ignoring, philosophical idiolect where possible – whether it hails from historical or contemporary debate – it tries and explains some pertinent issues in law. Among these are how law relates to politics, morality, and religion; what is involved in following (obeying, applying, enforcing, enacting, etc.) legal rules; in what sense we may speak of legal knowledge and argue that it is a respectable academic discipline; and a few others.

So this is a book in 'jurisprudence', that half-way house between law and philosophy? In a way it is. In another way, avoiding a term like 'jurisprudence', without ignoring its contents, is precisely paradigmatic of what I try to do. I have been teaching at the crossroads of many traditions in legal and philosophical thought, indeed even at the crossroads of ordinary and professional languages. If I would announce to talk 'jurisprudence' I would be misunderstood by Dutch, Belgian, French, and other students, who will associate it with the body of judicial decisions in a certain jurisdiction. Students coming from a German or Italian background would have similar problems, though for them *Jurisprudenz* or *giurisprudenza* are primarily synonymous with learned law rather than anything else. In their own languages, these words are tantamount to something like 'legal science' (*Rechtswissenschaft*; *scienza del diritto*) which again sounds rather odd to common law ears. Moreover, as all meanings, these also are largely contingent on context.

Of course, I could point out the various idiolects in the case of 'jurisprudence'. But my worry is a different one: I deliberately prefer to stay in-between. I will take liberty to switch between traditions and locations of thinking, and try to be consistent when it comes to language. As a consequence, I sometimes take inspiration from authors who are hardly read in the Anglophone world, or at least not in philosophy departments, or at least not in high-ranking philosophy departments. Perhaps this is a 'Dutch' book in more than one sense, in any case one that comes from a small country exposed to many linguistic, legal, and philosophical cuisines. I must confess that I have never been able to tell the difference between 'Sein ist nicht Seiendes' and 'Existence is not a predicate'.

I have reason to be grateful to a list of people far too long to mention their names here. I trust they remember the occasions. But some colleagues have been of special importance. First of all my research group at Tilburg University, with senior researchers Hans Lindahl, David Janssens, and Daniel Augenstein. Their open and critical attitude has been an invaluable source of motivation and inspiration on an almost daily basis. Our somewhat remarkable position in the School of Humanities never prohibited most appreciated contacts and cooperation with the Law School at Tilburg, and I have felt privileged to work with legal scholars like Herman Schoordijk, Jan Vranken, Marc Groenhuijsen, Anton van Kalmthout, Sacha Prechal (now at the CJEU in Luxemburg), Linda Senden (now Utrecht), Monica Claes (now Maastricht), Sjef van Erp (idem, now Maastricht), Jan Smits (idem), Willem Witteveen, Willem van Genugten, Maurits Barendrecht, and many others. I learnt a lot from long-standing contacts with colleagues abroad, some of whom became dear friends. I commemorate with great respect the late Hector-Neri Castañeda, the late Alexander Peczenik, and the late Sir Neil MacCormick. I am deeply indebted to Jan M Broekman and Stuart Silvers (my PhD supervisors). I have greatly valued the conversations with (in alphabetical order) Zenon Bankowski, Emilios Christodoulidis, Carrol Clarkson, William Conklin, Alessio lo Giudice, Bernard Jackson, Petra Gehring, Carole Lyons, Irina Dimitrievna Mishina, Alexander F Miskiewicz, Stanley L Paulson, Johan Vanderwalt, Scot Veitch, Bernhard Waldenfels, and Neil Walker. I owe Heidrun Peters (Greifswald) for all the years we could share so much more than the Tempus Project required. I would also like to thank Phyllis Lewis and Kay Caldwell for skillfully copy-editing my texts (and those of quite a few of my PhD students) at so many occasions.

Introduction

Lawyers philosophise more than they think, though perhaps not when they think they are philosophising. They may make poor philosophers when they indulge in *Reflexion auf eigenes Tun*[1] after office hours, recalling their first year jurisprudence course. But they often demonstrate fascinating wit and, indeed, wisdom in arguing their professional proposals, i.e. when they are doing the job they are trained to do. This book teases out some fundamental questions about law with due regard to what lawyers think. But it does not necessarily frame these questions, nor does it answer them, in terms that lawyers would deem useful for daily practice. Avoiding both philosophical idiolect and dialect, i.e., the idiosyncrasies of a specific author, school or circle, it rephrases them in a language of broader contemplation than the solution of a case. It prefers to ask not only what the law is, but also why it makes sense against a background of sense that we seem to adopt. It thus targets a group of readers different from legal practicians, namely students for whom law is an area of academic research. They are the agents who intertwine deep thinking and practical wisdom. The point is whether this entanglement will usher in confusion or insight. If the latter, both philosophy and law may profit, though not without a number of conceptual translations. If the former, law will continue as just another default institution, philosophy as a set of intellectual puzzles. It should be obvious where I prefer to put my stakes. Let me say something more on this entanglement of law and philosophy, on the setup of the project that follows from it, and on the didactic concerns behind it.

---

[1] K Larenz (1979 [1960]) XI: 'Die Methodenlehre einer Wissenschaft ist deren Reflexion auf ihr eigenes Tun.'

1. THINKING LAW

Law is not just an object of thought; it is also, itself, an exercise in thinking. There is no point in denying that there are huge differences between legal and philosophical thinking. One of these is that lawyers are trained to come up with a solution for every problem, where philosophers are passionate about finding a problem for any solution. Another is that lawyers propose their solutions under the pressure of conflicts that should be ended or precluded. Philosophers since Plato, by contrast, explore their problems in the conflict-free environments of a *sym-posion*, which could go on forever if the participants would not take this 'drinking together' too literally.[2] A third one is that lawyers cast their preferred solutions in the mould of 'doctrine' (common law) or 'dogma' (civil law), striving for authoritative status. Philosophers, however, appeal to ultimate truth; if need be to truth about whatever is true, good, or beautiful; at the very least to the sceptical truth that there is no ultimate truth.

These differences have a long history, hailing back from Antiquity. In Ancient Greece, real knowledge was to be expected only from philosophy. Philosophy in these days comprised nearly every pursuit of truth, true accounts of the world out there as well as accounts of what is truly the world out there, or what is truly human in that world. But encompassing as it may have been, philosophy did not engage every problem in life. Typically it did not entail practical problem solving pursuits such as medicine and law. There was no point in denying that these were important in their own right, as they dealt with the maladies of the human body and the body politic, respectively. They stored prudent ways of curbing these maladies, generalising over treatments that had turned out to be successful. But, though certainly skilful, such pursuits did not amount to establishing real knowledge. They remained at the level of *doxa* or *dogma*, i.e. the level of 'opinion' as distinct from knowledge. This, at least, is what philosophers wanted their disciples to believe, and with the rise of doctrine in the Christian religion it became grist to the

---

[2] Note that 'doing philosophy' in Antiquity was part of 'scholè', i.e. free time, time not necessary for labour.

mill of the theologians.[3] By the time the first universities in Europe emerged and philosophy had become ancillary to even more reputed knowledge, namely the knowledge of God and salvation, clergymen were not allowed to read either law or medicine. So when you now visit the library of the Strahov monastery near Prague, for instance, you may admire the marvellous Room of Philosophy and the even more splendid Room of Theology. You will see that these two halls of knowledge are linked by a corridor with books on medicine and law on either side, akin in epistemic status as skills geared to practice, and distinct from all endeavour geared to the contemplation of real truth, such as philosophy and theology. But on the other hand, already in those days there must have been more down-to-earth people who saw that medicine and law were the forms of knowledge people would pay for, and that could bring considerable amounts of money to those who mastered them. Or so we may infer from a little poem:

Dat Galienus opes
Et sanctio Iustiniana.
Ex aliis paleas,
Ex istis collige grana.[4]

Yet, in spite of these differences between philosophy and law, historically entrenched and currently sensed, the distance between law and philosophy has never grown so big that law becomes a mere object of philosophical thinking. It harbours itself a form of thinking, like all cultural phenomena do, such as art, or science, or the economy. Surely, therefore, there is philosophy of law in law, as perhaps Charlie Brown would say. Since philosophy itself is nothing more or less than thorough,

---

[3] Thus, the words 'dogma' in its relation to ecclesiastic 'orthodoxy' appears rather late in the history of (Christian) theology. Originally 'dogma' in law and medicine meant a thumb rule for practice, put down on the basis of generalised experience.

[4] 'Galenus' books provide resources; so does Iustinianus' code of law. From other disciplines you will collect straws, but from these real corn.' [my translation; BvR] Cf. M Herberger 1981, 161, the book on which the paragraph above is largely based.

systematic, critical thinking, it should recognise similar efforts of the human mind made elsewhere, even where they are embedded in received methods, established institutions, and political constellations. Indeed the best basis for a philosophy of law is one that is not voiced by philosophers but by legal scholars and practitioners. They sometimes think thoroughly, systematically, and critically when they are doing their jobs as lawyers pushing the limits of their craft. Philosophers should try and rephrase on the larger blackboard of human reason what lawyers do when they do top-law, rather than apply a sort of philosophical *savoir critique* to whatever they think that lawyers are doing.

In general, philosophy is not there as a supplement to cure and care. As the French philosopher Merleau-Ponty famously said: 'Philosophy is not a hospital.'[5] In the case of law it does not contain norms where positive law runs out. It does not provide answers where law has questions. It holds all the questions and answers of law but in a different and more encompassing conceptual framework. Seeing this framework does not make one a better lawyer in the technical sense of the word. It may make one a more prudent lawyer, more prudent than the prudence of law – jurisprudence – usually entails. So relating to philosophy may indeed educate students to become better lawyers in a different sense, the politico-moral sense of the word: less dependent for their thorough thinking on set methods, solid institutions, and powers that be.

2. OUTLINE

The overall structure of these chapters is governed by the answer to one question: what is so compelling about law? What is it about in the end, such that we cannot afford to cut loose from it and say that we can do without it? The answer will be found in the moral core of the concept of justice. Which is not to say that I regard law as a specific part of morality; on the contrary, morality will turn out to require that I do not. I will go on to sort out what follows from there with regard to two

---

[5] M Merleau-Ponty 2000, 366.

important aspects of law's appearance in socio-political life, namely (i) that law emerges as *positive* law, and (ii) that law presents itself as *knowledgeable*. The former characteristic means, roughly, that law is an artefact made by political authority; the latter that positive law may be scrutinised and challenged as far as its validity is concerned. I will regard these two aspects as constitutive parameters of a legal order claiming *bindingness* – and being received in its claim.

I start out, in Chapter 1, from a particular pattern of discourse, sometimes even referred to as 'a theory' one may find in legal textbooks and other treatises that offer a general introduction to law or some area of law. I call it 'contractual naturalism' and reject it for two reasons. One is that it does not explain some facts on the ground about law. Another is that it is conceptually incoherent. Chapter 2 will argue an alternative account by offering two radically oppositional principles, which mutually intercept each other's weight. True, each of them itself is built on solid ground. But the whole construction of the arch they form is only partly dependent on this solidness. The delicate interception of the two columns as they bend towards each other is far more characteristic of the supportive forces in the arch than the separate basis of the respective columns. In Chapter 2, I will indeed argue that the idea of law involves the irreducible antinomy of two principles of socio-political life, or two ways in which we have to conceive of the relationship between 'I' and 'others', or 'we' and 'others', as 'giving others their due'. Between these two conceptions is a deep chasm. There is no third and higher principle, which can serve as a bridge to connect the two. In fact, it will appear that even the metaphor of the one and only keystone as a distinct entity must break down, as we will discover that the law can only exist in the construction of the arch itself. So we may imagine, pushing the new metaphor to its limits, that the law is not the arch, but the process of constructing the arch.

The way in which law appears in socio-political life will evidence this process in various forms, which we will have to explore. I mentioned the most pertinent ones already very briefly. On the one hand, there is law as the outcome of an authoritative political act by which 'the law' is set, enacted or 'posited'. On the other, there is law as an object of knowledge that allows judgment concerning the validity of what is posited as law. The former will be dealt with in Chapter 3, where the keyword will be 'authority'. It will prompt us to a deeper understanding of the rule of law and its basic tenets. The latter is the topic of Chapter 4. The term 'validity' will draw centre stage here, after detailed investigations into the relationships between fact and norm in law. These two primary or pertinent forms will manifest the two mutually opposing and intercepting principles already mentioned. That is no doubt the most important thing. But, to make important things a little more complicated, they will turn out to be also interdependent in manifesting this interception. That is what is shown in Chapter 5, when we will address the issue of legal rule-following in a broad sense, encompassing interpretation and decision-making.

3. DIDACTIC CONCERNS

The plan I submitted is rather self-willed. It deviates from what one could call 'the beaten track' in the literature and tries to find some less travelled passages. Though this betrays some dissatisfaction with contemporary legal philosophy, it is not a reason for ignoring the great questions, the well-known divides, or the systematic links to other disciplines. Therefore, as we go along, enough famous topics and issues will present themselves for discussion to get reliable knowledge of the field. For the views involved will not remain in the distance, but disclose themselves as real obstacles on our way. It would be foolish to neglect them before we decide in which direction to continue our investigation. This will give us plenty of occasions to get acquainted with the different questions and possible answers in 'thinking law', and a few of its neighbouring areas as well. To announce just the main issues: Our initial and most pertinent question about the meaning of law will carry us into the complexities of the conception of man in law, of the ideas of freedom and equality, thus dealing with the relationship between law and morality (Chapters 1 and 2). Then we turn towards law and politics, where we will meet with the problems of state and society, democracy and authority, statutory law and violence (Chapter 3). The next part concerns the necessary preconditions that allow law to present itself as both the mode and the object of some sort of respectable knowledge (Chapter 4). These preconditions have to do with the notion of validity in general, the intricate interdependencies of facts and norms, the idea of (scientific) knowledge and the relevance of logic to law. The reflections on the structure of legal interpretation in rule-following (Chapter 5) refer to all the above, though coloured by the intriguing relationship of law and language. So, to sum up, law and morality, law and politics, law and science, law and language: these are the links and areas, which our project cannot afford to neglect.

As this book chooses to present radical thinking on law as an actual process of asking, arguing and answering, it will be unsatisfactory in another respect. It is not an encyclopaedia in which one finds basic information about the famous names, the professional jargon, the present debates, the schools of the past, the classifications and the periodisations. What I want to do is to demonstrate how one may think one's way through law, acknowledging other ways. I even prefer to demonstrate an attitude of 'never stop asking' over one of 'giving information', although I am ready to admit that you cannot do the former without the latter. So, yes, I will be making a pose. In order to picture what is fascinating in thinking law, I shall almost pretend that I invent the arguments myself while I am in fact pressing the footprints of real masters of thinking. I take the risk that the pose will look spasmodic at times. Those who have already dug deep into some real philosophy will soon discover that I do hardly anything but quoting; so that this book, in the final analysis, is a parade of great philosophers after all.

Be that as it may, it is fair to say that these pages are not an introduction into philosophy of law in the sense of a preliminary exercise. It is already the thing itself: a philosophy of law in the double sense of the little word 'of': a philosophy *by* law as much as a philosophy *on* law.[6] Inevitably, then, this book, unlike a computer manual, is in important ways circular. Computer manuals are useless when they presuppose on their first page what they explain on their last. They are algorithmic in that they solve well-defined problems in a finite number of steps to be carried out in a linear order, whatever the number of loops they may contain. This book is different from such a manual, as all philosophical books, as well as all legal books, perhaps even all *real* books, are. Real books prompt their readers to anticipate the last page when they are reading the first, and to remember the first page when they have arrived at the last one. Ways of thinking are not programmed instructions. They are, in the didactic sense at least, circular, not linear. What is important is to develop some sense of direction, in order to distinguish the vicious from the healthy wanderings.

[6] Cf. (GWF Hegel 1807 [1999]), 9.

1. Legal order

In this and the next chapter I intend to investigate what we have to think as the necessary and general keystone of our concept of law, or in less solemn words: what law is about in the end. While the second chapter will engage in placing this keystone, the present one will mainly prepare the place by deploying some critical arguments. It will attack a pattern of thought that dominates a good deal of thinking about law. The latter will be our starting point, because it presents itself ever so often in legal literature when it comes to articulating the reasonableness of positive law tout court. This pattern I will call contractual naturalism, which admittedly is 'rather a mouthful'.[1] It founds the legal order on the authority of the state, the authority of the state on the allegedly universal consensus about security demands of life in society, and these demands of social life on the natural needs of human individuals. Thus, it starts out from some allegedly nature-given facts: individual strivings for satisfaction of certain needs. On that sole fact it erects the buildings of society, state and law via two transitional moves: from individuals to society and from society to authoritative government. These transitions are conceived of as contracts.

I want to argue that this pattern cannot be regarded as a coherent line of thought to understand the concept of law. Firstly, I set out in greater detail where and how we meet this pattern in the literature. Then, secondly, I will defend the thesis that it is highly improbable that the legal order we are familiar with would swallow this pattern lock, stock and barrel, if it were to make sense of some features of its own discourse. Thirdly, I will argue the claim that the pattern itself contains important inconsistencies of thought, which make it conceptually untenable.

---

[1] As JL Austin (1970) 182 put it with regard to 'linguistic phenomenology'.

1. … AND THERE WAS LAW

In contemporary western legal literature there is this stable pattern of buzzwords, slogans and phrases that purports to explain to laymen (first year students, for example) why law is 'binding', i.e. why it not only imposes obligations on us for what it takes to be good reasons, but also persistently backs up these obligations by measures that make us comply willy-nilly. I will come back to the meaning of 'binding' later on.[2] Suffice it to stipulate here that I take law to be binding in the sense that it does not just order under threat. It claims to order for reasons that can be acknowledged and shared, but it makes sure that you will also comply if you do not share them. Moreover, 'making sure' is not tantamount to coercion. There are other ways to make people do what you order them to do, and the law uses them, e.g. offering them alternatives they cannot refuse. Also coercion is not tantamount to applying violence. There are other ways to coerce people, e.g. force them to refrain from specific behaviour by technological devices.[3] Now the question I propose to focus on is why we can understand that there should be this specific way of imposing obligations on people? What are the reasons for having an institution that requires certain behaviour for reasons, without caring too much whether the reasons are shared as long as it can make sure that the requirements are met?

To this question, I venture, we have a dominant though puzzling answer. It can be revealed by simple research. Let us go to the law school library and pick from the shelves all books of the last fifty years with titles bearing a fair resemblance to 'Introduction to law'.[4] Let us take some time to analyse the argumentative lines by which the concept of law is introduced in each of them. With few exceptions, what you will find[5] as a general pattern is a series of seven steps, which aim at bringing

---

[2] Cf. Chapter 3 and the last section of Chapter 4.

[3] Cf. EJ Koops (2008).

[4] Rather than listing all the books I checked I give a few paradigms. As the experiment is easy to reproduce, I will only submit that they are representative.

[5] The pattern is beautifully laid out by the most 'popular' introductory book known to me, by a Dutch professor of criminal law Enschedé, with the title

us to an understanding in western culture of what law is about. Here they are, marked by thumbnails of the steps that are to be taken.

(1) Life is dangerous
Individual human subsistence is constantly jeopardised regarding its basic needs, by security risks in the form of external catastrophes, internal discord, sheer loneliness, foolishness, callousness, or a hazardous mixture of these and other factors.

(2) Living together to live at all
Surviving under these circumstances requires living together in a sustained order, in which experiences of surviving are shared, passed on or corrected, as the case may be.

(3) Coordination required
In order to prevent this arrangement from falling back into the dangerous situation under 1), agreements on how to behave (norms) have to be coordinated, as they are not spontaneously shared:[6] not everyone has the same opinion and not everyone performs their part of a deal.

(4) Sanctions
If norms are to be effective in the required way, they need sanctions, in various degrees of explicitness and severity, e.g., social control, fees, penalties.

(5) Power
Sanctions are only effective if they are backed up by power, be it the power of words, of money, or of violence.

(6) Supreme power
But note that all people have *some* power over other people – a little or a lot. If we do not want the game of power to collapse into

---

Look! Law (CJ Enschedé (1984)). Captions 1–7 are more or less derived from this book.

[6] Cf. Ovid's sketch of 'The Golden Age', where there was no law since everyone performed his or her part of living in society 'sponte sua', i.e., spontaneously.

the right of the strongest, there should be supreme power: government or state authority.

(7) Law
What supreme power orders for the sake of protecting the person, the goods and the mutual confidence of everyone subjected to it, is law.

Now we are allegedly able to grasp why the normativity of law 'stands to reason': it is an ordering of society, stemming from a supreme power that is willing and able to protect the personhood, the goods and the mutual confidence of everyone subjected to it in a sustainable way, established by and large in accordance with the preferences of the society involved, for the sake of everyone's subsistence.

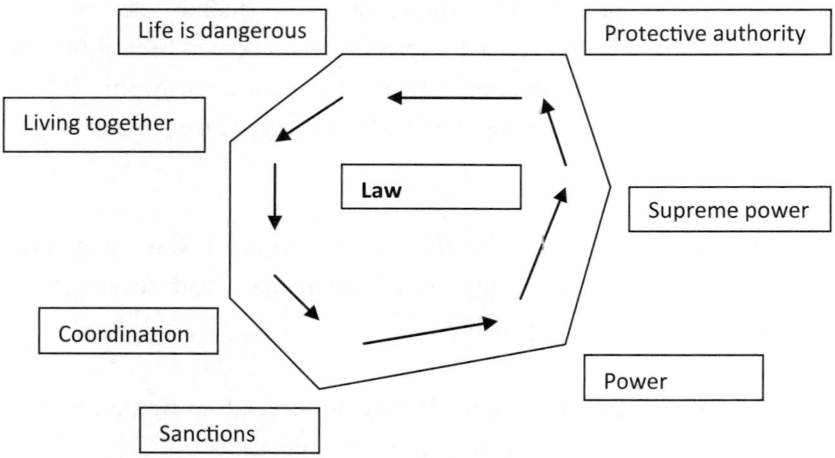

Figure 1.1 The heptagon of law

2. THE HEPTAGON OF LAW

This heptagonal pattern forms the widest perimeter of the 'philosophy of law' advocated by most legal subjects. Let's call it the heptagon of law. The edges of the heptagon are the way-points of their debates on any topic you may think of: fundamental rights, civil disobedience, principles of contract law, social security in the welfare state, the sense of punishment, the organisation of public administration, etc. It would be naïve to think of it as a layman's philosophy in the sense that it is only the banal form of a more sophisticated argument. It is not just the simple speech of the popular literature or the mass-media. It is also the basic argument of academic introductions. Many a casebook or dissertation that cares to be explicit on the concept of law makes appeals to this scheme. Arguments mounted by constitutional courts in support of their decisions on questions of legal principles follow a similar structure. And yes, yours truly – who believes that he is about to present some devastating philosophical arguments against it – could not escape from it, that night some bastards flung a brick into his bedroom. At the very least we must concede that the heptagon of law is a persuasive and dominant pattern of discourse.

Some might say that this is neither surprising nor embarrassing, as great philosophers of the past have reduced the meaning of law to this very core. In fact, the situation is much more complex. It is fairly safe to hold that the heptagon bears a faint resemblance to what classic authors like Grotius, Pufendorf, Hobbes, Locke, Rousseau or Kant have written. But it stands to the thought of these philosophers as the clergyman's sermon to biblical texts. It is the lumpy result of coagulating words, processed by the 'official' readings of heterogeneous writings, and sublimated to a truth about law by the priests, politicians, and pedagogues of the legal orders in place. It has very little to do, for instance, with the explicit statements of, let alone the original inspiration behind, the idea of the social contract in the seventeenth and eighteenth centuries. To substantiate this claim in full, however, would exceed the limits of this book, as it would demand a long digression into the history of legal philosophy.[7] In the course of our investigations there will be occasions to explain at least some arguments in its support. In the meantime we may

---

[7] I submitted the evidence with regard to Rousseau's work in B Van Roermund (1999; 2000a). Let me also add that contractualism, in origin, was often a *critique* of (some forms of) naturalism: cf. Hobbes' critique of Aristotelianism, but also Rousseau's critique of naturalism in Hobbes.

establish that this unifying, legitimating discourse is part and parcel of the reality of law as it presents itself in society. That in itself requires explanation.

But let us first scrutinise the heptagon in fuller detail. As announced above I will refer to it as contractual naturalism and define it as follows.

Def. 1.1 *Contractual naturalism founds the legal order on the governmental authority of the state, governmental authority, in turn, on the societal agreement regarding elementary demands of living in society, and, finally, the elementary demands of social life on natural needs of human beings as individuals. The transitional links from individual life to social life, and from social life to state life are contractually structured.*

Whence the labelling? Contractual naturalism attempts to understand law from a blank or 'zero' stage of human subsistence, in which there is not only no law but also no society, and in which everyone has to take care of himself in order to survive. In that situation, sometimes called the chaos, the jungle, or – in classic terminology – the state of nature, individuals are conceived of as distinct entities with certain inalterable and inalienable properties, capacities, interests and, above all, needs. They are distinct in the sense that each of them, independently of every other, strives to self-preservation. Self-preservation supposedly consists of the realisation of these characteristics, primarily the satisfaction of these needs. The strivings of the independent agents in this situation will get stuck in incompatible efforts and oppositions, individual shortcomings and deficiencies, or radical isolation. The threat of universal destruction lurks in the background as a permanent source of motives for action. The only possible escape from this threat and its eventual realisation is for the individuals to unite into what is called a society. The uniting act is conceived of as a tacit mutual agreement, a contract to which each of them enters as a party. What they thus decide, each for themselves, is to pass over from a non-social situation to a social one.

There are, it is said, two ways of conceiving this transitory move. Either the individuals take their decisions out of a rational insight into how the wanting nature of human beings is to be preserved by establishing a society; or they decide on the basis of calculated self-interest to harmonise everyone's preferences with every other's preferences preserving priorities as much as possible. As the former conception roots in some reasoned account of what constitutes a human being, it may be called rationalist, while the latter, departing from everyone's will to satisfy certain needs, may be called voluntarist. I will, however, ignore that distinction and concentrate on what the two have in common. The common issue in both is that their points of departure are regarded as given. This is the crucial point in relating both accounts to 'nature', even though 'human nature' means one thing in a rationalist conception ('man properly speaking') and another thing in a voluntarist conception ('men factually speaking').

Once the heptagon has situated the individuals as united into a society, it attributes to them a definite awareness of the precarious character of this stage. They may resolve this predicament by conferring all authority in their society to a supreme power or sovereign; either in virtue of the unanimous insight that this is going to be the best form of life for all of them (rationalism), or in virtue of the common will to convert the risk of constant opposition of powers into the power of one instance that is to determine how society is to be ordered (voluntarism). The sovereign is the necessary implication of either of these variants. His will is 'the law', be it that this willing is contingent on the will of all particular beings who have engaged in establishing the societal bond. This implies that the sovereign should care about their well-being in terms of a 'general interest', and that he would exceed the limits of his power if he were to rule on the sole basis of his own benefit. Thus, the state emerges from society, as a specific relationship between sovereign and subjects. This transition, too, is contractually structured: it is conceived of as a mutual agreement between society and some instance of power, which thereby becomes sovereign.

Thus, the official doctrine of contractual naturalism features a twofold contract: the contract of association (which the individuals make with each other to institute a civil bond or body politic) and the contract of authorisation[8] (which this political body makes with a powerful agent to install supreme power and legal authority in one fell swoop). It seems easy to articulate the modern idea of the rule of law in the heptagon by framing the contracts in specific terms: the conditions set for the performance of the sovereign have the form of fundamental rights ascribed to individual people in virtue of their personhood, while the mutual recognition of everyone's personhood is expressed in the well-known restriction clauses on fundamental rights, such as 'everyone's responsibility before the law'.[9] Be that as it may, the logic of the heptagon is to model the two crucial transitions by shaping the agents as parties that mutually bind each other. The point of these two moves is that man as an individual will fulfil his or her basic, natural needs by making these contracts and complying with them. That, to repeat, is why I choose to call the heptagon both 'contractual' and 'a naturalism'. It infers the reasonableness of law from a set of demands which 'nature' (of man and his environment) is supposed to impose. These are presented as

---

[8] The classical term is 'submission', which I think is less appropriate, not only for methodological reasons (as I try to explain the reasoning of the agents involved) but also for historical reasons, for instance in view of the text of the Catalonian Oath, dating from the tenth (!) century) and clearly authorising in tone. In the early Middle Ages Barcelona was governed by a Council of One Hundred, representing nobles, merchants, and artisans. The Council had to answer to the count king of Catalonia and Aragon, but he did not rule his realms absolutely. He was seen to rule by contract and not by divine right. The leaders of the Council swore the remarkable and unique oath of allegiance to the monarch of Catalonia and Aragon: 'We, who are as good as you, swear to you, who are no better than us, to accept you as our king and sovereign, provided you observe all our liberties and laws, but if not, not.' Cf. R Hughes (1992 (1991)) 103, and http://iberianature.com/spain_culture/culture-and-history-of-spain-c/catalan-aragonese-oath-of-allegiance/, accessed July 19, 2011.

[9] As the characteristic formula in the Dutch constitution goes; cf. however a similar provision to the effect that fundamental rights can be restricted by formal law is to be found in Art. 52.1 of the Charter of Fundamental Rights of the European Union: 'Any limitation on the exercise of the rights and freedoms recognised by this Charter must be provided for by law and respect the essence of those rights and freedoms. Subject to the principle of proportionality, limitations may be made only if they are necessary and genuinely meet objectives of general interest recognised by the Union or the need to protect the rights and freedoms of others.'

necessary properties and relationships, which escape human manipulation and precede all cultural shaping. The contracts are there to map these natural demands on to a legal order.

At first sight the heptagon seems air-tight: it looks like a perfect frame around two focuses in balance. On the one hand there is the need for orderliness in society based on 'nature', on the other there is the norm to respect everyone's right to the protection of his values, i.e., his person, his good and his reliance on agreements with others. The plea for order is complemented by a criterion of orderliness, and what on earth would be more suitable for that role than the condition that everyone should find his due in the protection mentioned? Inversely, where could respect for everyone's right to protection of his or her values find a better place to start from than in an ordered society?

3. THE KNURLED EDGES OF THE HEPTAGON

On closer examination, however, we may doubt whether this discursive pattern could function as the ultimate keystone of our legal order. Dominant as it may be in a variety of ways, it is hard to see how it can account for its reasonableness. To substantiate this doubt let me develop two sets of arguments. (a) Firstly, it is highly improbable that the heptagon provides an understanding of what a legal order is about if we look carefully at some fundamental characteristics of the legal order we call ours. Indeed, every lawyer with a minimally reflective attitude towards his craft will acknowledge that sometimes the law makes sense of states of affairs that would be utter legal nonsense if contractual naturalism would be all there is to the reasonableness of law. This I will show by a short analysis of how civil disobedience, fundamental social rights, and the categorical prohibition of torture are dealt with in our legal systems. (b) A second set of arguments aims to show that the function claimed for contractual naturalism is not only juridically improbable, but also philosophically inconceivable. To argue this thesis we will have to analyse the precise structure of the thinking we attribute to the agents allegedly involved in the heptagon. We will find that this pattern ascribes to them a set of reasonings that is utterly question-begging. In sum, I will offer one set of arguments from empirical analysis (section 3), and another from conceptual analysis (sections 4 and 5).

In the next three sub-sections on civil disobedience, social rights and the prohibition of torture, respectively, I follow a simple scheme of reasoning:

[P.1] If contractual naturalism would be the core of our concept of law, then it would be improbable that concepts like civil disobedience, social rights and the categorical prohibition of torture would make sense in legal practice as we know it.

[P.2] Now it is false to say that civil disobedience, social rights and the prohibition of torture make no sense in legal practice as we know it.

[C] Therefore it is improbable that contractual naturalism would be the core of our concept of law.

So what I will have to show is that in matters like civil disobedience, social rights and the prohibition of torture contractual naturalism cannot explain how positive law succeeds in making *some* sense of them. That is a weak claim, and deliberately so. What I want to show is that law is able to respond to some phenomena that are at odds with its official ideology, neither more nor less. I do not deny that, to the extent that a legal order comes under pressure and is challenged to appeal to this ideology, the scope for subtle response to such phenomena diminishes rapidly. I will point to this mechanism in all three examples.

3.1 Civil Disobedience

The question is whether a democratic order under the rule of law can make sense of civil disobedience on the basis of contractual naturalism? Well, it cannot. According to contractual naturalism, being deliberately disobedient in a legal order is non-civil by definition as it would amount to a crime. Better perhaps: it would bring out the very core of crime, and therefore be worse than crime. For civil disobedience does not just violate the legal order, it attacks it. It not only harms the rule of law but undermines it. Civil disobedience would have to be regarded as resistance to the legal order *in toto*. It should not just be punished on a par with other criminal activities, but repressed on a par with other forms of sabotage. Note that the issue is not whether civil disobedience is feasible from a moral point of view. It may obviously be feasible for one who holds that moral or religious arguments override legal ones in matters of conscience. But then again contractual naturalism holds that moral attitudes, whether or not grounded in religious belief, are to be ranked lower than the duties imposed by the legal order. That the former are to find their integrating framework in the latter is a strong conviction in itself, and contractual naturalism holds that it should be the strongest. Being disobedient within this overriding order is an act of resistance by definition.[10]

Nevertheless, contractual naturalism takes civil disobedience very seriously, particularly in times of increasing political pressure, for instance under the threat of terrorism or during persistent economic crisis. A few typical arguments used by the heptagon camp are these.

(1) In a parliamentary democracy, there are certain procedures of decision-making. Only provisions that have passed these procedures enjoy the status of valid law. The procedures provide for ample 'hearings' of the needs and wants of citizens in matters to be decided upon.
(2) The principal impact of the citizens on such decisions is by periodical elections of representatives (e.g., parliament), be these elections mediated or not by the action of political parties.
(3) Whoever wants to interfere with this procedure of decision-making disregarding the two principles mentioned above, sets foot on the slippery slope of social and political disorder.

---

[10] In his 'political parable' (as *The New York Observer* called it) *Seeing*, José Saramago unravels the logic of this view, starting from the point when, on election day, 70% of the people in the capital city appear to have run to the polling stations only to cast a blank vote.

(4) Even if such interventions can be explained by the fact that the government itself has tampered with these principles and has shown itself the first to be disobedient (e.g., when the multi-party system, periodical elections, parliamentary powers and/or legislative procedures, the independence of the judiciary and the rule of law in general are put in jeopardy), there will only be legal recourse if the government can be held to account in the context of a more embracing legal order and, thus, a higher government. If there is none, there are only political or moral grounds to resist the government's orders, which is not tantamount to saying that there are legal grounds.

(5) Whoever evades or opposes decisions taken in the way described above should be tried before an independent judge. Whether he disobeys the law out of psychological, economical, political or moral motives, is irrelevant to the judge's reasoning supporting the decision on such a case.

To summarise: according to contractual naturalism civil disobedience is not just legally intolerable since it violates legal rules. It is first and foremost at loggerheads with the very idea of the rule of law, and therefore legally inconceivable. It is not just crime, it is high-treason.

Yet, since the late sixties of the previous century we have heard various pleas to the effect that civil disobedience denotes something, which *is* legally conceivable all right.[11] Though it should be punished, it is acknowledged as something compatible with, indeed even in some sense commanded or presupposed by, the rule of law. The basic argument is that (a) the order imposed by the rule of law is to be regarded, in principle, as the outcome of a political compromise, and (b) that in a democracy everyone should have the right to contest some specific rule of that order, provided (c) that he or she is prepared to pay a price for

---

[11] The term 'civil disobedience', though, is more than a century older (Thoreau). As a result of discussions in the 1960s, see for example, J Rawls (1973 (1971)); C Schuyt (1972); P Singer (1973); RM Dworkin (1977). For a later analysis cf. W Van der Burg (1986), or more recently CR Sunstein (2003).

non-compliance. To substantiate this ‘compatibility thesis’, proponents of the legal acceptability of civil disobedience put strong restraints on the behaviour that should qualify as compatible or in accord with the rule of law. Prominent among these conditions are the following.

(1) Legal procedures to make the contesting claims in question valid must be exhausted.
(2) There should be a conscientious motivation oriented towards the general interest and a well-balanced proportionality between means (action) and ends.
(3) The action itself should pay respect to the principles of the rule of law, as (a) no violence is used or advocated, (b) rights of co-citizens are respected as much as possible, and (c) activists agree to publicly face the authorities, to not resist arrest and to answer accusations in court.

Those who want to argue the compatibility thesis carry an impossible burden of proof within the conceptual limits imposed by contractual naturalism. For these limits rule that you cannot have your cake and eat it when it comes to civil disobedience. You cannot argue that, with regard to only one specific issue, the government has fundamentally violated the conditions of citizenship while arguing at the same time that with regard to all other issues the government has not fundamentally violated the conditions of citizenship. Like marriage, citizenship is a package deal and you cannot revise the conditions from issue to issue, even if after a number of issues you may conclude that the conditions for the package do not obtain any longer. But you cannot say that the conditions for civil disobedience do and do not obtain. It is either one or the other, as there is no such thing as a fundamental assault on citizenship, which is only partly a fundamental assault.

It is, therefore, not very difficult for heptagon supporters to nail conditions (1)–(3) to the cross. Counter-arguments typically go like this:

(1) In a parliamentary democracy legal means never run out. It may only take time before you get what you want. But do try your luck at the next elections.
(2) Appeal to the general interest which violates legal procedures is self-contradictory, as these procedures are there to guarantee a general weighing of interests in the first place; that the balancing should be 'conscientious' is a gratuitous piece of rhetoric as the appeal to conscience is only legitimate if the law refers to it.
(3) Whatever one says about respect for the principles of the rule of law while violating the law is unconvincing. No violence? Well, that's hardly a credit. Respect for rights of co-citizens? Not very persuasive as laws are there to warrant these rights in the first place. Cooperation in persecution and trial? A superfluous promise, as law enforcement does not beg for such attitude.

And yet, the practice of law is different, provided that, on the whole, political pressure is modest in the situation at hand. In some cases the police are more reluctant to arrest people than they would be if normal crime or, for that matter, sabotage would be at issue. For instance, they will give more warnings, wait longer, announce action, give time to retreat from the scene, etc. In others the Public Prosecutor may apply a discretion policy in prosecuting or dropping charges, which are milder than she could afford in criminal matters.[12] Even in countries with formal

[12] Cf. the policy rule in the English Code for Crown Prosecutors (January 2013, para. 4.2), about '(…) cases where it is clear, prior to the collection and consideration of all the likely evidence, that the public interest does not require a prosecution. In these instances, prosecutors may decide that the case should not proceed further.' In Belgium, since 1998 it is stipulated that the Prosecutor has to give reasons for dismissing a case. Cf. for the Dutch situation: 'The public prosecutor may have reason to decide not to prosecute a case and may therefore drop the charges against the suspect. This could be the case, for instance, if the police have not managed to collect sufficient evidence. In other words, this would be a technical reason for dropping any charges. But charges can be dropped for other reasons as well, in some cases as a matter of policy. Even if the police do have sufficient evidence, the public prosecutor can drop the charge if the offence was a minor one, for instance, and if the offender has made good the damage done to the victim. Anyone who is directly involved in a case may

mandatory prosecution (like Germany or Italy), such discretion policy factually exists, as it makes prosecution dependent on, for instance, the seriousness of the crime and the corresponding deadline by which it has to be addressed by the Prosecutor. In still other cases judges mitigate their sentences more than they would do in penal cases. All these forms of what one could call 'legal reluctance' are not so much inspired by lenience as they are by the uneasy feeling among officials that the activists 'may have a legal point' after all. In cases of civil disobedience there often is reasonable doubt and disagreement as to the question whether or not the disputed law is 'valid', 'legitimate', 'good', in a rather loose, but not altogether arbitrary sense of these words. Loose it may be; but it is, for instance, far from a purely moral sense. In many cases there is at least some legal backup. Sometimes activist and critical lawyers prove to be right years later, when a court of appeal rules that the government was wrong.[13] Also there is the legislator sometimes deliberating on changing the rules as an effect of civil disobedient action, showing it, thus, to be 'right' after all. Even in states where judicial review under the constitution is formally forbidden or restricted, an appeal to supra-national statutory law will frequently back up such allegedly 'loose' judgments and give them a proper legal framework. Haven't we witnessed the European Courts (both the Strasbourg and the Luxemburg Court) showing little respect for institutions, procedures and statutes, which national legislators thought to be in perfect accordance with the rule of law?[14] These cases prompt the conclusion that, to say the

---

object to the charge being dropped. If the Court of Appeal sees grounds for doing so, it can order the Public Prosecution Service to have the case heard in court.' Cf. http://www.om.nl/vast_menu_blok/english/about_the_public/what_does_the_public/, accessed July 19th, 2011.

[13] Cf. The decision of the Dutch Council of State (the highest administrative court in some matters) of July 18th, 2007 ruled that the government had no right, in 2006, to cut the trees in an area known as the Schinveldse Bos, which activists vigorously opposed at the time.

[14] Surely the Netherlands got its share, for instance, the refutation of the appeal to the Crown in matters of administrative law (one cannot appeal to the Crown as the judge of administrative action if he is the agent of administrative action in the first place, as he would then be the judge in his own cause; cf.

least, in politically disputed matters there appears to be legal scope for contestation, provided that the protesters are able to give evidence of what one could call their 'civil reliability'. They are allowed to show in a given case that, when it comes to a decision on the balance of reasons pro and con, there is little reason in advance to give the benefit of the doubt to the government. This conclusion suffices to lend support to the belief that tactic tolerance and principled prudence can hunt in pairs without merging into prudent repression or repressive tolerance.

However, when the pressure is very high, e.g., under the threat of terrorism, the gap between civil disobedience and civil unreliability becomes difficult to manage for governments.[15] Under these conditions, contractual naturalism legitimises such power to authorities as to ignore any evidence of civil reliability. Then it shows that this contractual relationship between power and people is ultimately lopsided: one of the parties always has the power to make the other party liable for non-performance, which is tantamount to saying that there was no contract in the first place. In that case we might as well ask what entitles such a government to call itself government.

In sum: contractual naturalism does not seem to tell the whole story of why law stands to reason, neither in relaxed, nor in critical situations.

3.2 Fundamental Social Rights

Like 'civil disobedience' the term 'fundamental social rights' – or, for short, 'social rights' – is one that lawyers could have dropped long ago if contractual naturalism was not just dominant discourse, but full-fledged

---

ECtHR 23 Oct. 1985, No. 8848/80 (*Benthem v The Netherlands*). Or the same Court's refutation to accept the Netherlands' interpretation of Art. 8 (family life) in *Kroon et al. v The Netherlands*, 27 Oct.1994, No. 18535/91, (cf. in particular para. 40 of the decision).

[15] Under these circumstances, one is a suspect before one knows. Cf. the Kadi saga (beginning with the Court of First Instance, T-315/01, and the appeal in Case C-402/05P (*Kadi v Council and Commission*) as a sequel to the UN Security Council's 'war on terror'; the illegal regime of Guantanamo Bay maintained by the USA; the omnipresent surveillance installed in the BRD at the time of the RAF attacks.

theory about the basis of our legal order. That contractual naturalism is dominant all right can easily be shown in the case of 'social rights' by pointing to the fact that the term is reluctantly used, or even largely avoided, when it comes to national constitutional legislation. The 1950 European Convention on Human Rights does not feature any social rights, nor does the UK 1998 Bill of Rights. The International Covenant on Economic, Social and Cultural Rights (1966) was signed and ratified by an impressive number of states, but the USA Senate has thus far failed to ratify it and the reservations made by other states have turned it into a list of wishful political thoughts rather than a legal instrument (with the right to leisure and paid holidays (Art. 7 sub (d) ICESCR) as the butt of it all). After the adoption by all Member States except the UK of the European Social Charter in December 1989 the UK succeeded once more in securing an opting-out clause on the EU charter of fundamental rights at the EU Rostock summit in June 2007. Two other Member States, Ireland and Poland, left the door open to opt out as well. The charter was designed to enshrine and protect human and social rights, but it was social rights in particular that Britain and others were opposed to. They felt it would threaten labour market flexibility, in particular by acknowledging the right to strike, working times and minimal wages, that it would overturn stricter domestic laws, and that it would make unions a stronger political factor. During the debates on the revision of the Dutch constitution (promulgated in 1983), it was decided not to use the phrase 'the right to…' in connection with such matters as employment, health, education, clean environment, etc., as it would suggest that individual people could hold this right against the government and could demand a job, a medical treatment, etc. as the case might be. Parliament preferred to see these matters as the objects of duties of care, which the state would owe to society in general.

This evasive attitude towards social rights, as distinct from political rights, is readily explained by the dominance of the heptagon doctrine. It accommodates political rights far better than social rights. Political (or 'classic') fundamental rights are liberty rights. Liberty rights discourse sits happily with the heptagon: they confirm, enforce and enrich its pattern.[16] Indeed, liberty rights create the conditions for its dissemination as, in the end, they point from individual freedom to supreme power. At first they pose as warranted spheres of privacy, i.e. of *terrae incognitae* where the state has no access. Thus they are alleged to shape the individuality of every human being. In this respect they pay tribute to the humanistic ideal of personhood, which Enlightenment took to be exemplified in every human being. But the picture changes rapidly. The belief in the individuality of each human being introduces the problem of infinite heterogeneity. It suggests that society is always virtually out of control, as (by definition) one cannot control what is infinitely manifold, singular and evasive of categorisation. This is where a contract of association comes in: how else could all these individuals possibly relate to and opt for each other, if it were not via the reciprocal structure of contract?[17] Contract seems to get the social relation moving. But then liberty rights also justify the institution of sustainable supreme power, i.e. of the state. Since compatibilities and incompatibilities between diverging forces have to be constantly assessed and monitored in view of integration, some agency should keep control over all these relationships. And how else could this control be justified than on account of a contract of authorisation writ large? Such considerations enhance the legitimating value of contractual naturalism: the government of the state will be regarded as an instance which has a contract 'with society' on a par with that which is preferred in society itself and which fits in ever so nicely with individual self-development.

Now 'social rights' are at odds with this line of thought. They re-introduce a conception of the individual that starts out from social roots,

---

[16] See N Luhmann (1981) 87: 'Die Fähigkeit subjektiver Rechte, Anspruchsgrundlage zu sein und als Subjekt von Spezifikationen und Konditionierungen zu dienen, bewährt sich am Ende in einer etwas unerwarteten Richtung: als Korrelat des Wohlfahrtsstaates.'

[17] See F Ewald (1986) 49–50: 'The ideal (…) continues (…) to inspire our politicians; it is that every social relation should take on the form of a contract. The contract becomes the bearer of all virtues. Thanks to its reign, justice will be achieved. "He who says contractual, says just." More, it is to be the instrument, which allows one to contemplate the disappearance of the State and its constitutional oppressiveness: thanks to it, Society could become self-managing.'

loyalties, responsibilities and capabilities rather than from liberties and warrants. Contractual naturalism presupposes that, at the end of the day, i.e. in cases of conflicting interests, individuals have waived the possibility to determine their social relationships themselves. Civil society, in this conception, is a residue, a leftover from state power, or at the most a supplement to state power. It is the state that ultimately decides how its citizens are 'members of society'. But when we refer to 'social rights', we seem to imply that at least social groups themselves author the core of this decision, in their reciprocal relationships, even in cases of conflicting interests. The phrase seems to express that in principle civil society itself, in all its heterogeneity, is in charge of determining social relationships. It is not the state delegating this to society but society claiming original rather than derived power. Indeed, in a very basic sense social rights are not claims over and against the state. The state is the wrong address for what they purport to produce. Social rights are claims on certain collective goods over and against other would-be members of society. Not the state, but those in control of the means of production, the entrepreneurs,[18] can create employment. Not the state, but those who know about scholarship and youth can deliver good education. Not the state, but those who cultivate the earth (farmers, miners, producers) can balance what we have to invest in, and what we may extract from it. Social rights are not just rights on important 'public' goods the state is in charge of. They are primarily rights that social groups have to make valid against other social groups. They have a horizontal impact to start with, though they are not private rights. But this is no reason to say that therefore they are not real rights and must be phrased as duties of care on the part of the state. The duty of care of the state is derivative of this primary 'horizontal' pertinence of social rights.

So what 'social rights' demand from the state is to put part of its legitimacy on the line. They ask the state to acknowledge that it has only relative authority in these matters and that, if it wants to exercise

---

[18] I take this term in the basic sense of those who are able to organise capital and labour in a risky endeavour of producing something.

authority, it cannot evade making political choices between conflicting interests, between opposing camps, between incompatible views of what is 'good' for society as a whole. That is probably the main reason why social rights fit so badly into the legal system: they jeopardise the idea of the state as the power that is neutral to the positions and interests of conflicting parties in civil society. For instance, as the right to employment is a claim made by workers against entrepreneurs – i.e. parties who have (partly) conflicting interest – the state cannot stay neutral. It will have to take sides in this conflict of interests. Either it appears as just another power in society, thus undermining the very idea of 'supreme power'; or it assigns the status of 'general interest' to one of the private interests around the block. Both options are unattractive from the point of view of contractual naturalism. So the idea of social rights destabilises contractual naturalism by challenging one of its basic tenets. The ordered triples of 'state', 'law' and 'general interest' on the one hand, 'society', 'market' and private 'interests' on the other, fall apart.[19] No wonder that constitutional texts either try to avoid the term 'social right', or have to face 'the death of a thousand qualifications' if they hang on to it.[20]

One would expect that contractual naturalism, if it were really celebrated as the one and only tenable view, would be able to ban not only the vocabulary, but also the very idea of social rights. This, however, proves not to be the case. In modern legal thinking, the idea of 'social rights' has been far from absent[21] and appears currently more and more effective.

---

[19] Cf. already P Rosanvallon (1984 [1981]).

[20] As the verification principle in logical positivism.

[21] Note that already in the 1930s the French lawyer and theorist G Gurvitch promoted social rights as a key concept in law. See his *La déclaration des droits sociaux*. Marx's critique of the 'bourgeois' character of all human rights is earlier, of course, but it did not usher in any new conceptual proposal in law, as it did with Gurvitch. It should be observed that Bentham, right after the French Revolution, launched the same critique of the idea of human rights as is commonly mounted against social rights, to wit they are claims against the state that no state can afford to grant. Cf. J Bentham (2002 [1795]). See also F Tanghe (1988).

(a) It functions, first of all, as a conceptual point of reference to track 'linking pins' in the system of rules, by which duties of care on the part of the state can be welded to 'real' rights which citizens can hold against the state in court.[22] For instance, the right to a humane level of subsistence is a state duty of care in the Netherlands, rather than a claim every citizen can make against the state. But it can be linked to a real right flowing from social security rules (regarding, e.g., social support (dole)).

(b) Secondly, capability rights[23] and liberty rights often function as mutual complements. That is to say that liberty rights have an in-built reference to what social rights express, and vice versa. Liberty rights do not only refer to things the state should refrain from. They also point to active duties of care, which the state has to comply with in order to refrain from interfering with individual autonomy and political participation. For instance: it takes a lot of political intervention to sustain a free press (as distinct from censoring it on the one hand and leaving it to commercial parties on the other).[24] It not only takes a certain level of economic welfare, education and cultural awareness; but it also requires active interventions to create and uphold diversity in news reporting. Inversely, social rights require the state not to interfere with individual freedom rather than not to intervene. Intervention is required where weak interests conflict with strong ones, e.g. so as to ensure 'fair competition' rather than 'free competition'. But the state has to

---

[22] Cf. EA Alkema (1981) 13, 15. Or with regard to enforceable social rights in a European perspective cf. D Pieters (1985). At present, the reports of every UN 'special rapporteur' on human rights are replete with suggestions. See, e.g., the annual reports of the UN special rapporteur on the Right to Health to the Human Rights Council / Commission on Human Rights, easily accessible via the webpages of the International Federation of Health and Human Rights Organisations. For a more procedural approach cf. M Tushnet (2009).

[23] On the capability approach to justice see M Nussbaum (2000; 2003); A Sen (1989; 2009).

[24] The 2011 phone-hacking scandal around Rupert Murdoch's News of the World caused the British government not only to begin criminal investigations, but also to interfere with Murdoch's plans to buy BskyB.

refrain from interfering in the sense that it should not ignore deep socio-political conflict by imposing governmental preferences on the conflicting parties. It should rather deal with the conflict itself.

(c) Finally, social rights function in legal discourse as a conceptual viewfinder to bring relatively new types of problems into a legal format. It is a category that can often be used to construe a case that would otherwise not register as a legal problem. Environmental law delivers clear examples of cases in which social rights discourse in the only way to express that there are conflicting interests at stake, which the law should hear. For instance, without social rights it is difficult to construe a case if you have (a) relatively isolated individuals, (b) with diffuse interests (c) which are hardly identifiable, let alone quantifiable in terms of money, (d) opposing tightly organised companies with very specific, financial interests on markets which no one can afford to stay away from (e.g. energy).[25] As soon as fundamental 'rights' are at stake, however, things become easier (too easy, according to some). Then individuals, however isolated from each other, can infer corresponding duties to respect them on the part of powerful opponents. They can launch class actions; file complaints about poor performance and expect there to be a court to hear them; argue liability and demand damages, offer proof and line up witnesses. Social rights prompts asking questions like the following: Being a Norwegian reindeer farmer, is my land 'adjacent to' the nuclear plant of Chernobyl in the Ukraine? What are the interests to be taken into consideration when the city of Basel negotiates pollution restrictions with one of its big industries along the river Rhine? What is our price for the hole in the ozone layer?

---

[25] Seminal in this regard M Cappelletti (1982); M Cappelletti and B Garth (1978). Within the framework of 'European citizenship' the EU publishes 'barometer' results on access to justice on a regular basis, e.g., 1999, 2004, 2009. For the state of the art cf. research done at TISCO, to be found at http://www.tilburguniversity.edu/research/institutes-and-research-groups/tisco/research/projects/micro/measuring/

To sum up: the vocabulary of 'social rights' strategically appeals to the same ideas, which inspired classic liberty rights,[26] but its stakes are very different. On the one hand, there is the idea that the state should refrain from certain things, in particular that it should abolish the claim that its duty requires the privilege to determine social life on the final count. On the other hand, there is the idea that the state should guarantee certain things, to wit socio-political participation and emancipation, especially for those who have not yet the opportunity to participate (future generations included). There is no hierarchy between these two: one is the condition for the other, and vice versa. But this intertwinement is inconceivable within the rigid pattern of contractual naturalism. As long as the state conceives of itself as mediating and integrating conflicting interests in society from the position of a 'pouvoir neutre',[27] it will not be able to conceive of emancipation in the strong sense. Integration as such entails already this claim to a neutral, overarching view of 'the whole' that is yet to be realised. Emancipation, on the other hand, is about making up for socio-political set-back of interests (and its economic effects)[28] caused by political domination. Or, to put it bluntly, emancipation is about undoing oppression. Now oppression is between the oppressor and oppressed. Between their interests there is no mediation or integration.[29] A socio-political choice of the state itself becomes inevitable, renouncing its neutrality. To the extent that a state makes that choice, it proves that the heptagon of contractual naturalism is not sacrosanct.

---

[26] As also Habermas points out in J Habermas (1992 [1992]) ch. 6.

[27] Although Benjamin Constant's term (cf. B Constant (1997) 324 refers to royal power within the state powers, it can also be used to characterise state power as such over and against other powers aiming to govern society at large, e.g., multinational business, religious organisations, etc.

[28] Cf. Feinberg's definition of 'harm' in J Feinberg (1984).

[29] For an incisive analysis of the case of South Africa and a more profound account of the non-integration between oppressor and oppressed, see Ramose (1991).

3.3 Torture

Here is my third example to illustrate that the heptagon cannot be the whole story of our legal order in the specific sense that it leads to all sorts of fundamental questions that cannot be answered in the terms it provides. Contractual naturalism cannot explain why in international (human rights) law as laid down in multiple relevant treaties there is an unconditional prohibition of torture. At the most it could give an account of a conditional prohibition, allowing torture only under very specific circumstances and on the basis of equally specific procedural conditions. It cannot be denied that conditional acceptance of torture is precisely what becomes tempting in practice under serious political pressure – which only shows that contractual naturalism is the official ideology of most legal orders: the more political pressure, the more ideological pressure. But the norm is that the protection against torture does not allow for restrictions, whereas other basic rights, e.g., freedom of speech do.

Meanwhile the literature explores lines of thought about torture that do derive from contractual naturalism. Richard Posner[30] observes that one of the consequences of the horrible 9/11 attacks on the WTC and the Pentagon is that governments are reconsidering their standpoints with regard to the use of torture to obtain information from suspected terrorists. He grants that 'torture' can be defined in many ways, but submits that in any case 'the infliction of actual physical pain to extract information' is torture.[31] For Posner, the question whether the constitution should (be interpreted to) permit torture in specific cases is a matter of '(…) balance between costs and benefits of particular methods of interrogation'. Admitting that costs and benefits need not be (entirely) quantifiable, he argues that sometimes the costs of torture can be outweighed by the benefits, '(…) if torture is the only means by which to save the lives of thousands, perhaps tens or hundreds of thousands of people', or even the life of one innocent person. All constraints on

---

[30] Cf. RA Posner (2006).

[31] Ibid., 292.

torture, e.g., that it should be applied only on authorisation by the government, that it should be proportional to the evil that is to be diverted and the chance that this will happen, etc., are to be put in this balance. Obliging officials to seek a judicial warrant Posner expects to be unrealistic and even counterproductive,[32] though throughout the argument he assumes that somehow 'executive officials' are exclusively targeted to take decisions and 'do the job', and that they can be held to account in retrospect on the basis of constitutional and other legal constraints.[33]

Posner anticipates three objections. Against the objection that torture is always wrong, he points out that sometimes a lesser wrong can and should be used to divert a greater wrong: he has no difficulty with the principle that the end sanctions the means, provided that the balance of costs and benefits is carefully construed. This also counters the second objection that torture is never effective; if this is true, the practice of torture is ruled out by putting up the balance. But perhaps it is not true under all circumstances. The last objection is that torture degrades the society in which it is applied (by the government). With this one Posner has a very short answer indeed: 'Torture is uncivilized, but civilized nations are able to employ uncivilized means (…) without sinking into barbarism, provided the danger is big, clear, and present enough, and the means appropriately effective.' He adds a telling proverb: '*Inter armes silent leges*', i.e., amidst weapons laws fall silent.[34] In other words, where there is war, there is no law, and vice versa.

This reasoning deploys entirely along the lines of what I called contractual naturalism. All the key terms of the heptagon turn up to do their job, though sometimes under slightly different lexical guises. It presumes, firstly, that all people prefer self-preservation over all other priorities as a basic 'need' that has to be fulfilled, and that the means to fulfil it depend solely on the outcomes of calculations over ordered sets

---

32 Ibid., 296.

33 Ibid., 297–298, where he turns against regulating torture by statutory law, so that the use of it will not conflict, for instance, with the constitutional protection against self-incrimination of a suspect.

34 Ibid., 294–295.

of preferences. Secondly, it appeals to contract. As in the case of torturing for information 'calculating the balance' does not have to be a quantitative exercise, as Posner himself admits; the outcome of the balancing amounts to nothing more or less than a negotiated agreement or 'a contract of association' on the legal admissibility of torture. Since, thirdly, the enforcement of this consensus is attributed to governmental authority on condition of respecting the balance between ends and means, we also encounter a contract of submission. So although it poses as an exercise in reducing law to economics,[35] Posner's proposal is a common sense mixture of assumptions on generalised 'human needs' that are allegedly 'given'; a utilitarian quasi-calculus on 'the greatest happiness for the greatest number'; and a rather classical legal defence of civil liberties as a warrant against 'ad hoc' balancing. For at the very end of his argument Posner concedes that '(…) once one starts down the balancing path, the protection of civil liberties quickly erodes.'[36] He thinks that it is better '(…) to stick with our perhaps overly strict rules, trusting executive officials to break them when the stakes are high enough to enable the officials to obtain political absolution for their illegal conduct.'[37] Thus, apparently, even balancing itself should be balanced.

Let us not yield to the temptation to challenge this reduplication of the balancing metaphor. Suffice it to point out that Posner's format of arguing, precisely as a common sense amalgam, leaves large parts of relevant positive law unexplained. Perhaps the most important point is that in human rights law the prohibition of torture or 'inhuman or degrading treatment or punishment' is primarily an unconditional obligation imposed on the state. Though it is correlative to a right of legal subjects not to be tortured, the primary norm is addressed to the state. This is why it cannot be conditioned, in contrast to norms that primarily

---

[35] As is well-known, Richard Posner is the godfather of 'Law & economics', which basically holds that everything law can do, economics can do better. For a good summary of his views cf. R Posner (1990).

[36] Posner (2006) 297.

[37] Ibid., 298.

attribute rights to individuals (or groups). Take the European Convention on Human Rights (1950). Art. 3 ECHR formulates the prohibition of torture in a categorical way, and in this the prohibition of torture is on a par with the prohibition of 'slavery or servitude' (Art. 4.1) and some basic procedural rights like *habeas corpus* (Art. 5). It is not qualified in the Convention itself, and the Convention does not mention the usual restriction clause 'in accordance with a procedure prescribed by law'.[38] Again, the International Covenant on Civil and Political Rights (1966), Art. 7, rules unconditionally that 'no one shall be subjected to torture or to cruel, inhuman or degrading treatment or punishment'. Moreover, Art. 4.2 mentions this prohibition explicitly as one from which no derogation may be made under the provision of Art. 4.1 (the latter conceding that in times of 'public emergency which threatens the life of the nation' States Parties to the ICCPR are allowed to take appropriate safety measures).

The reason for this absolute ban on torture (and slavery) is that admitting torture (even under strict constraints) would amount to giving up on the rule of law. First of all, it is not difficult to imagine cases where the killing of thousands of people could be prevented effectively by torturing an innocent person, for instance the son of a terrorist who happens to know where his father is but not what he is up to.[39] And if the son refuses to talk, why not torture his fiancée before his eyes? Posner could say that such treatment would abhor so many people that it would always count as a cost rather than a benefit, and thus be rejected. But this is an empirical matter that has to be settled by experiment. So, firstly, one has to approve of the experiment and secondly, the experiment will probably demonstrate that there is a turning point where effective torturing even of non-suspected people is counted as a benefit rather than a cost if only enough people are saved. Now, if law does not protect innocent persons against the use of pain-inflicting physical violence on

---

[38] In contrast with, respectively, 'compulsory labour' (qualified by Art. 4.3) and 'the right to liberty' (which may be restricted by law on the basis of Art. 5.1).

[39] M Sandel (2009a) 39f mentions this scenario rightly as the more appropriate one to see what is at stake in torture.

the part of the government, who does it protect? And if the answer is 'no one' if the pressure is high enough, why have law in the first place? Secondly, even torturing a terrorism suspect is torturing someone who falls under the presumption of innocence. Referring to this presumption when you know that the suspect is the perpetrator and you are presumably able to stop him in the act by torturing, may sound highly artificial. But then law *is* a political artefact (as I will argue below) that can only exist by virtue of this and other presumptions. This is precisely why its existence is seriously undermined if every time push comes to shove, law has to give up on these presumptions. It makes law self-contradictory, thus unreliable. This is not a matter of balancing costs and benefits; it is a matter of being credible. More than anything else, the financial crisis of the last years has taught us that economic models that ignore credibility parameters in calculations are unrealistic. What Posner's Latin proverb suggests is that in some situations law becomes powerless and has to yield to the realm of action from which it originates: politics as the struggle for power over society. But it does not mean that law can sanction political action in emergency cases or give 'political absolution' in retrospect. The question left open is what more comes to law than politics if it is not just economic cost-benefit analysis? And in its wake comes the question that was central to this section: what more is to be said about law than the heptagon of contractual naturalism allows us to say?

4. CONTRACTUAL THINKING AND NATURALISM

From the examples given the presumption arises that our legal order knows more about its basis than it concedes when it is pressed to 'philosophise' about it under harsh conditions. It is, therefore, hard to imagine that contractual naturalism would be the whole truth in answering the question why we may call positive law 'reasonable'; i.e., remember, why we can understand what it is about in the end. This conclusion is a welcome incentive to now turn to a philosophical investigation in the proper sense. We are going to investigate whether or not the heptagon of contractual naturalism is thinkable, or rather re-thinkable. The 're-' would derive its specific ring from the strategy we are going to follow: we are going to try and think what the agents introduced by the heptagon allegedly think. We will find that their thoughts are inconsistent.

To aim at the right point let us rehearse the seven steps of contractual naturalism:

(1) Each individual wants to survive (self-preservation).
(2) Self-preservation requires living in society.
(3) Life in society requires order.
(4) Order requires sanctions.
(5) Sanctions require power.
(6) Power requires supreme power.
(7) Supreme power requires constraints: to care about the needs implied in (1) (security, property, reliance).

Perhaps a few caveats are in place to avoid misunderstanding. To state the obvious, this sequence is not a historical one. It is not an account of consecutive periods which mankind allegedly has lived through. Neither is it a description of events that, by hypothesis, have causally contributed to the rise of a society, a state, a government or a legal order. One who is interested in the history of a legal order will do some empirical research on museum collections, archives, excavations, etc. He or she may well discover numerous interesting causal intertwinements between a legal system and, for instance, its geographical conditions, its preferred division of labour and its distribution of goods, its process of cultural or political (dis-)integration, etc. Though the heptagon may look like an empirical theory, giving an account of how society came into existence is not what it aims at. It is an interpretational scheme, a symbolic structure that submits an account of the meaningfulness of the process in which a legal order takes shape. Nevertheless, it is a sequence of units of discourse: each step is supposed to prompt you to the next if you make a serious analysis of its concepts and their interrelations.

In order to validate this claim, it will be apt to note, firstly, that the whole scheme of seven steps develops from a very specific point of departure: the wants of self-preservation or survival in (1). This is also the point to which the whole sequence returns in (7) when restrictions on the exercise of supreme power are formulated. The strivings presented in this point of departure are conceived of as a sort of energy that is retained throughout the stages developing from that point. Secondly, it will be noted that the development itself is prefigured as a concatenation of two contractual transitions, which together produce the concept of law: from individual needs to living together (steps 1–3), and from living together in society to the exercise of supreme power under certain constraints (steps 4–7). It is, however, very unclear what this 'from … to …' phrase really means. Of course it is a prepositional equivalent of terms like 'requires' or 'implies', which we used earlier in our characterisations of the heptagon. But these terms have been obscure from the very first section of this chapter. They do not unravel how the transitions from that allegedly 'given' point of departure have to be understood. They just declare solemnly that there are such transitions. But how can there be?

Let us look at the two contracts in greater detail. If we interpret them as accounts of what law is about, we get something close to the following. The first contract – the agreement to associate as individuals – could be understood as a principle of coordination. The principle can be roughly formulated like this: We can conceive of society only if human relationships are understood from the principle that every individual refrains from an immediate claim on everything that appears instrumental to her own interests, but only if every other individual does the same. Only under such a principle can the relative compatibility of all private interests be tabled, in terms of the – all private interests overriding – general interest or common wealth. The second contract – the agreement to authorise supreme power – amounts to another principle, a principle of subordination that is to be accepted in the relationship between the co-individuals and the powerful agent. It is a principle to the effect that these individuals subordinate all the power in society to a supreme power over society, but only if this supreme power has regard to what each and every member of society takes an interest in: self-preservation. Or in less elliptic terms: that the relative compatibility of their interests be assessed, and effectuated accordingly, against the backdrop of their individual interests in self-preservation.

Now there is something awkward in these two contracts or principles of socio-political thought. They cannot evade the three ways of begging a question that Hans Albert famously labelled as the 'Münchhausen trilemma'.[40] Either they reiterate the problem and defer the explanation by one more step (infinite regress); or they presuppose what they try to explain, going round in circles (*petitio principii*); or they just stop at an arbitrary point (axiomatic or dogmatic 'just so' gambit). Take the contract of association. It expresses that the minimum requirement for living together is that everyone should waive the *a priori* claim to everything instrumental to her own interest, but only if everybody else does the same thing. Now let us take the perspective of thought of any of these individuals as agents capable of practical thinking. What would explain that such an agent would waive this claim? If it were really the case that everyone's step is dependent on a similar step taken by all others, nobody will take the first step and there will be no steps taken at all.[41] Then compatibility of private interests – the principle of association – will usher in infinite regress and never be acknowledged. To put it in shorter terms: then 'society would never come about' in the sense that society would remain incomprehensible. But suppose, inversely, that everyone would decide to take the first step because of what is in it for all, regardless of whether other agents do the same thing. Then the point of view, which we call the general interest or the common wealth is already acknowledged at a moment at which – by hypothesis – society was not comprehensible yet. The common wealth would have to drive the contract while the contract is creating the common wealth in the first place. Thus, in simpler terms, 'society would exist before it had come

[40] Cf. H Albert (1991 [1968]) 15.

[41] This is often the problem, for instance, in the disarmament negotiations. For a deeper theoretical analysis of the conundrum, see Margaret Gilbert's critique of agreements as an exchange of promises in M Gilbert (1996) 313ff.

about'. This, obviously, would amount to *petitio principii*: presupposing the very thing you are supposed to explain. Either way, the contractual model begs the question. It can only lead to 'just so' solutions taking their cue from factually existing society, which is only a third way of begging the question.[42]

The contract of authorisation does not fare any better. By hypothesis, the members of society subordinate all their power in society to a power over society, who in turn would commit himself to take care of their ultimate interests. But, reasoning again from the point of view of those involved, what would make this contract work? It can only be effective if society as a party to the contract is able to assess whether or not the sovereign keeps his part of the deal and to revise its promise if he does not. But, by hypothesis, this is impossible. If it is really the case that all power is transferred to the sovereign, society has given up even the possibility of judging by its own standards whether or not the sovereign complies.[43] In such a deal, there will be no meaning in any restriction on the performance of the agent invested with supreme power. So why would society enter into it? The contract would never get off the ground as it would infinitely be deferred. Inversely, suppose the contract would leave some scope for autonomous judgment of society about the actions of the sovereign. Then, indeed, society would have kept at least some of its own power. But that would contradict the hypothesis that was made from the outset, namely that all power would be absorbed by supreme power. We would in fact suppose that the supreme power was limited (by a pre-contract), or that there would be only 'so-called' supreme power in as far as society would agree to assign it to someone provisionally. The contract would already have been closed before it could be closed. In other words: the contract would be presupposed rather than explained – clearly going round in circles. There is, of course, the possibility to argue

---

[42] Various parts of this argument may be rephrased in a more technical way by contemporary game theory. On one interpretation of the Prisoner's Dilemma, it is about situations 'in which it is difficult to get rational, selfish agents to cooperate for their common goal'. (S Kuhn (2009) (spring edition)).

[43] This is why Winston Smith, in George Orwell's 1984, has to yield to the power of Big Brother by giving up on simple arithmetic.

that the contract is always with some factual power, relative to other powers in a given society; but that would be a 'just so' answer, and equally question-begging when it comes to understanding.

Discarding 'just so' answers, in both transitional constructs we arrive at the same conclusion: either the contracts are presupposed in the act of making them, or they will never be made in the first place. Either way they lack explanatory value as to the comprehensibility of the law. For they provide no good reasons for the agents involved to close, or to comply with, the deal.Thus they do not contribute to answering the question that governs this chapter: can we understand what law is about in the end? But the argument is not over yet. We may put our cards on the hope that the two contracts are just infelicitous rhetorical devices to convey the sound point that the very first step entails: in the end law is about self-preservation. Let us see if that is a tenable thesis.

5. SATISFYING NEEDS, SELF-PRESERVATION AND FREEDOM

The first step in the discursive scheme I dubbed 'contractual naturalism' was from a specific point of departure: the specific want to survive captured by the term self-preservation. The latter term is the more philosophical and, for our purposes, the more adequate one, because it reflects the point of view of the agents concerned with their *own* subsistence. For what the point of departure entails is neither a Darwinist observation on the survival of the fittest, nor some piece of advice from a sympathetic outsider about how to survive under harsh conditions, but the agony of someone asking herself as an insider: how am I going to survive in these circumstances? Thus, the point of departure entails the point of view of a first person relating to herself. The problem is, as it will turn out, that this point of view is not coherently carried through in the remainder of the argument.

The idea of the heptagon was to place such an agent at ground zero, where there is no question of existing law or, for that matter, existing society.[44] In that situation agents are conceived of as isolated entities with specific, 'natural' capabilities and needs. Though both capabilities (e.g., physical strength, eyesight) and needs (e.g., hunger or sexual urge), may vary over a relatively large scale, the idea is that the needs, in particular, are 'natural' in various respects. Allegedly, just as it has set maximum limits on capabilities nature has set minimum thresholds on needs, which are non-negotiable and inalterable. Human beings, for instance, need a minimum amount of oxygen to survive. It is commonly added, that some of these needs are not only inalterable but also universal – another connotation that comes with 'natural'. Moreover, in the practical perspective of an agent, needs are dominant over capabilities in the sense that agents will 'naturally' attempt to use capabilities of themselves and their environment to satisfy at least the most urgent of their needs. Living in a not too hospitable environment, as we humans do, some needs are felt stronger than others, as they are more relevant to bare survival. For example, if necessary, you can survive a month without music, but not without water. Thus, or so it seems, there is a set of 'basic needs', as distinct from 'additional needs'. The former rather than the latter come close to a universal or common 'human nature'. This is why, or so one holds, everybody has a claim to corporeal integrity, shelter, clothing, food and a few other things, even if these things can vary according to circumstances (e.g. climate).[45]

Notwithstanding this common ground, however, the quest for self-preservation is supposed to find its origin in isolation. The agents are 'individuals' or 'particulars' in the sense that each agent strives to satisfy their needs (minimally to preserve themselves) independent of any other agent. This may look a caricature, but the heptagon is only a model for the legal order, not a description of reality. If the model starts from individual agents in splendid isolation, it does not entail the view that

---

[44] From here to the end of this section, I basically paraphrase Hobbes' theory as found (with interesting differences) in T Hobbes (1651 [1973]); (1651 [1983]). My critique is in the next section.

[45] This is a basic tenet in HLA Hart (1961) 189ff: 'the minimum content of natural law'.

individual people are islands and that they are able to survive on their own. It merely pictures a relationship of independence from one another, in the specific sense of being not dominated by other agents.[46] In this very basic sense they may be said to be free: being independent of anybody else in the pursuit of satisfying one's needs. The contact they may have will be either wholly instrumental to or wholly apart from this pursuit – which is absolutely not to say that they instinctively or otherwise go after each other in constant fight. The order or peace they want will be wholly instrumental to satisfying the needs and avoiding risky confrontations that would be in no one's interest for surviving. Fear for one another is conceivable since one's own needs will not be satisfied easily if others may interfere at unpredictable occasions with unpredictable force. So there we are: 'freedom from want' and 'freedom from fear' are, in the final analysis, all there is to society and law, however instrumentally necessary these may be and whatever form they may take. Or so it seems.

5.1 The Basic Fallacy of Naturalism

This piece of reasoning is less cogent, once we realise that it is based on a trick: the trick of silently changing points of view. First we construct thinking agents in a situation, which we called ground zero or 'the state of nature': individuals without social relationships. Then we, as outsiders, attempt to think what they, as insiders, think. But at specific points in this interpretative or reconstructive process we merge our perspective from the outside with the agents' perspective from the inside. For instance, we use terms like survival and self-preservation indistinctively, merging 'our' knowledge about survival with 'their' quest for self-preservation. Now the first point is that self-preservation is a term, which *we* use to characterise *their* predicament as *they* see it. We may frame reasonable hypotheses about their view on the basis of what we know about surviving, but there is no *a priori* warrant that our views merge with theirs. In particular, from the fact that we can truly ascribe some

---

[46] Cf. P Pettit (2000).

particular view V to all individuals in a group G, we cannot infer the fact these individuals hold V in common or that they would think of themselves as the group who holds V in common. So if we establish that, in the model of contractual naturalism, all agents at 'ground zero' think the same, namely, that they want to be left in peace in the satisfaction of their needs, we cannot infer from that that peaceful satisfaction of their needs is what they hold in common.[47] The second point is that we cannot have it both ways: either we try to think what they think, distinguishing the two perspectives and merge them only on the basis of evidence, or we refrain from that distinction altogether and define their predicament as we see it. What we should not do is pretend that we can have our cake and eat it. It leads to nonsensical pieces of reasoning.[48] The third point is that, having carefully distinguished between the two perspectives and framing hypotheses about how they may merge, our evidence will be predicated on communication with the agents we are studying. If communication is impossible – and it is impossible in case they are just pawns in a model of our own invention as 'ground zero' is – we can only work on the basis of assumptions. But if we do that, we will find that we are trying to solve an equation with two unknown variables: what these agents are thinking and what they are thinking about. Here again we cannot have it both ways.

So we should make up our mind and decide what it is that we want to have access to: if we want to re-think what the agents at ground zero think in the world they live in and relate that to our thinking, we must refrain from inserting our beliefs about the world as something we can attribute to them. If, on the other hand, we are interested in the facts of the world as we know it under the assumption that they share it with us,

---

[47] Cf. from the fact that A, B, and C are all doing the same thing, namely painting my house, neither I, nor any observer, nor A, B, or C may infer that they are painting the house *together*.

[48] Known to the technicians of philosophy as 'quantifying into opaque (or: intensional) contexts'. Just one classical example: from [P1] John believes that he is the oldest man on earth, and [P2] The oldest man on earth is Santa, one cannot infer [C] John believes that he is Santa. The content of John's belief remains 'opaque' to us.

we should directly go to these and do science. For science is interested in facts; philosophy, however, in thinking. As we embarked on an exercise in philosophy, let us now track the thought contents of the agent characters that contractual naturalism put up.

5.2 The Need for Needs

To avoid misunderstandings from the outset, when it comes to what law is about I have no doubts that law has to do with interests or needs such as corporeal integrity, housing and food, for everyone, without fear for one another's behaviour. What I deny is that we can understand why this should be so by taking our point of departure in self-preservation, and that this point of departure is natural, innate, or nature-given in any sense of the word 'nature'. I am going to argue that we can only grasp the importance of needs if we put them in a wider perspective, in which the idea of freedom takes on other forms than the one which is allegedly linked up with self-preservation. It is from that more embracing idea of freedom that, in the end, we will be able to appreciate the freedom inherent to self-preservation.

Most people have an inkling of that wider idea of freedom, when they acknowledge that freedom entails not only the possibility to satisfy one's needs, but also the choice not to satisfy them. The human need for food may be undeniable, but a person can choose to starve herself to death in a hunger strike for a good cause. The need for corporeal integrity may be obvious, but a person can choose to join the army and risk dying for his countrymen. The need for security may be evident, but one can choose to leave a safe place and head for adventure. You may respond that what these persons do is to postpone and manipulate an immediate satisfaction of primary needs (e.g. food, sexual intercourse, protective housing) in order to get greater satisfaction from the fulfillment of secondary, but more deeply felt needs (eternal life, honour, happiness). That may be so. But the very fact that they can say 'no' to the satisfaction of primary needs suffices to raise serious doubts concerning one of the basic tenets of naturalism: to wit, a universally valid distinction between primary and secondary, basic and additional, needs. If primary needs are no longer the ones identifiable as those which people are most anxious to satisfy, the term loses its significance as a point of departure for societal order, as the cause of the social contract, or as the ultimate basis of law. Moreover, if all sorts of needs can turn out to be primary, the notion of freedom comes into a different light: it is equally important that people can want to satisfy their needs as that they can want to not satisfy their needs. Having this choice itself is important. Thus, giving people the opportunity to make this kind of choice will qualify as a more basic principle of societal ordering than giving them the means to satisfy their allegedly primary needs.[49]

This first inkling, however, is only a premeditation of what seems to be the real point. The real point is that the satisfaction of individual needs like 'food' or 'shelter' does not constitute in any sense a stronghold for social ordering between agents. Most humans will say that they do not need whatever food or shelter, but a certain quality of food and shelter. They will also be inclined to interpret the needs of those who cannot reflect on their needs (babies, mentally disabled people) in terms of the quality they would require for themselves. But they will not be inclined to specify the criteria for quality in advance and in general. They will rather want to have a say about what will satisfy their needs in the specific situation in which they find themselves. For instance, they will agree to be brought into a state of unconsciousness if they need surgery in order to live longer, but they will not agree to be brought into a state of coma in order to be fed by state-of-the-art food from a machine and live longer. Moreover, they will realise that there is no point in specifying every single aspect of the way in which they want to see their needs satisfied, firstly because there is no end to it, secondly because the more instructions they give, the more escapes they offer to those who are supposed to comply with them. Sooner rather than later they will end up saying two things: (i) that what they want is to be treated in a 'humane'

[49] We will see in a few moments how the legal order deals with this opportunity of choice.

way, and (ii) that they always want to have a 'free' say in what that amounts to in the case at hand.

So when we talk about needs, we have in mind neither a certain biological minimum (enough to keep you on the safe side of the ridge between life and death), nor a socio-economic minimum (an allowance that will make you enjoy your pension for not more than two years) that could be normative for how society should be organised. Biology may be able to tell us what a person needs to eat and to drink in order to survive as an organism. But it will never be able to tell what an organism needs to eat and to drink in order to survive as a person. What we understand by a human organism and, thus, by human needs, is a political rather than a biological question.[50] Similarly, economics will tell us how a society may proceed in distributing scarcity. But it will never be able to tell which distribution of scarcity, hence what society, has to count as civilised. Again, that is a political question, and we better make sure that we participate in the process that is meant to answer it if we want to satisfy our needs in the long run.

Satisfying primary needs of life is not only part and parcel of freedom in the sense of non-domination, it also presupposes freedom in the sense of self-determination or autonomy: freedom to determine one's needs, to relate them to a life-plan, to set proper standards of satisfaction, and to distinguish between primary and secondary needs by virtue of political choices rather than by virtue of biological facts. This, in turn, entails that fear and freedom from fear do not find their origin in needs discourse. Needs discourse cannot establish to what extent one has reasons for fear. Sharing and testing these reasons is essential in order to organise protection and freedom from fear. Needs do not tell how society should organise these processes of sharing and testing. A list of needs that have to be satisfied is itself a product of a specific order in society. To put it in another way: politics (the sphere of establishing, institutionalising, and accounting for social order) has a relatively independent status in relation

---

[50] Some would even venture to say that it is a philosophical question. That seems to me a quick jump to surpass the debatable character of the question.

to satisfying needs and lifting scarcity. Or in sound bite format: no self-preservation without self-determination.

5.3 Self-preservation, Self-determination and Self-awareness

Suppose you are lying in bed, lethally ill, and you fear the prospect of more suffering and loss of dignity. You decide not to eat and drink anymore, in spite of the fact that you feel hungry and thirsty. On the basis of what do you make this decision? It is not on the basis of the needs you feel. You do not even feel the overriding need not to eat or to drink in spite of the needs you also feel (as you would perhaps do in extreme cases of anorexia). The wish to die is not a need to be satisfied but a desire to be fulfilled. Self-determination is important to fulfil that desire, but it cannot be the ground of the decision. You take the decision on the basis of who you want to be, everything being considered, i.e., on the basis of who you are to yourself, in the end.

Look again at the point of departure of the heptagon. Agents at ground zero are (pictured as) 'isolated' or 'particular' in the sense that each individual strives for self-preservation, independently of each and every other agent. The relationships they have with each other are presumed to be instrumental to that striving – which does not imply (as said) that the agents are in permanent conflict but solely that conflict is a permanent option. Now note that these individuals conceive of themselves as related to each other in only a negative sense: they see themselves as independent, as non-dominated. To that extent, their relationship to one another does not offer them any chance of articulating a positive account of their identities. The question is, then: how could these agents develop any idea of the selves they are to preserve in the first place? Or even more precise: how could we give an account of how they develop their ideas of a self in each case? In which terms could we conceive of their conceiving themselves?

To mean at least something by the word 'self' in self-preservation, they must ascribe to themselves certain qualities by predicates as simple as 'big', 'strong', 'smart', 'beautiful', etc. In order to develop these wants to be 'bigger' or 'stronger' than they are at a certain moment, they have to develop a measure of what counts as 'big' or 'strong'. Of course they do not need such a measure in order to grow bigger or stronger. They will need it in order to embark on self-preservation, i.e., in order to grow bigger or stronger than they know themselves to be. They cannot afford to point their fingers into the air shouting 'I, I'. They will have to articulate their identity adding: 'I, who am/is strong like THIS', or 'I, who am/is in pain like THAT', etc. It is not a coincidence that we read these relative clauses hovering between the first and the third person singular. The third person in this case substitutes an 'I' that is referring to herself via the detour of a third instance. This awareness of a third instance – call it 'reality' while the first person may call it 'other-than-me' – is already presupposed (logically speaking) before contractual relationships come into play and before authority over these relationships is attributed to a supreme power.

One may think that I am making too much out of reflexive thinking or willing. Why not regard the 'striving for self-preservation' as a phrase which we as full-blooded social and reflective beings use, not the allegedly non-social agents at ground zero? Why not avoid a lot of questions by saying that the latter, indeed, do nothing but follow their instincts, which are – as we, not they, can see – directed towards continuation of life functions via processes of exchange with their environment? Yes, we might say that. But then we have left the enterprise we have embarked upon: to try to understand what allegedly non-social beings think regarding their existence, regarding themselves, regarding the 'self' that provides identity for their existence. Thus, we will get trapped when we try to proceed from step 1 to step 2 in the heptagon discourse. This step, recall, presupposed that pursuing satisfaction of needs would be frustrated, because the individual beings would get stuck in the mud of antagonism, loneliness or sheer want; and that the way to escape from the imminent decay of all would be to order society on the basis of mutual consent and support. So they decide to transcend their non-social stage and transform it into a social one. But then, by the very hypothesis of the heptagon, they surely are thinking, judging, and willing for themselves. Then social life, apparently, is not conceived of as one of their natural instincts, at least not in the same way as other urges are. If it were, the heptagon rap about independent entities would make no sense. Nor would the one about the order of social life be an issue. If agents would socialise by instinct, then a well-defined order, or a perhaps a well-defined disposition to develop a certain order, would be inherent to their biological wiring and it would hardly be a problem. A sort of natural homogeneity would result from it, similar to that we find in a beehive. But that is not what naturalism holds. It tacitly exchanges bio-functional programmes for practical thinking, and then there is no escape from reflexivity. So let us continue to work from within the hypothesis of beings, who will have to frame some idea of who they, themselves, are from the experience they gain of themselves as striving to satisfy their needs.

Will they be able to articulate this more or less warranted identity, given the hypothetical characteristics attributed to them? I think not. Note that, by hypothesis, they are not aware of themselves but as agents who experience certain urges called needs. Consequently, they will think of the world around them in general, and of other agents in particular, as one huge reservoir of things that either serve them well to satisfy these needs, or come in the way of satisfaction. Now, a world that is nothing but an immense reservoir of possible satisfactions and dissatisfactions for some first person 'I', is in a specific, but decisive sense not different from this 'I'. Such an 'I' will necessarily and exclusively refer to his environment as something at his disposal, either to reject or to use it, not as something that exists in its own right. He conceives of this world as 'his', and of himself as 'the owner'. The world presents itself to him as one huge screen on which he can project his needs. The screen will only reflect what he projects. Think of what happens to us if we feel the need of all needs and have to find a place somewhere soon. We may be in the heart of, say, Rome, but we could not care less. The whole city suddenly turns into one big reservoir of places that are or are not suitable to answer the call of nature. For an agent who is defined by his needs alone, the world becomes a mirror in which he can only detect himself. But then we must conclude he will not be able to distinguish himself and to ascribe certain qualities to himself in any warranted way. There will be nothing left different from him, for him to test his claims against. He will have no awareness of himself that is not reducible to his instantaneously felt needs or (dis-)satisfactions. All his ascriptions will be suspect in the sense of originating in nothing but his own needs. So he will not gain any reliable idea of a self from his experiences in satisfying his needs. But if he has no reliable idea of himself, what could self-preservation possibly mean for him? Or self-determination, for that matter? He is prevented from any way of relating to his needs, however urgent he may experience them. Indeed, he takes major risks, even death, by just going after his needs.

The upshot of all this is a second conclusion, over and above the one that marked the end of the previous section. Not only do we have to acknowledge that one cannot afford to let another agent determine one's needs, i.e., that self-preservation presupposes self-determination. We also have to take into account that one cannot relate to and, thus, determine one's needs in view of self-preservation or, for that matter, self-determination, by reference to these needs alone. More: we must acknowledge that the very idea of self-determination encounters the same predicament as self-preservation. Both self-preservation and self-determination presuppose self-awareness; and reliable self-awareness presupposes an instance that is the other of the self. Naturalism does not provide such an account.

6. SUMMARY

The foundations of our legal order turned out to be phrased in always the same pattern of discourse: contractual naturalism. This pattern becomes apparent when, at moments of crisis, this order is challenged by political pressure. Notwithstanding its dominance, it is not determinative of the legal order in all its respects. What counts apart from, or indeed against, contractual naturalism can be traced by analysing both its contractual transitions (contracts of association and authorisation) and its naturalistic point of departure.

Even the most benevolent interpretation of the contractual structures brings out that they have no explanatory power: they either assume what they are supposed to explain or they defer the explanation *ad infinitum*. They are, at the most, a repetitive rhetoric of what seems to be a highly valued apposition to the point of departure: non-domination in self-preservation. But this freedom does not find its ground – though it may find expression – in satisfying primary needs. For one thing, freedom to determine these needs precedes self-preservation in any organisation of society. For another, self-preservation – in whatever political form of self-determination – presupposes an awareness of oneself that cannot be derived from the experiences and acts of satisfying needs alone.

2. Justice, rights and human dignity

Having rejected a naturalistic conception of self-preservation, along with its contractual architecture, I may well find myself double-trapped. Am I really saying that in order to pursue self-preservation we have to exercise autonomy, as the term self-determination suggests, and then that in order to exercise autonomy we have to touch base in self-awareness that is calibrated against reality? The first trap would be collapsing autonomy into heteronomy: Is something 'other-than-me' going to tell me who I am? We may try to avoid it by shifting to reverse gear and collapsing the meaning of self-awareness into self-determination after all. I shall investigate this hypothesis in what I take to be its strongest form: a model of social life that is radically based upon ultimate self-determination by every first person agent (section 1). Often I will simply use the (italicised) pronoun *'I'* (and related pronouns) to indicate this perspective. At first sight, this model seems awkward indeed, as it appears to enthrone power in its most absolute and arbitrary form. Indeed, it takes us back to the point where the heptagon suggests proceeding from a contract of association towards a contract of authorisation if we really want to survive as masters of our own lives. But are these contracts inspired by a realistic conceptualisation of how power operates? What if we would learn from Machiavelli (and others) that power is exercised, first and foremost, by strategic self-restraint? Perhaps, generalised self-determination would usher in a relatively stable order in society, instead of producing arbitrariness and chaos? Thus we will be exploring the idea that law might just be the guardian of a well-balanced order by virtue of the solid mechanisms of power. In the end, however, I will argue that, although power in general may have this in-built tendency of self-restraint, *political* power in particular tends to appeal to a totalitarian conceptual framework in order to install this balance, thereby disturbing it. If that conclusion stands, we will have failed to understand law from this peculiar model of generalised self-determination. So we will have to reset the discussion and start anew at the point where this chapter began. If they cannot be merged into one model, we will have to accept a conceptual gulf between self-determination and self-awareness and ask what kind of distinction this is?

Here is where the second pitfall has been lurking all the way long. How can we expect any philosophical profit from concepts like *self*-preservation, *self*-determination or *self*-awareness in a reflection on the meaning of law? Should we not, rather, trust our intuitions that the law, whatever it may be, has to do with the relationship between *I* and other(-s), not with that between *I* and *myself*? In order to avoid this trap, as well as to fully face the pertinent question set out in the previous paragraph, I will argue in section 2 that self-awareness of any first person referring to herself as *'I'*, already entails both orientation and reference towards what is for this first person 'the other', the other person in particular.[1] The reflexive relationship between *me* and *myself* already always presupposes the social relationship between *me* and *you* so as to be well-founded. Indeed, the concept of a polity, as an ordering of social relationships, will appear to be inherent to well-founded self-awareness. I will, moreover, explain why this orientation remains ambiguous and, therefore, insufficient, as it is easily contaminated by ideological biases. In the end, however, we will be left with two equally respectable, but diametrically opposite accounts of this presupposition (section 3). The core of this chapter, and indeed of the whole book, will appear in section 4, when I will argue that the idea of justice is precisely bound up with living this antinomy[2] between two accounts or principles, that we should

---

1 Here I join Taylor's view that there is an 'essential link between identity and a kind of orientation' C Taylor (1989) 28, although it takes me more steps to conclude that the link is ultimately a moral one.

2 I will use the term 'antinomy' in a way that is only superficially related to Kant's so-called 'dynamic antinomies' in his Transcendental Dialectics, where it indicates an opposition between two sets of arguments inspired by radically incompatible principles (*Widerstreit der Gesetze*), thesis and antithesis. Cf. I

not give up either one of them, nor let them merge into a higher synthesising order. The imperative to live and uphold the tension between two opposing principles of social relationships will turn out to be the key to understanding what a legal order is about. This finding has critical merits: now we know what to investigate when a political constellation claims to be a legal order.

1. SELF-DETERMINATION AND THE BALANCE OF POWERS

1.1 Contradiction?

Why would there be a contradiction between the notions of self-determination and self-awareness? Didn't I argue in the first chapter that self-determination entails self-awareness as a necessary presupposition? In trying to give an account of what is normative in social relations I said two things. Firstly, self-preservation requires self-determination, since ultimately no other will be allowed to determine the needs of an agent (without his consent) if this agent is keen on self-preservation. Secondly, both self-preservation and self-determination require self-awareness independent of one's needs; how else would a first person know what is there to be preserved or determined in the first place? These two theses nourish the impression that there is indeed a hierarchical order since, ultimately, self-awareness seems both presupposed in and instrumental to self-determination and self-preservation.

But things are not that easy. Although I have not said very much yet about self-awareness, I have stressed that it implies a commitment to objectivity. Now that is a very solemn word indeed, but I will use it in a rather straightforward and minimal sense: I take it to mean a commitment to steer away from whims, arbitrariness, illusions and delusions in what one thinks oneself to be. Self-awareness aims at saying what one is 'at the end of the

---

Kant (1781/1787 [1975]) 401 (A408–409/B435). Cf. Radbruch's use of the term in G Radbruch (1973 [1932]) 164 ff.

day', and accepting the burden of proof that one did not choose one's own grounds for granting such a claim. Short of this condition, self-awareness would not be different from self-conceit. The reason why I did not accept the view that self-preservation can be defined in terms of needs was precisely that no one can determine who he is in any reliable way by virtue solely of his needs. To put the same point differently: inherent to the pursuit of self-preservation is the intention to refer, via one's needs and one's desires, to what one 'really' takes oneself to be, as distinct from what one fancies oneself to be. Of course, this intention itself does not warrant the success of the effort. All I am saying is that the attempt to satisfy one's needs already implies reference to what is not merely one's needs or one's arbitrary, immediate and 'free' idea of oneself. Self-awareness in this sense is already dependent on the capacity to think of something other-than-the-self as a warrant for the self: 'sources of the self', as Charles Taylor calls them.[3] But if self-determination is dependent on self-awareness and self-awareness is, in turn, dependent on the awareness of 'something other-than-the-self', then self-determination is dependent on this awareness of something other-than-the-self as well. Or again, if self-determination has something to do with freedom, it is not the freedom to determine oneself as one fancies, but rather the freedom to postpone such determinations until 'the end of the day', i.e. until one has considered their feasibility in the light of grounds that one truly believes (mistakenly or not) to escape from sheer projections.

So the fundamental aspect of freedom is not that an agent is able to ascribe to himself property or preference *X* rather than *Y* as he chooses, but that he can choose either *X* or *Y* on account of *everything else* he has reason to believe with regard to himself. Thus, he poses as an agent who is not absorbed by the sum total of his immediate experiences, but as one who is interested in the feasibility of these experiences as *his*. Freedom is the capacity to account for whatever one would like to say or to do with regard to oneself. The appropriateness (the 'proper-ness') of that account

---

[3] Cf. his discussion of 'inescapable frameworks (ch. 1) and 'the transcendental condition' of identity in ch. 2 (C Taylor (1989) 38).

is not one's 'property', i.e. not something that one can decide at will. In principle, such an interest relates to everything that appears to be the case and to the ultimate grounds why it would or should be the case. In this very general sense, then, a human being is not free to say of himself or to act for himself as he likes. If self-determination has something to do with autonomy, then it also has something to do with the awareness that the *autos*, the self, has to be accounted for in terms which it cannot determine itself. Thus, deep inside autonomy hides a principle of heteronomy: not what we factually think to be or want to do is the norm, but rather what we actually are or do.

One might well feel uneasy about this whole argument. Imagine an agent who has to give an account of his identity in some ultimate sense. For instance, realising that he is male rather than female, he wonders what this entails, how he should respond to this or that sexual desire he experiences, whether he should have children, how long he is going to put up with the incompetence of his boss, and (in the end) what it takes 'to be a real man'. It would not help him very much if there were a ready-made concept of manhood (or of human nature) available, as he would still have to work out to what extent he should accept it as applying to *him*. All the same he will have to establish, on particular occasions, whether he is on the right track or not, whether he has achieved certain goals or not. Where and when there is reason to celebrate, how and when a new challenge presents itself – these are the kind of things that he has to determine about himself, both in his private and in his public life, without there being any pre-established truth he has to subscribe to. But if that is the case, we are back at self-determination: We are in fact saying that he conceives of himself as a being that has to (provisionally) determine his identity over and over again. To put this in a slightly different way: the content of self-awareness of such an agent is that he is a being that determines himself. So, we may conclude, there is no such thing as a principle of heteronomy hiding inside self-determination or autonomy. The ultimate self one is aware of refers back to self-determination. So it is self-determination after all that the legal order has to put up first.

Isn't this all abstract quibbling, far from any real legal debate? As a matter of fact, the two positions set out above are at the heart of many a far-reaching legal policy discussion. Obvious examples are parliamentary debates on euthanasia and abortion, eugenics and stem cell research, or classical freedom of speech in light of (vigorously expressed) offence taken by religious groups. Less obvious ones are those on social security, arms control, or exploitation of energy resources. Here I will only briefly review the most obvious examples.

- In countries where the legal acceptability of euthanasia is an issue, camps pro and con are often divided along the following lines.[4] The pro-camp argues for legal acceptability of euthanasia under certain conditions, taking into consideration that human dignity entails in some sense a right to self-determination. The con-camp, too, argues from human dignity, now understood as a person's relationship to his ultimate ground of existence, from which they infer that neither the beginning nor the end of life could be regarded as a matter of self-determination.[5] The gap between the two positions is one between two opposing interpretations of human dignity, commanding autonomy or heteronomy respectively.
- A major debate in public research policy is whether stem cell research should be funded as long as these cells have to be harvested from cells that form the initial stage of an embryo. In a long article Starck[6] has argued that harvesting these cells amounts

---

[4] Some 25 years ago, the Dutch report by the governmental committee on euthanasia – preparing Dutch legislation on euthanasia – was divided along these lines. For a more extensive analysis of the positions in the report, see my (1987), as well a slightly revised version in Chapter 3 of my (1997).

[5] The latter view is not necessarily one of religious denominations, let alone of a conservative stand. The controversy on autonomy as a guiding principle re euthanasia and assisted suicide emerged again in the famous decisions HR 21 June 1994, NJ 1994, 656 (*Chabot*) and HR 24 December 2002, NJ 2003, 167 (*Brongersma*) the Dutch High Court had to decide whether 'unbearable suffering without any prospect' could be merely psychic, or whether it could consist of the mere conviction of a person that his or her life was completed.

[6] C Starck (2006).

to a violation of Art. 1 Grundgesetz (Gg), declaring that human dignity is inviolable. As the *Bundesverfassungsgericht* in its *Solange*-decisions[7] has made ample reservations with regard to the supremacy of European law in the German Federal Republic when it comes to the level of human rights protection, the principle of loyal cooperation between the European Union and its Member States[8] brings with it that funding stem cell research should stop; or so Starck argues. He takes the view that lumps of cells capable of developing into a human being should be treated with equal respect whether they are inside or outside a uterus. Indeed, the reason why Art. 1 Gg is applicable is that they should be ascribed personhood or selfhood. His opponents defend the view that we are free to determine what we want to protect under the human dignity clause and what not. They say that we should use that autonomy to weigh the pros and cons of stem cell research, for instance with regard to therapy, cloning, etc., and that this is also a matter of respecting human dignity.

- In an intriguing book[9] Sandel has gathered several policy problems circling around the same issue: should we strive to create the perfect man? He targets the view that if we have the means to make the (more) perfect runner, singer, scientist, etc. we should feel free to use them. Pursuing these policies, this view says, is not that different from curing imperfections like contagious diseases, improving on feed and food, removing potentially dangerous genes and germs, or following our preferences in having a baby boy or girl. Sandel argues that we are not free to decide who we are, but that we are free to acknowledge who we are. He shows that if

---

[7] Cf. *Solange-Beschluss I* (1974 – BVerfGE 37, 271 ff.); *Solange-Beschluss II* (1986 – BverfGE 73, 339). In line with these decisions the overall attitude of the German Constitutional Court towards European law is characterised by some by the ominous 'solange' condition, cf. its 1993 decision re the Maastricht Treaty (BVerfGE 89, 155) and its 2009 decision re the Lisbon Treaty (BVerfGE 123, 267). Cf., respectively, R de Lange (1994) and J Ziller (2009).

[8] Now Art. 4.3 TEU.

[9] M Sandel (2009b).

autonomy is just a matter of setting and following preferences, our moral categories will boil down to good and bad luck. We would have to give up on such elementary distinctions as suffering and prospering, compassion and joy, guilt and innocence.[10]

- Though played in a different key, the debate on freedom of speech is another example of reversed charges in the autonomy–heteronomy gambit. In the Netherlands, Theo van Gogh was murdered, and Ayan Hirsi Ali threatened with murder, in 2004 by a fanatic Moslem man because of the film they made. As *Submission* criticised fundamentalist Islam attitudes towards women, and in particular the female body, by pictures that were meant to be shocking, some Moslem groups took it as an insult of the Koran. Though no one in the public debate following upon the murder was of the opinion that Mohammed B's deed was justified, there was (and still is) a clash between those who think that there is no limit to freedom of speech apart from 'clear and present danger' for public order, and those who think that one should not deliberately insult people in their religious belief. In other words, some people think that everyone should respect what counts as the paradigm of heteronomy, to wit religious belief, even if it is the belief of others; while other people think that everyone should exercise full autonomy in what one wishes to respect.

These examples show that we are talking real politico-legal controversies when we point to elements of both autonomy and heteronomy in the idea of self-awareness. The level of discussion may be a general one, but that in itself does not mean that it is 'abstract', in the popular senses of 'vague', 'far-fetched', 'irrelevant', or 'scholastic'. On the contrary, it is abstract in the wholly different sense of being pertinent to a number of contexts.

---

[10] See also M Sandel (2009a) 261: 'A just society can't be achieved simply by maximizing utility or by securing freedom of choice. To achieve a just society we have to reason together about the meaning of the good life, and to create a public culture hospitable to the disagreements that will inevitably arise.'

1.2 Self-determination and Malleability

Now, as I said at the beginning of the last subsection, one solution to the problem would present itself if self-awareness could be reduced to self-determination after all. Let us see what happens when we take self-determination as a principle of social organisation, politics and law. Although in the end we will have to concede that this would foreclose any understanding of law in society, we will learn a great deal about why law makes sense as we proceed.

Embarking on that road we should decide firstly not to stop at halfway houses. Once we have chosen to take self-determination of every individual human being as a principled point of departure, we should not appeal to countervailing principles harking back to grounds other than self-determination, in order to avoid radical consequences. We should not introduce at any point the legitimacy of a supreme power, a general harm principle, a golden rule of formal morality (don't do to others what you won't let others do to you) or an overriding duty of substantive morality (compassion with the poor or the weak). For if we would allow such principles to restrict the axiom of self-determination, we in fact subscribe to the former, not the latter. From the view that *I*, as every other being, have a right to self-determination it does not follow that another being has a right that *I* restrict my acts of self-determination. Of course, one may deny that *I* would have such a right. Then one has a different view about the ultimate basis of law. That is fair enough, but for the moment – and for the sake of the argument – we have chosen to depart from self-determination as offering such a basis.

The point of departure seems unpromising enough. It will be readily objected that self-determination of everyone will throw society into chaos, as it entails that everybody goes for the exercise of sheer *power*. The latter is true, but does the former come in its wake? It is true that the exercise of power is the core of self-determination in its pure form. Even without implying that self-determination in a political sense is the paradigm of self-determination in all possible senses (for instance, in interpersonal relationships), self-determination implies the primacy of the first person over and above any other person from the point of view of this first person himself. Regardless of whether an individual, or a political agent like 'the king', 'the people', 'the party', 'the company' or even 'mankind' is referred to,[11] the indexical terms *'I'* or *'we'* with regard to self-determination function to ascribe pole position to oneself over others when it comes to ranking interests and beliefs.

But does chaos follow from this? Is not the fear that it does aroused by too simple an idea of the mechanics of power? Thinking about power, our first inclination is to associate it with frenzy feelings of superiority, exhibitions of dumb force and whimsicality. But we should not confuse power with the arrogance or stupidity of some people in power, even if the latter annoy us most. There are even institutions to protect people in power from becoming over-arrogant. Kantorowicz reminds us of one in the Roman Empire:

> When, on the day of his triumph, the victorious Roman imperator rolled on the chariot drawn by four white horses from the Campus Martius to the Capitol – a living god clothed in the embroidered purple toga of Jupiter Capitolinus, in his hand the eagle sceptre of the god, and his face painted red with cinnabar – the slave riding with him on the chariot and holding the golden wreath over his head, whispered to him: 'Look behind thee. Remember thou art a man.'[12]

I submit that, indeed, power is restricted by laws, even if these are not laws in the normative sense, but rather the laws of power in the strategic sense. These laws describe, explain and predict the course of power phenomena in terms of causes and effects. They allow us to predict that the most probable general pattern, which these phenomena will exhibit, is one of well-tempered order rather than chaos. Why?

The mechanics of power seem to produce a kind of societal behaviour which, brought into a simple formula, boils down to this: every agent

---

[11] Daily experience teaches us that all of these 'persons' are 'I-' or 'we-users': the crown enacts a law in majestic first person plural, the people sing the anthem in its popular counterpart, the party closes the meeting (and the ranks) by the 'Wake up …' of the *Internazionale* – using the first person innuendo inherent to every command.

[12] EH Kantorowicz (1997 [1957]) 496.

capable of practical thinking[13] will improve on his position in the short or the long run, on the basis of well-understood self-interest: it is a default way to retain or regain some minimal degree of self-determination for the sake of self-preservation. Of course, no law or principle *forbids* them to reach for extra power as soon as emergent or benevolent circumstances incite them to do so. But the chances that they *will* are to be estimated less high, once we realise how agents in power conceive of themselves and how they work from this self-conception. The crucial point is that power cannot be conceived without the category of 'equilibrium' or balance, and that the exercise of power even has some in-built tendency towards equilibrium. This is what Machiavelli has taught us, and it made him the godfather of modern political theory.[14] It is also what Hobbes, a few decades later, acknowledged when he radically departed from the Aristotelian, teleological view of power and developed the outlines of a new political philosophy on the basis of a mechanical view.[15]

Power has little to do with arbitrariness. Arbitrariness is the enemy of the very thing an agent in power is up to: continuation of power. The fastest way to lose power is to exercise it in a whimsical, unpredictable and inconsistent manner. Both parents and politicians know that. They realise that they will lose control soon after they have started to treat their subjects, or their children, in arbitrary ways discarding similarities and differences. It is easier to see how and why, when we give up on thinking about power as some sort of substance, of which some have little, others much; some sort of matter which lingers around here in big, there in small heaps. Foucault has reminded us of a different picture; one that Nietzsche already tried to hammer home, and Machiavelli before

---

[13] To repeat, practical thinking in the sense of thinking what is to be done by some first person '*I*' or 'we'. On the relationship of first person singular and first person plural see below subsection 1.3.2.

[14] Note that all this balancing, for Machiavelli, counts as 'the art of war', even if it is not actually 'waging war'. Cf. Machiavelli (1513 [1961]) ch. XIV. Below I join the Machiavelli interpretation submitted by C Lefort (1972), in particular ch. IV, 2 (Sur la logique de la force). Cf. note 16.

[15] Although there are of course many differences between Machiavelli and Hobbes, one of which is that the position of the philosopher and the prince are much more distinct in Hobbes than they are in Machiavelli.

Nietzsche.[16] Why not see power as currency, like money is – something necessarily circulating if we see our lives as a permanent trade of properties counterbalancing each other for all sorts of contingent reasons (self-preservation, excitement, weakness, etc.), and, thus, also something that evaporates into thin air if we do not trade (anymore)? We may imagine that this currency of power is subject to inflation, revaluation, devaluation, and crisis. We may regard it as in constant flux, in which, at particular times and places, certain points are defined in function of its motion. One who 'has' power at one moment in time (e.g. a bishop in the Roman Catholic Church), may find himself 'powerless' at another moment, because the parameters of power have changed, sometimes even overnight. We can only grasp the core of such processes by seeing power primarily as the way in which agents in society map capacities and properties on to a form of equilibrium.[17] Without conceiving these capacities and properties in terms of equilibrium, typical strategies of power like disturbing, restoring, resisting, maintaining, mean nothing at all. They carry equilibrium with them as their interior accusative: what else could be disturbed, restored, resisted or maintained if not equilibrium? It is really all very much at hand: one is strong, another smart, a third cute and a fourth adorably helpless. None of these potential actors has any power in or of himself. Power is created only when any of them (or a fifth one) begins to compare and to weigh these properties. They are not comparable of themselves, they have to be named and defined in specific ways in order to become comparable. This is what we call a

---

[16] Instructive texts are M Foucault (1988). For Nietzsche cf. V Gerhardt (1983), to which text I will return below. For Machiavelli cf. C Lefort (1972) 355–356: 'La question: qu'est-ce que la puissance? n'importe donc pas. Ce que Machiavel donne à penser, en premier lieu, c'est seulement le conflit ou les conflits qui opposent des acteurs pourvus d'une puissance plus ou moins grande; ce qu'il juge *naturel ou ordinaire*, ce sont les relations qui s'établissent entre eux, du fait de leur puissance respective dans les conditions particulières où ils sont placés. De là vient que se posant comme pur observateur il se pose aussitôt comme pur calculateur et que son discours établit peu à peu une équivalence entre ce qui est, nécessaire et conforme à la raison.'

[17] For equilibrium as a basic term in analysing the tributariness of our legal order to bourgeois culture and the categories of power, see Broekman (1982 [1978]), especially ch. 10.

cultural process: a process that sets the standards for what balances what. Only in virtue of such a process can it be claimed (and tested) that men are *stronger than* women, that a smart woman *can beat* a strong man, that somebody is gorgeous, *but* stupid, etc.

Maintaining such comparability and manipulating the equilibrium successfully presuppose order, rules, neatness, circumspection and ratiocination, averages and normalities. To that extent and in that sense, the main law of power resembles the principle that is often regarded as the main principle of law: treat equal cases equally. The presupposition of that principle in the minds of all agents involved is that all are *relatively* equal in power.[18] Power can only function by tactically recognising its relativity.[19] Thus it becomes important to understand the different aspects of the key-words *relatively* and *relativity* in order to get hold of the complexity of power relationships and to see how this complexity can explain their tendency to produce a factual well-tempered equilibrium. The following law-like statements frame these aspects, paraphrasing the relative character of power in various ways.[20]

(1) Power only exists in *a relation between agents*. It does not primarily reside in any of them. It is only productive in as far as it circulates between them in claims, recognised, granted, or denied. There is always a minimum of reciprocity in the power relation between *X* and *Y*.

---

18 That is what Hobbes pointed out in *Leviathan*, ch. 12.

19 Cf. again concerning Machiavelli C Lefort (1972) 353: '(…) il ne suffit pas que celui qui s'est emparé du pouvoir domine ses adversaires par la violence; celle-ci risque de se retourner contre lui dans la mesure où elle exite leur résistance, sans lui permettre de trouver des appuis (…).' 'De l'analyse de la situation dans laquelle se trouve placé le prince nouveau au lendemain de la conquête, il ressort que son action a un double caractère: elle va dans le sens de la plus grande et dans le sens de la moindre violence.'

20 The following is derived (in part) from V Gerhardt (1983), who analyses Nietzsche's account of power in terms of equilibrium. Cf. F Nietzsche (1878 [1982]) *Menschliches, Allzumenschliches*, II, 2 para. 22. In the *Nachlass* [1879: 41 (42)] we read: 'Zur Beendigung des Kampfs ums Dasein entsteht die Gemeinschaft. Das Gleichgewicht, ihr Gesichtspunkt.' I also use Foucault's analyses, as referred to in note 16.

(2) Power-in-relations is *dependent on knowledge*. In order to exercise power it is necessary to estimate one's own and other's options and opportunities for action. In order to make such estimations one has to articulate and interpret them. In order to articulate and interpret them, one needs a framework of schemes and categories.

(3) The properties that are to be balanced against each other are always *quantitatively underdetermined*. One can neither make a full list of relevant properties, nor a perfect scheme of what balances what.

(4) Part of the exercise of power is, therefore, to *incessantly develop new points of view* for quantification, such that reasonings about an achieved or to achieve equilibrium are spread over a conceptual area as large as possible.

(5) All of the previous tasks are not to be performed from the standpoint of an external observer, but *from an internal standpoint*, i.e. the standpoint of the terms of the relation (the participating agents) themselves.

(6) The borderline between internal and external is not a static but *a dynamic one*; it can shift depending on whether the exchange between the terms is conceived of as one between different parts of a larger whole, between a part and the whole, between the whole (system) and its environment.

(7) Expressing or concealing such estimations is itself a *recursive* factor of power in the relationship.

(8) The equilibrium is perceived always as *instrumental* and therefore *provisional*. Its ultimate perspective is asymmetrical from the first-person point of view of each agent. It will not be sufficient for him to have his power recognised at a certain place and time, for what he is up to is recognition at a yet unknown 'next' place and time. The present situation will only interest him in as far as it contains the elements to preserve his dominant position over others in the future.

(9) However, all strategic changes can only be framed, calculated and carried out if the agents maintain a certain background order to

> which they refer as their *unalterable conceptual and factual framework*. Though it may change in point of fact, it cannot be the object of changing strategies. Otherwise, the very idea of strategy would lose its sense for the competing parties, as no equilibrium and, by the same token, no action would have any meaning at all for themselves.

Summarising the main points I am making here. (i) Power exists only in the relationship between first person agents, precisely in as far as they think of their properties and capacities in terms of equilibrium. (ii) Because they perceive such equilibrium from an internal perspective, which, moreover, is always instrumental and provisional, they will develop a certain amount of order or equilibrium as a framework of strategies.

On the basis of these two reasons I submit that, from a first-person viewpoint, 'absolute power' is an oxymoron.[21] Power is crucially dependent on denying absoluteness and on acting accordingly. If agents claim absolute power, this is because they believe that this will make them better off with regard to other claimants. So they conceive of it as relative. To exercise power means: to bear in mind one's limits along with the idiosyncrasies of what is other-than-oneself in the strong sense, i.e. what cannot be reduced to a function of the self. Everything that is different from the self from a first-person viewpoint (things and other people), i.e. everything that is not reducible to what the self says it is, is a risk factor for the self seeking to stay in power. If it is not taken into account, it may strike back. It is really an old wisdom: If human beings

---

[21] Of course, absolute power is not self-contradictory from an observer's viewpoint. If you take Weber's definition of power: the chance to pursue one's will against the wills of others, regardless of the grounds on which this chance may rest – absolute power may be taken as the limiting case in which this chance is 100%.

want to exercise control over 'nature' they will have to start by obeying its laws – laws to which one is always already subject.[22]

By this line of thought the operations of power are not so much based on actual war of all against all as they are on a sort of generalised economy of power for the sake of life. This permanent negotiation process is to be regarded, not as something, which a legal order has to superimpose on 'the state of nature', but rather as the very core of the latter, i.e., as a basic fact of human life at the most elementary level we are able to lay bare.[23] It suggests that these law-like facts of life will offer us for free what we meant to conquer by moral effort. But surely, the rudimentary moralist in us might protest, you admit that the exercise of power does not incite, by its in-built laws, the participants to give up their first-person perspective as an *a priori* legitimate one, and to recognise the perspective of others on a par with theirs? That is true, and I will come back to this. All I have argued was that power is predicated on a tactic, instrumental and provisional recognition, as part of any agent's long-term strategy to take or keep pole position in the struggle for power. I explicitly admitted that the asymmetrical perspective of *'I'* over others remains. If you want to reject that as half-way recognition, or even as deferred denial of the other's interests, that is all right. But then again it matters, not only how persistent the denial is, but also how long the deferral. Who would tell, in the end, the difference between infinitely deferred denial and principled recognition of the other's interests? A well-tempered order of society may come in the wake of such incessant deferral.

Is such an order indeed the upshot of universal self-determination? I doubt it. Perhaps there are too many memories of totalitarianism sanctioned by legal orders (its colonialist variants included), for us to put faith in the conclusion that absolute power is absolute nonsense, or that power

---

[22] Rousseau put it briefly: 'The strongest is never strong enough to remain the strongest, unless he transforms his force into law and obedience into duty.' (J-J Rousseau (1762 [1964]) I, 3.)

[23] In this view, the model of the social contract as proposed by Hobbes and Rousseau (himself) would boil down to a purely theoretical discourse by a philosophical observer, not containing any directive for (political) agents.

is exercised by recognising its relativity. But I have no reason to condemn it by moral judgment. For if this is the best account of power we can buy, morality has little to complain about. The role morality has to play would be far more convincing, if there were reasons to believe that the description of power given above has overlooked something as law-like in the mechanics of power as anything said up to now. Indeed, I suspect that there is such mechanism, and it is part and parcel of how *political* power in particular works.

1.3 The Social Imaginary of Political Power

Suppose it is true: without the internal perspective of equilibrium in social relationships, thinking in terms of power cannot exist. But is this internal perspective sufficient for the agents in the relation to exercise power *in a political way*? That is a pertinent question, because it was political power in particular that we were concerned with in investigating self-determination. The answer, I submit now, is: no. Although the same may be true in some cases for exercising other forms of power, e.g., economic or psychic power, it is true for all cases of exercising political power that the internal perspective has to yield to what is *for the agents* an external perspective in order for their acts to be effective. Shortly, we will look at the arguments for and the implications of this claim in greater detail. But let me first sketch some examples of what I have in mind.

1.3.1 Some examples

A rather illuminating exercise is to analyse the programmes of political parties in an election campaign. Here I generalise over what I found in analysing their rhetoric in my own country. First, they will typically refer to 'what society expects from politics', 'what our time needs most', or 'what the people in this country really want'. This is a common element in all programmes. It shows that political agents imagine themselves to operate not on their own account, but on behalf of some specific society, considered as a whole. But then the programmes diverge: each of them goes on to make specific reference to what this society, properly speaking, *is*, i.e. to what constitutes this specific society's identity. Religious parties will articulate this identity as a divine creation, and frame their own role by virtue of this identity, for instance, as 'stewardship'. Orthodox socialist parties will explain that this society is meant to be 'classless', liberated from exploitation, repression and discrimination of the poor: the realm of freedom, as Marx put it. They will ascribe to themselves the role of the vanguard in the struggle for freedom. Social democrats will be more modest: they will usually refer to the heritage of the social welfare state, which they promise to protect. Liberal parties – i.e. liberals in the economic sense, which in some civilised countries are called conservatives or republicans – tend to refer to some form of 'the invisible hand' (the mechanism of the market), which they want to give way to for the benefit of individual development and creative initiative. These different images of society, diverging as they may be, have something very peculiar in common. As one can see, they all go to great pains to locate the essence of society in some realm beyond actual society: a transcendent, invisible, utopian, past or future image which makes the actual society transparent to itself as something it 'really' is, only not yet, or not anymore.

A second set of examples may be found in the history of political ideas. During the absolutist periods of the *Ancien Régime,*[24] the king was not just an individual human being. He was also, and more importantly, a symbolic figure in which the nation could articulate itself as a delineated whole, as Kantorowicz has documented convincingly. Though mortal as a human being, he was immortal in this second quality, which was as corporeal a condition for existence of the state as the first. His power was believed to derive not from his own merit or force, but from God (*droit divin*). That is why the nation would accept him as its king in the first place.[25] That is also why he would believe that, as a mortal individual, he would be held to account for his reign and be judged, indeed trialled, after his death. The French Revolution is commonly said to have put an

[24] I use the term in a general sense, which is not restricted to France. It refers, roughly, to the period until 1800 in Western Europe.

[25] Cf. e.g., Kantorowicz (1997 [1957]) 218.

end to the *Ancien Régime*. But whatever it put an end to, it was not to the symbolic reference to a point beyond society, from where this society believes to derive its identity. Throughout the history of Modernity the notion of 'the people' – central to democracy – kept referring to something 'introuvable', as Rosanvallon put it:[26] there is no sociologically perceivable referent of the people as it is represented in political discourse.

For a third set of examples we may turn to the accounts of revolutionary movements as offered by political science. At the moment of this writing, in the course of 2011–12, we still have to wait and see what will come out of the revolutionary 'spring' in various (and varying) Arab countries like Tunisia, Egypt, Yemen, Libya and Syria.[27] But what we see in Egypt and Libya, in particular, is prototypical: The success of the revolution is accompanied by utter disorientation, because at the very moment the enemy is defeated, the political identity of the movement is put in jeopardy. Since they have derived their common identity mainly from the struggle against the repressor the revolutionary factions have framed divergent (and often vague) ideas about the political programme to be realised after the dictator has been ousted. Sometimes, the spearheads of the revolution find new enemies in their own midst: the revolution devours its own children, as it is said, as in the years following 1789 in France or those following 1917 in Russia. In the present Arab context, a radical interpretation of Islam in political terms (as Salafi movements advocate) gains popular support, not only because, for decades, it has been the only source of social relief for many in poverty-ridden regions, but also because, different from old military and young protesters, it provides a trans-social imaginary of society.[28]

---

[26] Cf. P Rosanvallon (1998) 18 and (concluding) 363n.

[27] As Marc Lynch writes on the Foreign Policy blog (June 13, 2012) 'There is widespread agreement that, as Jillian Schwedler puts it, "it's just too early to really make substantive headway of the sort that would allow us to either challenge or support existing theories of revolutions and regime change."' http://lynch.foreignpolicy.com/posts/2012/06/13/political_science_and_the_arab_uprisings, accessed November 4, 2012.

[28] Cf. M Lynch (2012).

1.3.2 From the first person singular to the first person plural

The first problem of any political enterprise, indeed of the political enterprise as such, is to present an image of society as related to this society *itself*, as present to *itself*, as recognising *its selfhood or identity*, that is: to become transparent to itself and to acknowledge *itself* as a limited whole that remains 'the same' over time.[29] Every agent – individual or group – who claims to play a political role or to perform a political act, has to relate this role or this act to what he considers to be 'the whole' of society. Of course such agents can focus on only one issue (e.g., the environment) or act for[30] the benefit of only one group (e.g., senior citizens). But then they have to argue that such issue or benefit would be key in serving the interest of society as a whole. To put this in another way: political agents have to presuppose that there is 'already' constituted some limited, definite and ordered '*we*' different from 'others'.[31] As a first person singular they have to picture society as a first person plural. They have to attribute an identity to this 'we', from which their own identity, programme and ideology as political agents are to be derived. Of course, an outsider may point out that this attribution is nothing short of sheer projection, wishful thought, or false belief. But then, what has this outsider to do with the politics of the society he is criticising? His very position as an outsider disqualifies him as a member of the society involved, and makes his criticism irrelevant, if not inimical. With regard to the internal 'we' of society he is 'the other', if not 'the foe'. Once he has himself become part of the 'we', he has to play the game.

The name of that game is social imaginary. Its basic rule is that no agent can afford to imagine the identity of the society he is referring to as

---

[29] This section is inspired by Claude Lefort's insights, in particular the chapter 'La permanence du théologico-politique' in C Lefort (1986). It also profits from an intriguing analysis by M Weyembergh (1988). See also B Flynn (2006), and Dallmayr's preface to this book.

[30] On the concept of representation as 'acting for' see HF Pitkin (1967).

[31] Cf. Lindahl's analysis of the Preamble of the (consecutive versions of) the TEU, where the contracting Member States of the European Union postulate a delineated 'Europe' preceding their constitutive act. (HK Lindahl (2003)).

something constituted from within that very same society. For any place 'within' society is a private place in the eyes of other agents: a place from where certain private interests and positions are defended. It is therefore suspect. Any claim of articulating the whole of society or the general interest of society which is reducible to such a place, disqualifies itself as a political claim. The agent putting forward such a claim would not qualify as a political agent at all in the eyes of other agents, indeed, not even in his own eyes. Since any place within society is, by definition, a particular place from which no member can identify the whole of society in a credible way, the only other way to acquire credibility for such identification is to make reference to some point connected to, but outside society. Regis Debray[32] has even submitted that this is the political counterpart of Gödel's theorem in logic: no system can exist without closure, but also no system can close itself from the inside, i.e. by the mere use of the elements of the system.[33] Society as a whole presupposes society with a hole: the 'trou fondateur' (Debray) by which it can escape into what it regards to be the trans-social realm. Horizontal closure is dependent on opening up to a vertical dimension. These two dimensions can only be reconciled by having a substitute of the vertical, transcendent reality present in the horizontal, social reality. By calling it 'a place' Lefort emphasises that this symbolic 'beyond -' is a variable. It can take on a variety of values for concrete staging, as long as these are values of this place, i.e. of this basic exteriority of political power with respect to the society it claims to manage.[34]

This is not to say that, from any point of view, political thinking requires theistic religious belief. It is to say that, from its own point of view, political thinking must acknowledge a trans-social source of power

---

32 R Debray (1981) 261ff. The same notion draws central stage in R Debray (2009).

33 JP Van Bendeghem (2004) has forcefully argued that this is utter non-sense as far as Gödel is concerned and I am quite prepared to believe him. It does not, however, affect the drift of the argument made here.

34 C Lefort (1986) 265: 'Le pouvoir, avant même qu'on l'examine dans ses déterminations empiriques, s'avère ce pôle symbolique; il manifeste une extériorité de la société à elle-même, lui assure une quasi-réflexion sur elle-même.'

in order to establish the social. Indeed, as an empirical matter of fact, many peoples of the world pay tribute to this general thesis by referring to their 'creator' in their anthems and in their foundational history. But in the context of this section the relevant fact is that even in a politically secular age, this creator is created by the social group in order to enable the group to enter into a relationship with itself. So in this sense, creating this vertical dimension is dependent, in turn, upon the horizontal joint action consisting of shared representation. At the same time, however, the group will renounce or disclaim that it is, itself, the creator of its creator and profess the belief in a trans-social reality.[35] It will act *as if* beyond society there is something authoritative, where power originates, on behalf of which political agents operate. This special symbolic scenery is a condition of political action as long as it imagines itself as ordering society *tout court* (rather than *a* society).

Under the secular conditions of Modernity such a logic of political representation becomes highly ambiguous. Lefort stresses that there are two fundamentally different ways of coping with it on the political level itself.[36] The first one is to hypostatise the symbol at the heart of this staged exteriority. That is to say, to give it a concrete, ontic prefiguration, and to attribute the origin of power to some real person or instance, which is believed to be the incarnation of the transcendent world in the immanent world the agents live in, i.e., the social world.[37] It may go by various names, such as 'the chosen', 'the party', 'the *Führer*', 'the avant-garde', etc. It presents the agent in charge as the representative, indeed the embodiment, of the very selfhood of society as an actual unity, of which 'ordinary' people would have no idea if they could not actually point to such a concrete figure. Thus it creates a divide within the immanent social realm between the partisans who know about the proper self of society and the masses who do not; or between those who,

---

[35] Cf. A Van de Putte (1987) 408.

[36] Cf. C Lefort (1981; 1986) 21; 269.

[37] Lefort explains that this is not what happens in 16th–17th century absolutism: the power of the prince is regarded as deriving not from the person himself, but from God (*droit divin*), to whom the prince would be (and in many cases indeed *feel*) responsible.

by virtue of such knowledge, are destined to command and those who, by lack of such knowledge, are destined to obey. This is the hallmark of totalitarianism, as Hannah Arendt also observes.[38]

Going against the grain of political power, the second way to cope with the postulate of a trans-social 'beyond' is to retain its symbolic character. The faint awareness that such point is not legitimated by the sole fact that it is postulated, may be remembered, cultivated, and even given institutional form. This is what a democracy tries to capture. It is, for instance, the essence of general and periodical elections.[39] At regular intervals in time, the general interest is calibrated against a count of individual votes based on a completely opaque, perhaps even absent, relation to the common wealth. Moreover, whatever the past performance of the elected, at the end of their term they return to the ranks of the electorate. Such institutions lend form and substance to the idea that in a democracy 'the place of power is empty', as Lefort puts it.[40] This is not to say that it is vacant, nor that it is non-existent. The first would trigger an ever so

---

[38] H Arendt (1973 [1951]), part III; cf. the motto on p. 303 ('Normal men do not know that everything is possible') and the analysis on p. 324.

[39] C Lefort (1986) 28–29: 'Rien, en outre, ne rend mieux sensible le paradoxe de la démocratie que l'institution du suffrage universel. C'est précisément au moment où la souveraineté populaire est censée se manifester, le peuple s'actualiser en exprimant sa volonté, que les solidarités sont défaites, que le citoyen se voit extrait de tous les réseaux dans lesquels se développe la vie sociale pour être converti en unité de compte. Le nombre se substitue à la substance.'

[40] 'Incorporé dans le prince, le pouvoir donnait corps à la société. Et, de ce fait, il y avait un savoir latent, mais efficace, de ce qu'était l'*un* pour l'*autre*, dans tout l'étendue du social. En regard de ce modèle, se désigne le trait révolutionnaire et sans précédent de la démocratie. Le lieu du pouvoir devient un *lieu vide*.' (Lefort (1986) 27) Again: 'Voilà qui montre bien en quoi il [i.e. le lieu du pouvoir sous la dictature de Staline; BvR] se distingue du pouvoir tel qu'il se définit dans les sociétés démocratiques. Là il s'avère déjà social en ce sens que l'origine de la souveraineté est placée dans le peuple; mais la manifestation de cette souveraineté est rigoureusement soumise à des procédures fixées par le droit. (…) La même raison fait que le pouvoir est en droit borné et qu'il ne peut se confondre avec la puissance de ceux que l'exercent; et la même raison fait encore qu'il n'y a pas de peuple en acte, en dehors de l'opération réglée du suffrage et qu'il n'y pas de pouvoir susceptible de l'incarner. Le lieu du pouvoir se trouve ainsi tacitement reconnu comme un lieu vide, par définition inoccupable, un lieu symbolique, non un lieu réel. (Lefort (1981) 125–126; cf. Lefort

vehement struggle between competing parties to occupy the place,[41] the latter would scatter them over ever so many factions,[42] i.e. private interests they can hold on to, because there is no point in making compromises. In either case decision-making potential in the group is lost. The parliamentary impotence in the Weimar Republic has clearly demonstrated what happens when a democratic forum conceives of itself as a place for perennial discussion. Soon enough the call for a strong agent who is able to represent society's 'better self' will sound and democracy will be tempted to yield to totalitarian reflexes.[43] Compared to the latter, democracy is the more artificial, and therefore the more demanding and costlier form of organising political power. Ignoring the symbolic character of exteriority is its default inclination by virtue of a simple political logic: representing the whole is equated with representing actual unity and representing actual unity is equated with representation by one – the One.[44]

I promised to investigate the mechanisms of power. Admitting that they revolve around the concept of equilibrium, and that they may even tend to lead to well-tempered order in society, I surmised that we may have overlooked some mechanism characteristic of political power. I now submit that we have found it. And, indeed, it casts serious doubt upon our initial hypothesis on generalised self-determination. We tried the hypothesis that, although power entails a mere tactical recognition of others by the first-person agent and, thus, a final denial of the former's interests by the latter, this final denial would never come about as it would be involved in infinite deferment. But things look very different indeed if we include the representational imaginary of political power in our picture. Let me concede that, 'absolute power' is oxymoronic, as

---

(1986) 265ff.)
On the problem of translating 'vide', cf. (B van Roermund 2009).

41 As Freud reminds us of in S Freud (1912–1913).

42 Cf. on the perils of factions *The Federalist Papers*, No. 10, in A Hamilton, J Madison et al. (1999 [1787–1788]), and in a similar vein J-J Rousseau (1762 [1964]) II, 3; IV, 1.

43 Cf. P Van Haute (1992b).

44 Cf. C Lefort (1976).

power (i) is a reciprocal relationship between agents, and (ii) is dependent on knowledge-claims in permanent shift. But we have discovered that political power has to 'stage' a knowledge-claim of its own with regard to its very source, to wit that the latter is to be found in a realm that transcends the society that is to be ordered in total. Political agents can fight about the properties of this source, but they cannot refrain from referring to one. Implicit in their intentions to order society as a whole is the claim that they are able to refer to a point from where this whole is identifiable precisely *as* a whole.[45] Thus they are under the permanent temptation to immunise their favourite source against alternative options. They are tempted to do so by pointing to some concrete incarnation of the exterior source that defines the society they pretend to order as an actual (rather than a virtual) unity. They want to believe that society ascribes the place of power to and derives its identity from a Leader, a Party, or an Avant-garde, whom you can see, touch, join, and follow. This incarnation, on the one hand, represents the one and only essence of 'the people' while, on the other, it places itself over and above any of its members, thus '(…) finding in his "*I*" the law of all things and all knowledge, and acknowledging nothing but his own self.'[46] This is, says Lefort, the core of totalitarianism.[47] It is a discourse of self-determination squared: individual self-determination collapses into the self-determination of only one agent, who makes self-determination present for the whole of society to see, rather than representing how it could guide the individual members in living social relationships.

---

45 Hence I disagree to some extent with H Arendt (2003 [1993]) 9: 'Politik beruht auf der Tatsache der Pluralität der Menschen.' To capture plurality politically, reference to the whole wherein plurality is a fact, seems inevitable.

46 A Van de Putte (1987) 425, explaining Lefort.

47 Cf., for instance, 'Plus précisément, la représentation – qu'il faut bien nommer fantasmatique – d'une société rapportée à elle-même dans toutes ses parties, délivrée de l'opacité qui tenait à la division des intérêts et des passions, mobilisée par la tâche de son auto-édification et dans le but d'éliminer tous ceux qui conspirent contra le pouvoir du peuple, cette représentation n'implique-t-elle pas la position de quelqu'un détaché de tous, tout agissant, tout voyant, omniscient, grâce à qui se nomme le peuple-Un. (C Lefort (2007) 878.)

If power cannot be absolute, political power can certainly be totalitarian. Totalitarian power is not absolute. It does not claim that it can do anything in society; it claims that it represents society in the flesh. In the secular age we live in, totalitarianism is a permanent fascination of political power at large. It is simply an attractive way to get rid of the imaginary and provisional character of political discourse in an era when the faith in a 'real' transcendent world has disappeared. Totalitarianism gives in to the law of gravity of political power, while democracy is the sustained effort to escape from it.

1.4 The Lures of Self-determination

At the beginning of this section, I asked if self-determination, rather than self-preservation, could be an anchor point to understand what is reasonable about law. For self-preservation, conceived of as the pursuit of satisfying one's vital needs over time, presupposes self-determination. No one in such pursuit, I said, should let another agent determine his needs, and the ways they are to be satisfied, as long as he maintains an interest in the quality of such satisfaction. And although I added that both self-preservation and self-determination presuppose a conception of the self by the first person (self-awareness), I yielded to the objection that this is perhaps mere conceptual humbug, as human self-awareness might boil down to the awareness to be a being that quintessentially determines itself. So self-determination became our point of departure, as we promised not to stop at halfway houses for the sake of moral concerns.

Quite apart from moral concerns with totalitarianism, at least two salient difficulties regarding self-determination as a basis for politico-legal order are to be noted. Firstly, totalitarianism seems to be the political reflex of a social order that celebrates self-determination as the ultimate principle in social relationships. Am I now mounting the thesis that liberalism leads to totalitarianism? Not at all. No liberal in her or his right mind will defend individual freedom in the sense of radical autonomy; they will always invoke principles deriving from socially shared freedom, such as the principle of equality in freedom or the harm principle. This, however, points us to the question where in our account of the social relation between *I* and other(s) one may find a stronghold to resist the inherent logic of political discourse? Is an alternative account possible, one that does not celebrate but liberates our capacities for self-determination by disclosing how they contribute to an order that makes sense to us? Secondly, self-determination as a principle by which we may understand what sense law makes fails at a basic test of reasonableness on two accounts. The first is a negative account: nothing is reasonable that, in advance, sets its own criteria of reasonableness. A more positive, though perhaps less incisive, account would amount to the general idea that reasonable is any first person who lets something count against themselves, even if they are not forced to do so by a second or third person.[48] This is, for instance, what scientists do when they try to falsify a hypothesis, or, for that matter, what hikers do if they want to check the path they follow against the map. The totalitarian agent, however, '(…) finding in his "*I*" the law of all things and all knowledge, and acknowledging nothing but his own self',[49] believes he can afford to let nothing count against him. Thus, he cannot qualify as reasonable. Now, to the extent that radicalised self-determination gives rise to the concept of such an agent, it would be unreasonable and provide no anchor point whatsoever for understanding the reasonableness of the legal order. It does not explain why law makes sense, which is the purpose of this chapter.

This, of course, is neither to say that law has nothing to do with self-determination, nor that the balance of powers which it may bring about is irrelevant to the concept of law. Both are extremely important and relevant, as we will see later on in this and other chapters. All we have established now is that unqualified self-determination is a tricky foundation for erecting the conceptual building of law. This does not exclude that a more adequate conception of self-determination can play a

---

48 This is a slightly altered version of Gadamer's definition of 'openness' in H-G Gadamer (1975 [1960]) 343, which I will return to in section 4.2. Indeed I will hold that justice is nothing more than 'politics opening up towards what counts against its closure'.

49 Cf. subsection 1.3.

prominent role in it. To find that more adequate conception, we have to return to the beginning of this chapter, when I proposed a short cut to avoid the rather solemn notion of self-awareness. We cannot evade it anymore. In fact, we have come already within its range, as we detected that politics is dependent on a society staging the framework of its self-awareness as a common, though trans-social point of reference for all its members. Here again, however, we first have to remove the lures of totalitarianism.

2. SELF-AWARENESS AS RESPECT FOR HUMAN DIGNITY: THE TOTALITARIAN ACCOUNT

At the beginning of this chapter, I mentioned a second pitfall, more treacherous than the compatibility or incompatibility of self-determination and self-awareness. In order to be reliable, self-awareness entails, in any case: taking 'the other' into account; i.e., acknowledging a perspective that cannot be reduced to the perspective of the first person agent. Such phrases are highly ambivalent at the inter-personal level. An agent can easily refrain from immediate reduction of the other to his perspective while attempting to assure his grip in the long run. For him, i.e., from the angle of his pursuit of power, this would just be an exercise in patience or resilience. He would not have to give up, on the final count of things, his perspective in which the whole of reality, social reality included, is subordinated to him as a first person. Taking Machiavelli's advice he would just hold back for a while and instrumentalise his self-constraint for the sake of his long-term targets. This attitude would be crucially different from one by which the agent allows the perspective of the other to count against him. If we want to disentangle this ambiguity philosophically, we have to show that self-awareness entails not just recognising 'the other' as irreducibly *different* from oneself, but rather recognising the *normativity* of such a difference. We may call the latter 'principled recognition' in contradistinction to the former, which may be called 'strategic recognition'. In the end I will conclude that anything short of principled recognition amounts to a form of totalitarianism and injustice.

2.1 Recognition of the Other at False Bay

It may seem that a first person agent can bring objectivity to his self-ascriptions by acknowledging, albeit implicitly, that both he and the other are of the same kind, that they share a set of predicates that neither of them can monopolise, for instance (being a) 'human being'. If I believe (a) that I am tall for a human being, and (b) that you are a human being, and if you admit to me that I am tall, I have good reason to believe that I am tall for a human being. I would have less reason to believe so if I believed that you were a giant. Let us call it the strategy of the common denominator.

To see it in greater detail we may take our cue from Rousseau's story on the origin of language[50] – a story which is remarkably parallel to the one he tells in another discourse[51] on the origin of society.

> A primitive man, on meeting other men, will first have experienced fright. His fear will make him see these men as larger and stronger than himself: he will give them the name of *giants*. After many experiences, he will discover that the supposed giants are neither larger nor stronger than himself, and that their stature did not correspond to the idea that he had originally linked to the word giant. He will then invent another name common for them and himself such as, for example, the word *man* and will retain the word giant for the false object that impressed him while he was being deluded.[52]

The strategy appears to be a two-pronged one. The first is the introduction of the human vs. non-human dichotomy as the paradigm of the

---

[50] *Essai sur l'origine des langues*. The basis of my argument in the next paragraphs is P De Man (1979) ch. 7, although my interpretation departs from his at some points. I read Rousseau's text in the Pléiade edition (J-J Rousseau (1753 [1995]) and used De Man's translation.

[51] The *Discourse on the Origin and the Foundations of Inequality Among Men* (J-J Rousseau (1754 [1964])

[52] J-J Rousseau (1753 [1995]) ch. 3, 381.

self–other distinction, preceding any conceptualisation. The story suggests that, for any first person, seeing some other as *different* from him makes him think of this other person as non-human, and the non-human as a virtual threat prior to any threatening experience. There is simply no reason why the first-person agent should be afraid of her and express this fear by calling her a giant; for, as Rousseau points out elsewhere in his essay, the primitive man does not conceive of quantities yet. For him, the properties of size and strength do not in any sense refer to an objectified world that counts against him; they are, instead, projections of his own *a priori* fear and distrust. The name 'giant' just summarises the reactions of a first-person agent to his encounter with a segment of reality. In order to have this reaction of distrust, however, the agent must already maintain a specific topology. He must think that whatever the giant's behaviour looks like *superficially*, this other being is *basically* a threat. Or he must think that behind all the *outer* properties there is an *inner* property ('animosity') lurking in the *back*ground, which threatens him regardless of what he hears or sees in the *fore*ground. The agent can always uphold this presupposition of an ever-imminent danger, for no matter what the other agent, the alleged giant, does, it may always be regarded as either a sign of this inner property or a disguise of it – and, thus, a sign after all. Hence there is no necessity for that agent to call other people 'not-giants' or 'not-enemies'.[53] But this is only the first half of the story.

The second strategy consists of replacing the qualitative distinctions sustaining the friend–enemy scheme by quantitative criteria. Fear can be withdrawn and domesticated when, 'after many experiences', the first-person agent develops a criterion from *his* perspective for what counts as 'large' and 'strong' in relation to these entities. This enables him to measure the supposed giants by *his* standard or rule, and claim that by virtue of *his* standard they are *relatively equal*. Thus, what Rousseau's story on the origin of language shows is that a predicate like 'man',

---

[53] Notwithstanding Rousseau's critique of Hobbes in *The Social Contract*, this description of the origin of language is very similar to Hobbes' description of 'the state of nature', where human agents are a virtual rather than an actual threat to one another.

rather than being objective between agents, is the product of a sequence of transformations commanded by a first-person viewpoint *I*.

Once these transformations are completed, i.e., once *I* have succeeded in reducing others to positions in the world as defined by *me*, *I* can safely engage in bargaining a contract.[54] To become social, by this conceptual model, *I* firstly have to establish that no one is different from *me* in any *radical* sense. Having established this, *I* can go on to recognise any of the others as another 'I-sayer' without much of a risk. But of course, this does not at all imply that *I* have given up my attitude towards the other as a virtual threat on the basis of nothing else than first-person impressions. Well, on the contrary; why would *I* care whether the other is different or not, unless from the suspicion that she may well constitute a threat? Only then *I* can proceed to falsify this bias and find out that the risk is limited. As a result *I* can handle my fear, suppress my distrust, and transform these into social energy without losing the idea of a possible attack from his side. Ascribing 'human dignity' to an entity is therefore not *in itself* contradictory with remaining in control over what counts as human and what not. Indeed, attributing this predicate is compatible with, may even be a form of, treating this entity in the last resort in terms of power. Whether this ascription pertains to basic properties, including human rights, or to an inner essence does not matter in this respect. It boils down to a preference for one ontological fetish over another.

So, by calling someone 'man', 'human' or 'fellow human being', indeed by ascribing to her human dignity according to a common denominator set from his first-person viewpoint, an agent does not imply that this other agent is acknowledged in *her* existence as irreducibly different from him. By bringing her on a par with 'him' without taking any earlier history into account (e.g., by reassuring her that 'we're all human beings…') he has deprived her of her alterity. Henceforth he is in power to return it to her on his terms. He can do so without fear since, if need be, he will always be master in deciding to retreat to the prior scheme of human and non-human. In the final analysis, calling someone

---

[54] Cf. J-F Lyotard (1981) 29ff.

'human like us' may be a way of regarding her as either supra-human or infra-human, angel or demon. This is precisely what women criticise when men claim that gender should not be an issue since 'we are all humans'.

2.2 Law after Auschwitz

Contemporary philosophy[55] has raised this very problem of a prematurely claimed common denominator in a much more radical way, namely in the face of 'Auschwitz' as the apex of totalitarianism. Is, after Auschwitz, an unsuspected 'we, humans' possible as an *a priori* of society, culture, and law? Can this common ground be postulated, after Auschwitz, as a point of departure or articulated as a basic experience? What the proper name 'Auschwitz' refers to – if it is a proper name at all, adds Lyotard[56] – has poisoned the concept of 'living together' by unpaired cynicism. It has transformed political order into a legally sanctioned division between those who ought to live and those who ought to die. It has shown that it is possible to address people as 'humans', only to condemn them to death as 'sub-humans'. Even those who survived 'Auschwitz'[57] have experienced themselves as being excluded from mankind. This is, to be sure,

---

[55] Notably Adorno in *Negative Dialektik* (1966); see in the third edition (1982) the first of the *Meditationen zur Metaphysik* with the famous title 'Nach Auschwitz' (pp. 354ff.). Lyotard's essay is, in fact, an extensive commentary on Adorno (T Adorno (1982 [1966]) 354ff). (Nach Auschwitz), rejecting Hegel's conception of dialectical philosophy. In a similar vein J Derrida (1972) 144: 'Ce qui est aujourd'hui difficile à penser, c'est une fin de l'homme qui ne soit organisée par une dialectique de la vérité et de la négativeté, une fin de l'homme qui ne soit pas une téléologie à la première personne pluriel.'

[56] Much more than a proper name for a camp (let alone a village), 'Auschwitz' has become the referring device for the complex of extermination that consists of crematoria, gas chambers, camps, railways, planning, management, commanders, secretaries, propaganda, fellow-travellers, etc., that together (but not necessarily jointly) acted in the belief that their political power was totally right, even where it failed to be absolutely powerful.

[57] 'What is at issue here is not, of course, the difficulty we face whenever we try to communicate our most intimate experiences to others. The discrepancy in question concerns the very structure of testimony. On the one hand, what happened in the camps appears to the survivors as the only true thing and, as

not an intellectual conceptualisation of Auschwitz; it is what we can hear by listening to those who narrate their memories, as in Claude Lanzmann's film *Shoah*. They report about the experience of sheer alienation felt every day since they got out of the camp, the experience of being *alone* in this world. This is not the experience of someone who does not trust anybody anymore. It is, rather, that of someone who does not see or sense anybody anymore, as any basis of living together has lost its conceivability to an infinite shame.[58]

The cynicism of 'Auschwitz' is indeed beyond comprehension. To get a sense of only its most superficial forms it is necessary to realise that the holocaust was staged neither as an act of war, nor even as a process of political technology, but as a matter of justice done in the name of human dignity. Entering the camp was getting access to justice. If on your way to Weimar you decide to visit nearby Buchenwald, you will see it: enter the camp and turn around to the entrance. There it is: 'Jedem das Seine' – 'to everyone his due'. Both the victims and the survivors were subjected to the cynical lie of a norm which first addressed them as legal subjects – only to then tell them that they *ought* to die.[59] Obeying the

---

such, absolutely unforgettable; on the other hand, this truth is to the same degree unimaginable, that is, irreducible to the real elements that constitute it. Facts so real that, by comparison, nothing is truer; a reality that necessarily exceeds its factual elements – such is the aporia of Auschwitz.' G Agamben (2002 [1999]) 12. Surely survivors have lived in more places than the camps of Nazi Germany, like the Gulag or South Africa.

[58] Deepening an analysis by Levinas, Agamben (G Agamben (2002 [1999]) 105) writes: 'To be ashamed means to be consigned to something that cannot be assumed. But what cannot be assumed is not something external. Rather, it originates in our own intimacy; it is what is most intimate in us (for example, our own physiological life). Here the "I" is thus overcome by its own passivity, its own sensibility; yet this expropriation and desubjectification is also an extreme and irreducible presence of the "I" to itself. It is as if our consciousness collapsed and, seeking to flee in all directions, were simultaneously summoned by an irrefutable order to be present at its own defacement, at the expropriation of what is most its own.'

[59] Lyotard observes that the content of the norm addressed to the Jews was: to die. Not to die as a choice from alternatives or an inescapable fate, but as the consequent of a legal antecedent, namely their Jewishness. It was not: 'to die, rather than to escape' – the choice Socrates made. Nor was it: 'to die, rather than to surrender' – like a general would command to his soldiers in war. It was: to

norm would be recognising that they had to die, much as they did not consent to it. For it is conceptually implicit in the enactment of a norm, that the norm-giver commits himself to a common denominator (or 'nature') between himself and his addressees. The Nazis used this bond of a common denominator to betray it, i.e. to convey the inferior nature of the Jews as a legal fact, which could have only one legal consequence: the *Endlösung*. The minutes of the Wannsee conference[60] reflect that, indeed, this final solution was discussed as an issue of law enforcement. Both antecedent and consequent of this duty were embedded in the presupposition of its enactment: a common concern of the authorities and their victims to obey the norm in the name of human dignity. The victims of Nazism were invited to confirm the validity of this norm and, thus, of their own death, by virtue of the alleged fact that they were a disgrace to human dignity by their very existence.

Since Auschwitz, any phrase containing 'human dignity' carries the burden of proof that it does not disseminate such cynicism, in order to be acceptable in giving an account of a legal order. This pertains, in particular, to those political positions that identify the legal order with some common good or public interest.[61] If law is tantamount to the public interest of a polity, there is no reason why its members would be interested in those who do not yet belong to it. They will simply not

---

die as a legal duty, as a normative consequent unfolding the legal meaning of an antecedent fact. That fact was the allegedly sub-human nature of each and every Jew. Cf. J-F Lyotard (1981) 293 ff.

[60] The 'Final solution' was conceived as a follow-up on the failed 'accelerated expulsion' policy of the Nazis, which formally expressed aim was 'to cleanse German living space of Jews in a legal manner.' (Cf. Protokoll der Wannsee-Konferenz von 20. Januar 1942, under II: 'Das Aufgabenziel war, auf legale Weise den deutschen Lebensraum von Juden zu säubern.').

[61] Bearing in mind Arendt's warning in H Arendt (1973 [1951]) 299: 'And this predicament is by no means solved if the unit to which the 'good for' applies is as large as mankind itself. For it is quite conceivable, and even within the realm of practical possibilities, that one fine day a highly organized and mechanized humanity will conclude quite democratically – namely by majority decision – that for humanity as a whole it would be better to liquidate certain parts thereof.'

register as 'human'.[62] It should not come as a surprise that so-called 'populist' versions of these positions reject immigration, multiculturalism, regional or global solidarity, or even monetary integration. But the burden of proof applies also to arguments which naively circle around popular terms like 'self-realisation' or 'self-development of the human person', this '(…) fundamental principle of bourgeois subjectivity without which Auschwitz would not have been possible.'[63] This is, first and foremost, a burden for political practice.[64] But no less is it a burden for political and legal philosophy, in as far as philosophy has to explore the conceptual directions in which this burden of proof may be carried. For at the very least we have to admit that acknowledging the dignity of another being as human, does not involve, by the same token, acknowledging the normativity of another being as different. To ascribe the predicate 'human' to another being can be a subtle way to deprive her of her alterity, to reduce her to what is already confirmed as, made akin to, or appropriated by the first-person agent: *his* concept of a person, *his* social contract, *his* culture, *his* world.

3. THE FIRST PERSON: CAPTOR AND CAPTIVE

Let me briefly recapture the line of thought so far. I took my cue from the belief that law is there to warrant self-preservation. Crucially I framed this point of departure as a concern of a first-person agent. Then I argued that, for such an agent, self-preservation can only be warranted if it is tied up with self-determination. Others will prefer the term 'autonomy', but I propose to stick to the slightly tedious term as it brings out what is at stake in both self-preservation and self-determination, which is the very idea of the self. I posed the question: What warrants the

---

62 Cf. HK Lindahl (2006).

63 '(…) [dieses] Grundprinzip der bürgerlichen Subjektivität, ohne das Auschwitz nicht möglich gewesen wäre: drastische Schuld des Verschonten.' (T Adorno (1982 [1966]) 356).

64 And so we may observe that the Charter of Fundamental Rights of the European Union does copy Art. 1.1 Gg (Würde des Menschen) from the Federal Republic's Constitution, but not Art. 2.1 (freie Entfaltung der Persönlichkeit).

reliability of an agent's self-awareness or selfhood? The answer was: the extent to which he can take into account a perspective that is not reducible to his first-person vantage point. Now our new question is: how can an agent acknowledge the normativity of the other, without landing at the false bay of a common denominator he has already appropriated? In the next sections I will argue that two radically different modes present themselves. Neither of these is viable in its own right, as it is always vulnerable to challenges by the other mode (as we will see). I will try to forge an opportunity out of this predicament, arguing that what we are looking for is precisely the opposition, indeed the contrariness, between the two. The mutual critique of the two modes will enable us to define justice and – what is more – to understand what law is about in the end. Accepting both principles is like appreciating that it takes two legs to walk: we can make progress by moving one provided that we rest on the other, but then we have to move the second and rest on the first. This iterative alternation will be the key to alterity.[65]

---

[65] I can only draw a few lines here in a wide-ranging debate that revisits some important issues in phenomenology, prematurely left behind about half a century ago and recently revitalised simultaneously from various corners. Inevitably I will have to abbreviate and simplify the discussion. Important protagonists were Heidegger, Jaspers, Marcel, Arendt, Sartre, Merleau-Ponty. Though the debate in fact never stopped, it was pushed aside by the rise of various strands of 'structuralism', 'analytical' philosophy, and 'critical theory'. Charles Taylor definitely renewed it in the Anglo-American world, while Dieter Henrich and Bernhard Waldenfels, for instance, remained faithful to it in the German context. It is interesting to see Habermas, towards the end of J Habermas (1992 [1992]), referring to Claude Lefort (a student of Merleau-Ponty's); to see Derrida continue his reading of Heidegger in J Derrida (2009) (12th session, for instance) whom he (nor Lyotard or Nancy) never left behind; to see Merleau-Ponty reappearing in current philosophy of mind (cf. S Gallagher (1995); M Rowlands (2010)). Those interested in a much more in-depth discussion of the relevant texts I refer to the important works of my Leuven colleague Rudi Visker to whom I owe much (Visker (1999); Visker (2004); Visker (2005)). Cf. also my reviews (Van Roermund (2001a); Van Roermund (2007)).

3.1 The First Person as the Ultimate Captor

What is law about if we take into account the understanding human agents have of *themselves* as part of the world they live in; the social world in particular? This understanding of human existence is at pains to avoid the kind of naturalism[66] that we encountered in the previous chapter. We cannot understand human existence as 'just a fact'. On the contrary, each and every fact presupposes an agent as fact-establishing. For instance, it is a fact that the earth is round. Neither the earth nor being round are facts. Particulars (like entities or events) and predicates are not facts in themselves. They become building blocks of facts by taking two steps: (a) Inserting a linking pin between a particular and a predicate; (b) warranting the link in view of truth as a preferred value. This is called thinking, and facts amount to the products of truthful thought, e.g., that the earth is round.[67] It will be readily admitted that establishing a fact is dependent on a framework of beliefs that we regard as already established, as well as on certain aims that humans pursue. For instance, although most Dutch and West-Flemish people believe that their country is part of the surface of the earth, as well as that the earth is round, they also believe (without contradiction) that their country is flat, and act accordingly on a daily basis. Moreover, both their belief that the earth is round, and their belief that theirs is a flat country, emerge from experience. To a large extent this experience (in particular the daily experience of one's country being flat) is entrenched in an agent's body prior to being raised to the level of conscious thought. Gradually tuning into my flat country, I-as-body discovers what it takes to run ten miles

[66] For a similar critique of naturalism (defined along similar lines, though in different wording) cf. C Taylor (1989) 30ff.

[67] This is surely not a combination of two facts. It may make sense to say that the proposition (or 'statement') 'the earth is round' only reflects a state of affairs in the world which is the fact itself, which then corresponds to the true proposition. But what is at stake in this chapter is not the difference between 'it is a fact that the earth is round' and 'it is true that the earth is round'. The point is that in both expressions some link between 'the earth' and 'being round' has to be *established* by human thought. Further discussion on 'facts' one finds in ch. 4, including also the relationship between facts and norms.

prior to any explicit self-instruction I can think of – knowledge I have to revise by going through similar tuning processes if I were to try to run ten miles in hilly country. Thus, what we see is (i) that thinking is intertwined with experience at the level of the body becoming gradually aware of his acting himself, (ii) that every belief, true or not, involves a thinker inserting the linking pin between an entity and a property, and (iii) that this first-person agent is there to stay throughout the whole corroboration process, as this is an exercise in thinking intertwined with experiencing. However, that this first person is omnipresent does not entail that he is omniscient or omnipotent. Precisely because he cannot be removed from establishing that the earth is round, he has to ascertain that the corroboration of his belief is not premised solely on his believing it.

In philosophy this specific capacity of an agent is often labelled by the term 'subject'. Being a subject is precisely that: being *the one who* experiences and judges in that peculiar double bind of 'attentiveness' between 'paying attention' (to the world) and 'attracting attention' (from the world).[68] The subject will not pay attention to 'the other around him' if this surrounding world does not attract attention, but then nothing will attract attention unless someone is attentive. It is tempting to add: unless someone is paying attention 'in the first place'. But that would be wrong as, properly speaking, there is not first and second place here. The to-and-fro between agent and world forms, according to Merleau-Ponty's favourite expression, a 'chiasm':[69] an intertwinement that has all the features of a Möbius strip where inside becomes outside and vice versa in an infinite loop. This Möbius strip of 'first person-and-other' is what

---

[68] Here I am indebted to B Waldenfels (2004).

[69] Cf. M Merleau-Ponty (1964) 172ff. I realise that I am mixing vocabulary from later phases in Merleau-Ponty's thought with earlier phases. But I do think that the very notion of 'chiasmus' is already present in M Merleau-Ponty (1945). Apart from its reference to the Greek letter χ there are connotations with 'chiasmus' (the trope of inversed word order in the second of two parallel phrases) and 'chiasma' (an interchange at corresponding points between homologous chromosomes). I submit that the picture of the Möbius strip better conveys the perpetual dynamics of the chiasm that Merleau-Ponty had in mind.

we are, not what we can enter into or retreat from. Thus, subjectivity implies: being 'at the origin' of sense and reference. Note that I do not say 'being the origin' of sense and reference, let alone 'being the origin of the world'. That would be sheer nonsense. The subject is *at* the origin of experiencing, and of affirming or negating, a world appearing while she or he is always already part and parcel of its appearance.[70] The world or 'reality' is only 'there' in as far as it is hooked by the 'here' of the subject and its referential gesture, but then the subject is only 'here' if it is in a position to point to 'something over there', setting itself at least at *some* distance.[71] Without pre-sup-posing[72] ourselves as 'at the origin' of referential gestures and meanings hooked by such gestures, we will find ourselves unable to discuss facts, or, for that matter, to conceive of the category 'fact' at all.

While an agent finds himself at the origin of sense and reference, and, thus, of experiencing and judging how the world appears, he is geared towards truth rather than towards falsehood. He does not keep a neutral position between two equally possible values, as if he were a Turing machine.[73] Thus, preference for truth is crucially dependent on reducing, as much as possible, the subject's self-willed constructions of what is 'other-than-*I*'. Openness toward the 'other' precisely *qua* other is *valued* by the agent as being indispensable for what he may consider as knowledge, including the kind of knowledge we have been persistently calling self-awareness. Knowledge, then, is dependent on acknowledgement; the 'other-than-*I*' will not remain altogether alien to the agent, on condition and to the extent that he will make it appear *as* 'the other' and not as something already familiar, appropriated, or otherwise 'owned'.

---

[70] Cf. also, in a different but related philosophical idiolect, S Hampshire (1959).

[71] Taking this position is a way of 'taking place' and hence of occupying a space which is impossible without making a bodily appearance. I am critical of the view that subjectivity collapses into sheer referential gestures without a bodily entrenched 'from –', as V Descombes (2004) argues.

[72] And we should take all prefixes seriously: a presupposition is to 'posit ourselves on top of some belief that we prefer to hold prior to any other belief'.

[73] C Taylor (1989) 50.

If it is true that the subject's being at the origin of sense and reference requires already the 'other-than-*I*', the other *agent qua subject* acquires a distinctive value. She will be, for him, the paragon of what is 'other-than-*I*'. The agent will be aware of her presence precisely because he cannot reduce her agency to a content of his consciousness. On the contrary, the other agent is experienced as being at the origin of sense and reference similar but opposite to my being an agent. Apparently, other things are significant for her than for him; the same things acquire significance differently between her and him; his pursuits interfere with hers. Her appearance can only mean to the agent that he is not the *only* one being at the origin of sense and reference. By that very token, the other's alterity is irreducible to the agent's awareness. That is why recognition of her subjectivity is constitutive of the ultimate reliability of the predicates the agent ascribes to him*self*.[74] As long as he does not take into account what the other has to say about what he says of himself, his self-ascriptions run the risk of being whimsical, arbitrary, and imaginary. To the extent that he tries to reduce her to a function of his pre-established orderings, he destroys the irreplaceable value the other has for him precisely by being *not* a part of his world, but the origin of a different world. In this way, the selfhood of the other is a value to the agent, indeed the ultimate value he can strive for. The other *as* other is the one who, in the end, makes his self-awareness reliable.[75] On the basis of this

---

[74] JE Smith (1991(1984)) 339 neatly captures Gabriel Marcel's view on this point: 'The recognition in question must come from someone who lies beyond and fails to coincide with my consciousness, my ideas, and especially the control of my will. This degree of otherness is required for the recognition to be something that I cannot command, no matter how fervently I desire it.' He adds a footnote that is even more pertinent: 'In *Being and Having* (…) pp. 104–107 (…) Marcel claims that we begin by attributing existence to the other – as a genuine other and not merely as my idea of an other – and then come to think of ourselves as not being the other. He makes a most perceptive interpretation of the *cogito* as a standing back and seeing myself as other, with the result that I appear as existing.' (348, n. 2). Much later, Ricoeur will write a majestic monograph under on 'oneself as an other'. Cf. P Ricoeur (1990).

[75] Cf. Merleau-Ponty (1947) 193: We '(…) need to have our opinions recognized by [the other] and to justify our choices before him.'

value one can understand why recognition of the other in her independence is normative. The agent can never subject the other totally as an instrument to serve his own existence without destroying the irreplaceable value the other represents. He has to acknowledge, respect, and indeed foster, the other's existence in a principled way, rather than strategically calculate on it.

3.2 The 'I' as the Final Hostage

And yet, this is not the end of the line. A Jewish philosopher made the world aware of a radical objection against this view: Emanuelis Levinas.[76] Western philosophy, says Levinas,[77] is a philosophy that departs from the insurmountable presupposition that nothing can be experienced, or thought, or said, or indeed performed, without a prefix *'I'* tacitly placed ahead of such proceedings. It refers to an agent who performs, experiences, thinks, or speaks, in the (tacit) awareness of doing all these things *himself*, i.e. as a first-person agent. Before something is thought, there is the thought of an *'I'* that thinks this something; prior to any act being performed, there is this source of a first-person agent, as a bundle of needs, interests, preferences, etc., to whom it is ascribed. This instance of the first person appears already before the other-than-*I*, a second or third person, can come to the scene. Anything other-than-I is only acknowledged in its existence within the ambit that is already ordered *for this I.* It only exists in as far as it is part of this *I*-world, and, thus, in as far as it is *of the selfsame order* as this *I.* Precisely when and

---

[76] Levinas (1906–1995) born in Lithuania and raised with Torah and Talmud, has lived in France ever since he went to study in Strasbourg (1923). He read phenomenology with Husserl and Heidegger in Freiburg, was a prisoner of war during 1941–1945, taught at several colleges in Paris until he became a professor of philosophy at the universities of (first) Poitiers, (then) Paris-Nanterre, and (later) the Sorbonne. Wikipedia provides a good biography at http://en.wikipedia.org/wiki/Emmanuel_Levinas; there is an extensive on-line bibliography at http://www.levinas.nl/ .

[77] In the following paragraphs I heavily compress a few lines from E Levinas (1974a), referring therefore to sections and subsections rather than pages. The present paragraph paraphrases *Totalité et infini*, Part I, Le meme et l'autre, 2 and 3, (e.g., p. 13 in fine).

where the other is regarded as the warrant of the reliability of *my* view of the world, this other serves *me* well. Consequently, the other is believed, by the '*I*', to be not different from the *I* in any radical sense. It exists on '*my*' conditions as a first-person agent.[78]

By this, Levinas neither means that Western thought is egocentric in the psychological sense, nor that it is egoistic in the moral sense of the word, namely that each and every individual is preoccupied with his or her own interests. He aims at a general diagnosis of our idea of 'thinking' – whether we think primarily of our own interests, the general interest, or even the interests of others. Even the disposition to, or the duty of, altruism can only be conceived by western thought as a thought content that originates in an *I* thinking. The western notion of thinking presupposes this *I*-that-thinks, thus putting it at the centre of world order before the instance of 'the other' has made its appearance. The only event which can affect the self-evident character of this order is the rise of a question: On what title was this order or hierarchy established by the *I*? Who has acknowledged this title if it was created while anything or anyone other-than-*I* was absent from the scene? Whose standpoint was it, from which the ordinal numbers were assigned to agents: first, second, and third person? Whose order is referred to by these ordinals? The answers to these questions are at least as obvious as the self-evident character of the *I*: it is the order of the *I*, for whom there were no others to acknowledge any title whatsoever at the moment in which it established its *I*-world. So there is no title, or only a self-proclaimed one – which amounts to the same thing. Even if it were true that nothing can be thought without an *I* thinking, even if the I could not escape from thinking the prefix '*I* think' ahead of every content of thought, it is not true, by the same token, that the *I* is *justified* in doing so. The idea of a title can only arise on the basis of a fallacy: from a necessary order to a justified order.

---

78 Cf. Ibid., I am not implying that philosophers like Merleau-Ponty (and also Marcel) did not engage this very problem of 'cartesianism'; well on the contrary.

Several points need to be elucidated here. First of all, what cleft can there be between a necessary order of thought and a justified one, if we have to admit that, in general, justification often amounts to showing the necessary character of an event or a state of affairs? Well, that is easy to answer: we have to distinguish between two meanings of 'justification'. The first one is linked up with what in western culture is called 'thinking'. In each thought content (whether it concerns what is the case or what is to be done) the act of thinking performed by the *'I'* is already presupposed, together with the *I*-based ordering of the world coming in its wake. This is part of the framework from which we cannot escape. The second meaning of 'justification' pertains to what is right (just) and wrong (unjust) with regard to acts. Not everything we have to do is thereby something we rightly do. Which is not to say that we are wrong in doing it. The only thing Levinas asks us to concede is that we are not right in doing ϕ on account of the sole thought[79] that we have to do ϕ.

A second point which stands in need of clarification is this. If in the *I*-world everything is qualified in such a way that it suits the *'I'*, how could something in this world have the power to challenge this very order? If the *'I'* puts himself ahead of everything existing, such that he sees the world developing from his own point of view according to what he defines as 'order', how could a question of title register?[80] Of course, it may be ventured *in abstracto* that the first-person's claim to a title for his order is not met. But whatever the instance that would make this claim, it would be, by definition, a powerless instance. Its properties would be *I*-determined properties. They are, therefore, of the kind that cannot really disturb or jeopardise the order of things as proclaimed by the first person. But that is precisely the only experience, which *is* in a sense disturbing for the agent: apparently, *he had no right* to order the world as he did, he just did it. He has not only proclaimed this order, he has also pre-claimed it, in the sense that he has made a premature claim.

---

[79] And note that we cannot say 'fact', as this regards a presupposition of thinking rather than a thought content we can corroborate.

[80] For a specifically legal context in which this question arises see E Christodoulidis (2004).

As a first-person agent he has designed a realm that he believes to be different from himself, before anything different is recognised. In other words, the *I has to admit* that, from its very first act of thought, the other-than-*I* had to watch powerlessly his creation of an *I*-world coming about.

A third and last point to elucidate is constituted by the reiterating expression 'experience'. This phrase is inadequate if it were to be taken to mean the experience of a phenomenon. What the '*I*' experiences is an oblique awareness of unease, at the most, as the whole world bends over to him, even where and when it appears as resistance. But the truly 'other' simply does not register, let alone register as resistance. The *I*-agent may only sense a challenge in the lack of resistance. Thus, the admission of being wrong rather than right, can only be experienced obliquely rather than made present in thinking. For each act of reflective thinking would reinforce the *I*-world, as it is intrinsically bound up with the way thinking is defined in the first place. The challenge can merely be felt as an uneasiness about a mode of thought in which, apparently, the other is pushed back behind the horizons of what the first person agent prefers to call 'the world'. So in what specific sense is the other an experience for the '*I*'? Here Levinas uses a famous formula, which he himself calls 'a plastic form' for what is in fact a disturbing awareness: the epiphany of 'the naked face' of the other.[81] Far from being a phenomenon, the nakedness of the face represents the other in as far as she is without protective coverings and without counteracting powers. It is the other without defence, as the predicate 'naked' emphasises. In this very defencelessness of the other '*I*' may sense the quality of disarmament: the '*I*' has expelled the other from the world in as far as he pushed her to the subordinated places of the secondary, or tertiary, person who matters.

---

[81] E Levinas (1974a), 22, 47, and Le visage et l'extériorité, 161ff. Levinas emphasises the plasticity of the face in an informative interview with France Guwy at http://www.youtube.com/watch?v=tQPjVT3WU5I&feature=related (French, Dutch subtitles); another interview (French, English subtitles) *The Right to Be* is at http://www.youtube.com/watch?v=mC0-E67XyG4&feature=related

Of course, these are reasonings at an extremely high level of generality. But they are not, therefore, deprived of concrete meaning.[82] I tried to say something about the 'points of view' which are most pertinently and pervasively involved in every piece of discourse or process of thought we can imagine. The *'I'* recurring in the paragraphs of this section was, as I have already said, not the index of a particular or an arbitrary individual person. It was the index of a position necessarily involved in discourse and thinking. And so were the indexes of the second and third person, referring to the position of 'the other'. This level of abstraction makes the model meaningful and critical. Indeed, it allows us to neatly and rapidly recognise the pertinence of patterns in everyday social life we are familiar with. We are all familiar with an individual *I*-world which we develop from our very first moments of experience, thought and speech, and in which we negotiate a hierarchy of loved-ones, friends, neighbours, colleagues, clients, etc. to which we feel ourselves related in a more or less intimate way, as the case may be. We are aware of the fact that this world is hierarchically ordered – for instance in terms of care and concern, shared or opposed interests, cooperation and competition – from our *own* point of view, and that we act in it accordingly. And note that, in that very awareness, we also are obliquely aware of the fact that this spontaneous and, indeed, inescapable order, is not, by the same token, a legitimate order. Some well-known moral puzzles stem from this oblique

---

[82] Without any reference to, but almost in unison with Levinas, H Arendt (1973 [1951]) has described what statelessness (in fact refugeeship) amounts to: 'The calamity of the rightless is not that they are deprived of life, liberty, and the pursuit of happiness, or of equality before the law and freedom of opinion – formulas which were designed to solve problems within given communities – but that they no longer belong to any community whatsoever. Their plight is not that they are not equal before the law, but that no law exists for them; not that they are oppressed but that nobody wants even to oppress them.' (295f) 'The conception of human rights, based upon the assumed existence of a human being as such, broke down at the very moment when those who professed to believe in it were for the first time confronted with people who had indeed lost all other qualities and specific relationships – except that they were still human. The world found nothing sacred in the abstract nakedness of being human.' (299) See LE Van Waas (2008); N Oudejans (2011).

awareness.[83] In a similar way, we will have no difficulty to recognise that the '*we*' of our socio-political order is globally structured along the lines of certain preferred values, in which we define knowledge, power and income. One does not have to be a Marxist to believe that a lot of social institutions are the superstructures of these choices and relationships, and to bear in mind that these (super-)structures systematically make victims. These victims are the feeble, the poor, the alien. As a class, they lose because the rules of the game were made without their consent or in their absence. It is not a coincidence that the world of the deprived and the alien is called 'the Third World', by those who have proclaimed *themselves* to be 'the First World'. The ordinal numbers are indices of subordination, as also the phrase 'the West and the Rest' conveys. Indeed the challenge of these naked faces on their desperate way to 'fortress Europe' is powerless but persistent: whence the authority or the title to determine which world comes first, second, or third?[84] Yet we cannot do otherwise.

Levinas radicalises the quasi necessary character of these social mechanisms by relating them to the grammar of what the philosophical tradition of the western world calls 'thinking the world'. He points out that our account of thinking reality starts with covering up the oblique awareness of the first person '*I*' to have trespassed over against 'the other', who never had a chance in the first place. Our deepest metaphysical convictions are accompanied by this profoundly *ethical* 'unrest' of trespassing. And as this is an ethical awareness, it also evokes the question: what should be done about it? Levinas's answer is that what the '*I*' senses in seeing the naked face of 'the other' is not only a powerless

---

[83] All sorts of so-called 'trolley dilemmas' in ethics are built on these I-related world order (buzz word: proximity). For instance: you are in a small boat with your daughter and her girlfriend. They both fall overboard and you have a duty to help. You know your daughter's friend cannot swim (while your daughter can), but you also know that the temperature of the water is so low that your daughter's condition will be critical as well within a few minutes. Who should you try to rescue first? A dramatic example is provided by William Styron's novel *Sophie's Choice* (1970).

[84] For an impressive spectrum of analyses see HK Lindahl (2009).

reproach, but also the evocation to try to repair the fault always already committed, by taking the position of the other, putting oneself in her place like a hostage and, consequently, enduring the consequences of this unfortunate position. Substitution should be the only, though always inadequate, answer to subordination.[85]

Why inadequate? We saw that the act of subordination does not result from wilful wickedness or weakness of the will. It is necessarily tied up with our account of thinking what is the case, or what is the right thing to do. That the *'I'* could not have done otherwise is not a sufficient reason to justify the act and to call it otherwise than trespassing. On the contrary, for Levinas it is a reason to enhance the incisiveness of his analysis by writing that, in fact, the *'I'* does not trespass over against 'the other' but over against 'the Other'. The capital 'O' indicates not primarily what Christian religion would call 'God'.[86] It is meant to express that the real other is the absent other: not the second person we may encounter in our social relationships but the third who does not register. The second person is the one who can be met by the first person in what we called experience. The second person is the one whose deprived status can be recognised by the first person. But should the first person act according to his recognition and try to undo the deprivation by substituting himself in her place, he would not have fulfilled his moral obligation to its full extent. The moment he arrives, so to speak, at the other's position at the edge of his I-world, his position becomes a new standpoint from which he proclaims a new *I*-world. And for this new I-world, there will also be a horizon, at which there will appear new victims of deprivation. The Other (as a third person) is the one *beyond* the edge of the first-person

---

85 Cf. (E Levinas 1974), with the 1968 essay 'La substitution'. Also, e.g., E Levinas (1991) 206ff.

86 Here I have doubts about R Visker (2005) 106: Visker believes that an 'experiment' on Levinas's position, by cutting out the word 'God' from his texts, would see them collapse into Habermas and Lyotard's views. I think that this experiment makes no sense unless you control for the meaning of that very word 'God', which for Levinas is a Judaic concept, by which he '(…) is not explicitly guided'. Cf. E Levinas (1991) 126: 'Dans la théologie juive – je ne suis pas guidé par cette théologie explicitement – Dieu c'est Dieu de la justice, mais son attribut principale est la miséricorde.'

world, while the other (as a second person) is the one *at the edge*. As soon as the first person moves toward the second, the edge moves, like a horizon, signifying that, for every change in the *I*-world, there will *always* be 'another other'. Consequently, substitution is an infinite moral pursuit, as the other is but 'a trace' of the Other.[87]

The scenery of the *'I'* being the hostage of the Other may make us worry about human freedom. And as our intuitions about the basic idea of law are very much tuned to law as the ultimate guarantee (Kant) or even the ultimate realisation (Hegel) of freedom, Levinas's account of the social relationship between the *'I'* and 'the other' seems to run counter to our intuitions. But let us be patient by paying closer attention to the idea of freedom involved in his account. The subject *'I'* cannot but conceive of himself, primarily, as 'une joyeuse force qui va':[88] an instance of power that relentlessly subordinates everything other to himself. Most theories of natural law see this original dynamic, this absence of any responsibility, as the paradigm of freedom, and proceed by showing that there is reason for the *'I'* – including every individual or group occupying the place of the first person – why one should limit one's power. Though these reasons may be accounted for by various strains of thought, the bottom line is that, by yielding to certain constraints, the core of the original freedom (no responsibility) can be realised. Not so Levinas's theory. He points out that in proclaiming his *I*-world, the agent is not free at all. He is dependent[89] in a double sense: firstly, he is encapsulated in this self-proclamation, as he encounters nothing which is not the echo of his ego; secondly, he is under the permanent though powerless summons constituted by the epiphany of the other. By contrast, in responding to the call of the other, the *I*-agent is able to stand on his own feet, rather than on the shoulders of those he subordinated. He is called upon to bear 'the weight of the world', but without being glued to

---

[87] E Levinas (1963).

[88] Or 'une force qui va', cf. E Levinas (1974a) 146 – a phrase from Victor Hugo, often used by Levinas, also in interviews. See E Levinas (1987) 200, n. 112 by Th. De Boer.

[89] Ibid., part II, C.

a standpoint he once and for all developed as 'his'. This is why Levinas speaks of a dazzling and difficult freedom, one that entails radical responsibility rather than maximal non-responsibility.[90] The only thing that can mitigate its effects on a person is the hope that others will know themselves to be responsible for *me* as *I* feel for them. But this reciprocity cannot be the object of a deal, or the condition of a contract, like it is in so many natural law theories. The first person *'I'* would destroy her independence if she would allow herself to sit and wait for the offer of reciprocity by the other. All there is, is the comfort of hope, not the certainty of assurance.

Levinas's philosophy may strike us as a philosophy of guilt – as an argument to the effect that one cannot get rid of an original sin. In a sense this is true, but we should be careful not to understand it from the Christian preoccupations that get so easily mixed up with western thinking, even when it is not expressly religious. Levinas admits that his argument leads to the conclusion that everybody is responsible for what he did not 'really' do himself. We may say that the others' misery is everybody's misery. No one in particular *deprived* the poor of their means of subsistence, or the aliens of their means of attracting attention. Nevertheless, their existence can only be qualified as deprived, or strange, from the point of view that dominates the world you benefit from, while they do not. Their existence defines your world in a negative way, as they mark the edges of it. But by that, their existence also constitutes an evocation or interpellation, and therefore an opportunity: there is life after you have been discovered to be guilty of that first-person ordering which, as we saw, is both inevitable *and* premature. The evocation to make a fresh start is the reverse side of the discovery that you are not in the right to do ϕ by the sole fact that you could not avoid doing ϕ. That is what substitution is all about: moving towards those who are at the edges of your self-proclaimed world and who will not register unless you become aware of the fact that it is you who made them not register. Then they register as those who did not register. The

---

90 Cf. E Levinas (1976 [1963]); E Levinas (1974a) Conclusions 11.

other is not a powerful judge, who can convict me on the basis of a law previously enacted between us. She is, rather, the victim offering reconciliation.[91] Her very powerlessness is the basis of her authority to summon the *'I'* and to question his order, thus opening up the perspective of the promise of justice. Therefore, the Other is not the limit of the first person's freedom, but its very basis. It is in this sense that the Other can be characterised as *a law* (or as I will say: a norm) for the *'I'*, rather than *a value*.[92] This constitutes the radical difference between the first and the second account of what we called 'the social relationship' – the relationship between the *'I'* and his 'other'.

4. FROM RECOGNITION TO A POLITICS OF RECOGNITION:[93] HANDLING TWO OPPOSING PRINCIPLES

4.1 Alterity and Alternity

In most theories of (natural) law, man's social being is grounded on the belief that the other, being irreducibly different from the *'I'*, is of the utmost *value* to the *'I'*. The existence of the other is seen as a necessary element in developing reliable self-awareness, freedom and dignity. Norms governing social relationships should therefore find support in and further this ultimate value. But as we saw in section 3.1, the basic presupposition of this line of thought is a specific epistemic hierarchy:

---

91 Cf. Van Roermund (2001b).

92 'Law is what I must obey. It may confer on me certain benefits, here the immunity that my life, too, is to be respected; but fundamentally I am *under* law.' (C Taylor (1989) 11).

93 I borrow this term from Charles Taylor without introducing the specific context of multicultural society. Where C Taylor (1994) 26 says: 'Due recognition is not just a courtesy we owe people, it is a vital human need', I regard this as tantamount to what I call 'the other as a value'. 'Politics of recognition' in my argument refers to the pragmatic negotiating of the antinomy I described. This makes my own account also different from A Honneth (1995). See also the discussion and Honneth's rejoinder in B Van den Brink and D Owen (2007) and his reply to critics A Honneth (2010).

the first person is the position *from where* the other is valued. In that sense the first-person agent precedes and governs the position of the other. Levinas's theory does not just reverse this hierarchy; it changes its very nature. What this theory says is that, prior to any other having any value from the first person's point of view, the Other constitutes a norm, indeed a *law* for the *'I'*. This, as we learned in section 3.2, is implied in the oblique awareness of the agent that his *a priori* valuing of the other is a self-proclaiming act.

But how ever fascinating and incisive Levinas's critique of western thought is, it cannot hide from two fundamental problems inherent to it.[94] Firstly, whatever Levinas is saying about the other's alterity – doesn't it remain true that the agent can only act upon her evocation by noticing her from his world order, the *I*-world? It seems that, indeed, this must be the case. The other is not able to confront the agent with an alternative order of her own. Were she able to do that, she would not be powerless (as, by hypothesis, she is). But if her appearance at the edge of the agent's world order has the potential to constitute only a tiny question mark for the latter, it does so on account of the agent's point of view. If the agent is able to read a summons in the eyes of the other, it is because the other is radically different in the sense of being *infinitely* different,[95] not *completely* different. Her alterity presents itself as a shifting horizon of duty, not as a realm beyond the boundaries of the I-world. Were the latter the case, she would also remain completely out of the agent's sight, out of his language, out of his history. She could not be the instance which disturbs the agent's order, unlocks its safety devices, dissolves its pre-established harmony. She would not, thus, enable him to start all over again to detect new definitions of order, safety and harmony. So if the

---

[94] These are problems which Levinas himself is very much aware of, and which he tries to circumvent by pushing philosophical language to its limits. His vocabulary sometimes becomes, as it were, recursive, for instance when he famously says that one has 'a responsibility that precedes responsibility'. At other times, it conflates the idiolect of western philosophy with the vocabulary of Jewish wisdom and faith. Then it becomes difficult to insert his thought in the vernacular of western philosophy.

[95] Cf. S Critchley (2007).

other discloses herself as the one who summons the agent not to kill her, to follow the trace of the Other and to grow to ever greater responsibility, she implicitly asks him to do what makes his order illegitimate in the first place: to (once more) ascribe to her properties, meanings and values deriving from the I-world.[96]

The same difficulty entails a second problem that is to be explained. We may ask: can the other really present a summons or a challenge to the '*I*' by virtue of her sheer alterity? To put it in another way: can the other embody the instance of 'the law' by virtue of its sheer alterity? It seems that it cannot, for the following reason. The legal scenery which Levinas creates to render the basic moral experience of the other as a radical one, presupposes already a specific relationship from the agent towards the other. It presupposes that the other is the one missed and desired by the agent. Without the presupposition of the agent longing for what is different from him, sheer alterity would not lead to the oblique awareness of trespassing in the agent's mind. The ordinal numbers of the first, second and third person would not be questioned as indices of a premature hierarchy, since the possibility of a more mature order than the self-proclaimed one would never dawn upon him. Only a precedent desire to be 'with' the other could explain why the epiphany of the other's naked face would disclose the agent's failure or fault, and evoke his new start. Above, I pointed to such a desire as a preference for truth preceding our epistemic endeavours; but surely this is not the only realm where our desires are not value-neutral. We also prefer the good over the bad, even when we define it in a very narrow sense and pursue a cause that others call bad. The point is that we are not indifferent towards the distinction between good or bad, otherwise the epiphany of the Other would not disturb us, even if it would register.

At the risk of creating despair regarding the end of this philosophical pathway, let me bring up a difficulty with these two difficulties. They are of the kind that not only undermine, but also reaffirm a Levinasian

---

96 This question is part of Derrida's critique of Levinas's position in J Derrida (1967); see, for instance, p. 219.

account. As to the first one: if to respond to the other entails infringing her alterity, doesn't this prove that Levinas was right rather than wrong after all? And as to the second problem: if it is asserted that the other cannot embody the instance of the norm unless the agent's desire for the other is presupposed, can one not object that this very desire presupposes, in turn, a norm constituting the difference between the I and what is other-than-I? Both points bring out that the primary mode in which the other discloses herself to the agent is that of a norm rather than a value. But if we concede these two points, we will feel urged again to undermine them by the kind of questions we began this section with – questions which come down to the bottom line that the primary mode in which the other discloses herself to the agent is that of a value rather a norm.

It may seem that, in this way, we are going round in circles. But that is actually an inadequate way of putting the problem. Going round in circles is something we do when the terms of the argument are continuous; for instance if we use the concept which we have to define in its very definition, or if we presume the truth of a statement which we want to argue for in the first place. In the present case the terms of the argument are not continuous at all; they are, rather, radically distinct and opposed to one another. This is our predicament: if we accept the truth of one side of the coin, we are prompted to deny it by virtue of the other side, but this very denial reinforces the initial truth we accepted, thus prompting … etc. When it comes to a philosophical account of what we have called the social relationship, that is to say: the generalised relationship between the first-person agent and the other, we seem to have found two opposite ways of reading the formula 'acknowledging the other as other', namely

(1) acknowledging the other as a value, i.e. a reality that we can judge and find 'good';
(2) acknowledging the other as a norm, i.e. a reality that judges us and finds us 'good'.[97]

---

[97] If professional philosophers are reminded here of the everlasting opposition between teleological and deontological accounts of morality, that is fine with me.

Note that the term 'norm' in the second mode is as pregnant of meaning as the term 'value' in the first. The latter is short for whatever appeals to us from our point of view; the former is short for what directs us prior to any reason we may have to comply with it. These two philosophical modes of reading what we could call 'normativity' are not at all far-fetched. Both the terms and their oppositional relationship form the basis of fascinating paradigms, images, symbols and narratives in our cultural tradition. We are 'between Athens and Jerusalem'.[98] Our culture remembers Odysseus's wandering, the Greek hero who – after coping with various guises of alterity – finally arrived where he once started (his *I*-world, home). But it finds itself also challenged by Abraham's exodus, the Jewish patriarch who obeys the law even if it asks him to sacrifice what has ultimate value for him (his son) and whose people follow the trace of the Other to the promised land. These two paradigmatic stories are by no means circular. We cannot, for instance, interpret the one in terms of the other and vice versa. They are radically opposed accounts of a quest, and acknowledging alterity is what this quest is about. Apparently, alternating these basic modes of alterity in the practice of the quest is our only way to live it. To put it in a brief formula, derived from George Steiner:[99] alternity is the practical mode of alterity.

This is what we have to bear in mind when we use a phrase like 'human dignity'. In order to avoid turning the other into a function of our dominant concept of man we should try hearing what we are summoned to by those who were pushed to the edges of the societal order derived from this dominant image of man: Norm precedes Value. But then again, if we want to hear that appeal we will find ourselves embarking on yet another detour in our return to our point of departure: what the other could mean to *us*, what we could *learn* from her in recognising her. Then Value precedes Norm in the interpretation of human dignity, only to find its scheme challenged again. This is not because we cannot lift the chair we are sitting on. We can, by simply standing up, making one step aside

---

98 As David Janssens puts it in his Strauss monograph (D Janssens (2008)).

99 G Steiner (1976) 222ff; cf. 407. Robert Cover refers to the same passage in his magnificent R Cover (1992 [1983]).

and take it with both hands, as Levinas would probably advise. It is just that we quickly get tired standing on our own feet. Yet the oscillation between the two poles of our antinomy is not meaningless. With each to-and-fro we have the opportunity to make a slight shift in reconfirming who we are in the end, mitigating its most aversive effects, deferring its harshest policies.

4.2 Justice as the Politics of Alterity

We are now able, finally, to say something about what law is ultimately about and why it makes sense. The quest for an answer departed from the hypothesis that law is a political artefact and that politics is about ordering society. Thus, in order to learn what law is about we should turn to what politics is ordering in ordering society: social relations as conceived from first-person agents to what is for them 'the other'. I reviewed various possible accounts of this relationship, to finally settle for one that does not reduce the other to a function of the first-person agent: the model of recognition. Within that model I pointed to an antinomy of two mutually challenging principles that we will have to negotiate in ordering action, thus in politics, incessantly oscillating between them. Politics as a politics of recognition, recognising alterity by practising alternity, is what I propose to call 'doing justice' – and law is the set of institutions that, in a given society, lends default form and substance to 'doing justice'.

I rejected various accounts of law for various reasons: law as an equilibrium of powers, as respect for human dignity in terms of a common denominator, and even as recognition of the other in her alterity as merely a vital value. I have taken up the latter formula and detected two opposite readings of it: recognition of the other in her alterity 'as a value' versus 'as a norm'. Submitting now an explicit definition of justice in terms of this antinomy, let me point out that 'antinomy' should not be confused with 'contradiction'. Contradiction is the deadlock of reasoning and reasonableness alike. If we find ourselves asserting that 'something x has a property ϕ' and then that 'x is not ϕ' *in one and the same respect*, i.e. with regard to some middle ground between the two assertions, we can safely say that we have left the realm of insight and argument.[100] But this is not the case with our two readings or 'principles' of recognition. Logically speaking their relation should be regarded as a contrast rather than a contradiction. From an epistemological point of view, however, one should bear in mind that these principles concern the most basic structure of the social relationship one can think of, as seen from either the first-person agent's or the other's vantage point. There is no middle ground between the two: no common or mediating truth from which they depart and which would allow us (indeed, oblige us) to bring them to a synthesis on a higher level. That is what makes the antinomy between the principles radical and irreducible.

But we have also seen that neither of these principles can stand-alone: one prompts an agent to the other and vice versa. As soon as one of the two would be attributed exclusive foundational strength, its claim would be undermined by arguments deriving from the other one. They harbour reciprocal challenges, even though it is true that one of the two – let us call it the Value account – is dominant in our way of thinking and therefore less easily challenged. They are not so much each other's conditions as they are each other's burden of judgment, to lend a Rawlsian term.[101] Rather than being 'equi-primordial'[102] they are 'equi-onerous' in charging each other with a burden of proof. This means that the opposition is not what philosophers call a purely 'transcendental' matter, i.e. a matter about the general and necessary conditions of our thinking (social) reality. It forms, informs and transforms social practice,

---

[100] We can, without contradiction, say that 'the room is dark, but it is not dark' when the first token of 'dark' means 'the amount of light falling into the room', while the second means 'the amount of light reflected by the room'. In a similar way, there is no contradiction in 'I ought to do A, but I ought not to do A', as long as we have not established that the two 'oughts' express obligations within the same institution. There can easily arise conflicts of duties, for instance, between what I have to do by virtue of my contract and by virtue of public morality. See Castañeda, *Thinking and Doing* (1975).

[101] Cf. J Rawls (1993) 54ff.

[102] Cf. Habermas's preferred term for the relationship between public and private autonomy, democracy and human rights in J Habermas (1992 [1992]; 1997).

thus revealing itself as a touchstone for ordering this social practice, i.e. for politics. Alternating points of view is something we *do* if challenged, and the middle ground we seem to find is never a conceptual and necessary fact or norm, but a contingent, provisional and consensual 'equilibrium' that is already disturbed at the moment it is achieved. The two principles in their polarity are conceptually necessary in the pragmatic sense: they are necessary to carry on with our lives rather than to carry on with our thinking: to carry on in spite of the risks lying ahead, of the suffering remembered from an oppressive past, or of the free riders among us. That is why they open up a space for history rather than ontology. They allow, indeed they prompt, agent and other to articulate what is *already* established between them, what is *yet* to be achieved, what is *prematurely* taken for granted, what should *never* happen again, what is hoped for *in the end*, etc. These are the categories that shape up the dimensions of present, past and future of their relationship. They structure its historiography as well as its ideology.[103]

This is, I think, the only adequate way in which 'history' can be accounted for within the context of politics, law, and morality – a problem we shall have to return to in the next chapter. Here already I want to prepare some space for a concept of history that allows for something to really *happen*. That is to say: one in which history is not bound up with regaining a paradise lost or conquering one beyond time, a realm from which all sense is believed to derive *a priori*. I believe that history has a pace (of making sense *and* nonsense) because the concept of a social relationship has two feet to walk on rather than one: two principles of recognition. They are essential in the practice, which aims at ordering the various forms that this relationship can take. That historical practice, as said, is called politics. It is within the framework of politics that justice – giving the other her or his due – can be defined in terms of the two opposite principles.

---

103 The background of my use of 'ideology' is P Ricoeur (1973; 1974; 1977).

Def. 2.1 *Justice is the politics that negotiates the two opposite principles governing the social relationship between the first-person agent and the other in such a way that it allows the challenging principle of acknowledging alterity as a Norm to count against the dominant principle of acknowledging alterity as a Value.*

In the natural law tradition of legal philosophy, such an explicit conception of justice is often called 'the idea of law' (the *Rechtsidee*).[104] If that suffices to label my argument as 'iusnaturalistic', I accept it. But note that I do not confess myself to a catalogue of norms or values that should be constitutive for the *concept* of law, as some natural law thinkers do. Nor do I imply or suggest that law is to be defined as a sort of 'minimal ethics' or a special branch of ethics if that would mean that in order to say what the law is, we need to rely on an ethical divide between good and evil. The only presupposition I introduced in this regard is that an agent tacitly knows about his preference for the good as distinct from the evil, the true as distinct from the false, whatever its parameters.

What I do claim, however, is that definition 2.1 allows us to take up everything we learnt in the preceding two chapters and integrate it into a formula, which hammers home a concept of law. For what definition 2.1 says is that – prior to its subdivision in distributive and retributive justice – justice is a specific political virtue that can be specified in the following sense.

(1) It is a political practice that acknowledges its point of departure in the first person. Taking up the social relationship between 'agent' and 'other' does take us into the realm of morality, only to ultimately leave it again as there is only a political solution to a moral antinomy. As said earlier in this chapter: politics starts out by delineating a 'we'. That is part of the 'grammar' or the 'logic' of each and every political act. Delineating a 'we', i.e., constituting a

---

[104] Cf. G Radbruch (1973 [1932]) 119ff.

first person plural is an action performed as a 'joint action' by a plurality of first persons singular. It does not require an extra ontology on top of what it takes to 'act together'. Hence a polity is not something different from the individual agents that take part in it; it rather is their bonding with each other the political way that constitutes the polity.[105] On that account it starts out with self-inclusion, hence exclusion of others, reiterating the dominance of the first-person position on the canvass of the plural.

(2) Justice is the political practice which takes on the challenge sensed from the position of those who appear to be pushed to the edges of the social order which this jointly acting 'we' represents, and it does so without being forced. We may say, therefore, that justice is a political practice that, of its own accord, brings out the *relative* character of the polis's justifying identity. By saying this much, we only reiterate in socio-political terms what Gadamer has called 'openness': '(…) the recognition that I have to allow something in me as counting against me, even if there were no other to enforce me doing so.'[106] If we understand 'openness' in this non-trivial way, we can bring the complicated definition 2.1 back to a simpler format: *justice amounts to the openness of a political order towards the premature, hence provisional, character of its identity*. Such a politics of recognition goes beyond political self-restraint in that openness is principled rather than strategic self-restraint.

(3) This also entails that doing justice is an infinite enterprise. How ever so often justice is done, one is never done with it: its pursuit is an infinite response to what calls on us from a shifting horizon. In other words, there will always be another other challenging the dominant view of what the inclusion of the other requires.

---

[105] This point is stressed by otherwise different accounts of joint action like ME Bratman (1999), M Gilbert (1996; 2006); C List and P Pettit (2011). See also B Van Roermund (2003a).

[106] '(…) die Anerkennung (…) daß ich in mir etwas gegen mich gelten lassen muß, auch wenn es keinen anderen gäbe, der es gegen mich geltend machte.' See Gadamer (1975) 343.

(4) As a political practice, justice cannot transcend the concepts and categories deriving from an initial identity, which it has to re-articulate in the very act of bringing out what counts against it. One of the implications is, that joint self-preservation and self-awareness are part and parcel of what justice aims at, be it in such a way as to challenge their pervasive force. In other words: contractual naturalism was not wrong in stressing the importance of self-preservation, it was wrong in immunising it as the bottom line of political practice.

Positive law, in my view, is neither more nor less than an institutionalisation of the above idea of justice, i.e. of this specific, open-closing, political practice. If we resume the phrases of our definition 2.1, we may frame its core by definition 2.2:

Def. 2.2 *Law is that institutionalisation of the political order in a limited society which – while integrating every member's autonomous claim to self-preservation – allows, on its own accord, something in it to count against the identity of this society, even if no other could enforce this challenge.*

By this definition I grant that law is a political artefact. What I do not grant is that it is reducible to politics. Once political action has wrought a legal order, the polity cannot cut loose from what the latter requires.

4.3 Exemplifying the Dynamics of Justice

How to illustrate the relevance of my conceptual point? No better example, perhaps, than the intricate relationship between democracy and human rights, in particular in the context of migration.[107] In legal documents of a foundational nature, democracy and human rights are often harnessed together. The Treaty of Lisbon, for instance,[108] chose to

[107] Part of the following overlaps with B Van Roermund (2009b).

[108] Amending the Treaty on European Union and the Treaty establishing the European Community, signed at Lisbon, December 13, 2007 (2007/C 306/01).

insert as Art. 1a: '(…) The Union is founded on the values of respect for human dignity, freedom, democracy, equality, the rule of law and respect for human rights, including the rights of persons belonging to minorities.'[109] Also, they are often imposed together as preconditions for entering the European Union, for instance in the case of Turkey's application, where a special rapporteur was appointed to investigate the matter and report annually.[110] Political rhetoric always makes sure of mentioning both in their juxtaposition, so as to compensate for their rather puzzling relationship. Campaigning speeches, presidential addresses, party programmes, etc. are there to prove it.[111] What is the uneasiness? The first paradox is well-known. If the people in a democracy have supreme power over the legal order they seek to establish, they cannot be bound by pre-established norms like human rights. Thus either human rights are at the mercy of the *demos*, or the *demos* is not in full power. An elegant and convincing solution to this paradox is offered by Habermas's proposal to see the two as co-original, i.e. as mutual conditions in the pragmatic rather than the purely semantic sense.[112] If people are to exercise supreme political power together there should be warrants that they do not have to fear about their subsistence, that they are secure when gathering to deliberate, that they are free to express their opinions, that they have access to an educational system to acquire relevant knowledge and learn the necessary skills, etc. On the other hand, in order to determine what should count as 'necessary', 'appropriate', etc., or what constraints there should be on free speech, free movement, free religion, etc., one should have a deliberation- and decision-making

---

[109] Cf. the insertion in the second recital of the preamble: '(…) DRAWING INSPIRATION from the cultural, religious and humanist inheritance of Europe, from which have developed the universal values of the inviolable and inalienable rights of the human person, freedom, democracy, equality and the rule of law (…).'

[110] See the relevant documents at http://ec.europa.eu/enlargement/countries/detailed-country-information/turkey/index_en.htm, accessed Nov 7, 2012.

[111] Just one example for all: President Obama's Cairo speech June 4, 2009, at http://www.whitehouse.gov/issues/foreign-policy/presidents-speech-cairo-a-new-beginning, accessed Nov 7, 2012.

[112] J Habermas (1992 [1992]; 1997) III (III).

procedure involving all those who are affected. Or again, on the one hand, fundamental rights, both civil-political rights, socio-economic rights, and even cultural rights, are primarily horizontal, i.e. they primarily root in inter-subjective or reciprocal relationships between would-be citizens. On the other hand, they can only be realised by virtue of vertical protection from the part of governmental authorities, who have to take care of this primordial mutuality. Thus, public autonomy (democracy) and private autonomy (human rights) hunt in pairs.

Habermas's view is very attractive and it has important implications for legal practice. For instance, it undercuts the orthodoxy of 'first' and 'second' (even 'third') generations of human rights. It makes very limited sense to argue about these rankings between 'political', 'social' and 'cultural' rights, let alone to build comprehensive political ideologies on them. Moreover, it provides a justification for human rights to become positive law only if and when they are qualified by restrictions flowing from formal (supposedly democratic) legislation.[113] Similarly, it gives some good reasons to exclude certain political parties from the democratic process, namely if they would use it to curtail human rights. Yet Habermas is right only up to a point with regard to public and private autonomy. Here is Hannah Arendt's warning:

> Since the Greeks, we have known that highly developed political life breeds a deep-rooted suspicion of this private sphere, a deep resentment against the disturbing miracle contained in the fact that each of us is made as he is – single, unique unchangeable. This whole sphere of the merely given, relegated to private life in civilized society, is a permanent threat to the public sphere, because the public sphere is based on the law of universal difference and differentiation. Equality, in contrast to all that is involved in mere existence, is not given us, but is the result of human organization insofar as it is guided by the principle of justice. We are not born equal; we become equal as members of a group on the strength of our decision to guarantee ourselves mutually equal rights.[114]

---

[113] Cf. The Charter of Fundamental Rights of the European Union, Ch II, Art. 52.1

[114] H Arendt (1973 [1951]) 301.

This warning signal is of no less practical relevance than Habermas's. But it can be validated only if we realise the exact tones that compose it. The first thing she says is that the distinction between private and public is invariably made from the pole of the public, not the other way round, and this preference determines the difference.[115] Obviously, it questions Habermas's thesis about the co-originality of public and private autonomy: this very co-originality finds its origin in the pole of the public rather than the private. Secondly, Arendt's warning is that, at the pole of the public, we cannot revert to the horizontalism of mutual recognition between agents. Her claim is precisely that mutuality cannot be primordial when it comes to law and politics. For all the importance the principle of mutuality may have in explaining what today is called 'shared intentional action', it always comes too late. Like social contract theory in general it ignores the question on what grounds the terms of these reciprocal relationships are selected. Indeed, there is a problem lying at the very heart of reciprocity: prior to reciprocal recognition it is already decided who is to be involved in the set of elements between whom reciprocity will reign. And this decision, by necessity, cannot be taken reciprocally or horizontally, without seriously begging the question.

So the drift of Arendt's critical – very Levinasian – observation is that, apparently, it requires a non-reciprocal account of the polity to respond to the membership issue. Indeed one gets one's rights on the basis of the membership of a polity, or more accurately, from a public realm already constituted, in the terms and on the conditions of that realm. More often than not this is a realm where one is invited to appear provided that one is trimmed in accordance with the image of a human being that this public sphere requires. The typical parameters of the 'national' public sphere are just one example, and nothing of the logic of the polity changes when these parameters are replaced by others, e.g., supranational parameters. This is why Arendt can say that, since the French

---

115 Cf. B Waldenfels (1994) 202ff.

Revolution, it has become gradually clear '(...) that the people, and not the individual, was the image of man.'[116]

This brings in a third challenge. Note that the term 'people' has to be taken here not as a predicate but rather as a name, i.e. as a dummy for a first-person plural position, a 'we' or – slightly more precise – the plural 'self' of this 'we'. To repeat: 'We are not born equal; we become equal as members of a group on the strength of our decision to guarantee *ourselves* mutually equal rights.'[117] It is by virtue of this collective self, e.g. by reference to national security, that officials tell torture from (mild) physical pressure or invasive interrogation. Similarly, by reference to the common wealth, they tell violations of privacy from protection of citizens or boosting GNP.[118] Similarly, by reference to a public doctrine of health, they tell illness from passion, from perversion, from handicap, or from 'those things that come with age (or with gender) and just have to be endured'.

To see the relevance of the three theses explained above I should point to the problem of granting asylum. The relatively secure and affluent countries of the world often have to take a decision, whether someone arriving at their gates should be admitted to enter, whether this person is a 'real' refugee or not, and if so, if she should be granted asylum. The legal framework for these decisions is pretty clear. But, as Oudejans has argued on the basis of extensive research of legal decisions and policy documents, it is the 'joint' composition of a plural self that is decisive of restricting, furthering, qualifying, conditioning, etc. immigration and asylum.[119] Moreover, empirical research in the Dutch context has shown that the set of shared values making up for a collective identity within the constraints of a specific political situation, is reflected in the parameters of what we count as a 'credible' story of an undocumented refugee or what circumstances we find 'pressing' for 'humanitarian' reasons. It is

---

116 H Arendt (1973 [1951]) 291.

117 Ibid., 301 (emphasis added; BvR)

118 Or GDP, for that matter. Whether the reference is to 'national' (N) or to 'domestic' (D) Product does not have to concern us in the present context.

119 Cf. N Oudejans (2011) and materials referred to there, including also T Spijkerboer (1999).

the ground for making a distinction between refugees and fortune hunters, often politely rephrased as that between political and economic refugees or 'migrants'. Last but not least, it marks the gap between welcome (well-educated) and unwelcome (poorly educated) immigrants. To put it simply: those who are 'like us' stand a better chance of getting what is meant to serve all humans who need it. It allows a polity to say, in point of fact, that some humans are more human than others.

In this respect, Arendt may be seen as tributary to Marx, who famously criticised human rights for being the rhetoric of alienation. Human rights discourse, Marx said, reduces full-fledged human beings to the abstract category of 'man', i.e., individual subjects without any societal identities. Thus, it allows officials to trade the free citizen of a democratic polity for the ready-made bourgeois of a capitalist society.[120] But Arendt's thesis is a more universal one: the bourgeois self-image of a people is just one example among others of a polity trading the rights of men with all their singularities for the rights of man as so many instantiations of an official image of man, purified from all that is alien. For a political regime '(…) the "alien" is a frightening symbol of the fact of difference as such, of individuality as such, and indicates those realms in which man cannot change and cannot act and in which, therefore, he has a distinct tendency to destroy.'[121] Note that it is not the threat to the public realm that is definitional of the alien: it is the alien that is definitional of the threat.[122] For Arendt it is the very coming-into-existence of the polity or the *demos* that creates the distinction between the plural self and the other, the own and the alien, the people and the population, the 'open society' and 'its enemies'.[123]

---

[120] A similar critique of human rights being attributed to 'abstract' entities rather than real human beings is vouched by Burke in an altogether different (conservative) political perspective. Cf. C Douzinas (2000).

[121] H Arendt (1973 [1951]).

[122] Here we are back with Rousseau's giants once more: the strategy of the common denominator as set out in section 2.1.

[123] Thus, though Arendt's definition of the polity as a public realm is admittedly more abstract than Marx's, it is also much more incisive than Schmitt's. Schmitt's definition hinges on the friend–foe distinction as one that has to be made for 'existential' reasons: an existing state that has to subsist.

But let us make no mistake. Arendt's analysis does not imply an immediate moral appeal to downplay everything that has to do with the public realm. It does not prompt us to reverse the charges and turn things around in the name of an alternative right-wrong distinction. Moral appeals can make sense only if they open up to this ambiguous realm of politics again. Arendt's account of the polity remains deeply 'agonistic'; i.e., it conceives of establishing a polity as an *agoon*, a battle.[124] What it shows, as said, is the ambiguity of the public realm, but only after it has acknowledged its necessity. Human rights are there, because the public sphere cannot articulate its own opacity. It cannot, in one fell swoop, set the boundaries that exclude the alien and deny that these are real boundaries. But it can do something else in setting the boundaries. Instead of denying that they are where they are, it can leave space for contestation, thereby admitting that it may not be absolutely right even if it cannot but claim to be right. This is why human rights are rooted in the same sphere, which they are supposed to protect you from: the political sphere. It does not make them 'nonsense upon stilts', as Bentham would have it.[125] It makes them part and parcel of that form of politics that acknowledges, on its own account, something counting against a specific polis. That is to say, it makes them part and parcel of law. Also, this is why human rights do not become positive law unless they revert again to politics by way of constraints that the polity may impose. By recognising human rights a polity confesses doubt on the boundaries it posits but not on its positing boundaries.

The ambiguities of the plural self spill over into two other directions: its representatives and its beneficiaries. Let me take beneficiaries first. As Arendt reminds us, the *demos* in Modernity is not only the reflexive mode of those who rule, it also captures those who are to profit from their own ruling. Although this may seem pretty obvious, it is in fact a

---

124 For an incisive analysis of Arendt's conception of politics see HK Lindahl (2006). On 'agonistic democracy' and its backgrounds cf. B Honig (1993a; 1993b), C Mouffe (1999); and Andrew Schaap in his Introductory essay to A Schaap (2009).

125 J Bentham (2002 [1795]).

separate conceptual turn taken, marking a separate mode of the act of self-inclusion. Since interests are mixtures of needs and desires, and since agents (collective agents included) have limited insight in what they really need and want, their ruling themselves does not logically entail that they will rule in their own interests. This is why we have to add this dimension of the political self in an analysis of democratic law-making (be it in legislation, administration or adjudication): the people rule themselves in their own (i.e. common) interests.[126] This is the main tenet of Rousseau's theory: it is part and parcel of a democracy that nothing is considered to be right apart from the common good.

But this tenet is precisely the source of further ambiguities, as Arendt reveals. If law is exhausted by this notion of the common good, one has to admit that good is what is good for the people, good for (an) 'us', even if this 'us' is 'as large as mankind itself'. And Arendt adds (half a decade after the end of the Second World War): 'Hitler's motto that "Right is what is good for the German people" is only the vulgarized form of a conception of law which can be found everywhere and which in practice will remain ineffectual only so long as older traditions that are still effective in the constitutions prevent this.'[127] The central ambiguity is this: on the one hand, within a society there is no appeal from the common good in the name of justice. Justice is what is good for all of us in our social relationships as politics orders them. But on the other hand, that is exactly the problem for those who are not within that polity, for instance those who are 'between polities' as stateless people, refugees, or

---

[126] Rousseau, was very much aware of this separate dimension. On the basis of his initial conceptual model, the people as sovereign citizens ruling themselves as obedient subjects, there is no need for human rights as rights of individuals over and against sovereign power. This is only logic. But not only does he concede, further down the Social Contract, that the people do need protection from the 'ineradicable' inclination of the administration (the 'government') to go after their private interests (which could be interpreted as support for a human rights regime). He also concedes that the sovereign people are 'often' unable to decide what they want. Cf. CS II, 6, towards the end, introducing 'the great lawgiver' juxtaposed to the sovereign legislator to teach the latter about their own interests.

[127] H Arendt (1973 [1951]) 299.

migrants. They either do not count yet, or not anymore. In either case they do not register as the beneficiaries of democratic law-making. If law would really boil down to nothing else than the common good, nothing in the name of justice could beat a situation in which no individual agent in the set of those who rule themselves can improve on his or her situation, i.e. nothing could beat Pareto-optimality as the definition of what is 'right'. In that line of thought, human rights would fall victim to what Schmitt blasphemously called 'the tyranny of values'.[128] Which is not to say that they would not stand for 'what we value most', but only that within a certain society they can be traded (admittedly under sufficient pressure) for other values as so many articulations of 'the common good'. Law would basically boil down to an economy of values, i.e. of more or less shared preferences determined by a 'we' always already determined. If we believe that to be a dangerous bet, we will have to concede that democracy is not able to cater for everything law stands for; namely for the doubt a polity should foster with regard to its own legitimacy. In other words, if human rights are part of the rule of law, it is not by virtue of democracy but by virtue of justice. If a human right would be just one articulation of the common good among others, it would be easily explained why people agree on trading, for instance, the right to privacy for the feeling of security, the right to asylum for a suitable immigration policy, the right to *habeas corpus* for revenge. I submit that my account explains the ambiguity of human rights: On the one hand, we cannot escape from defining them as 'good for us', i.e., as basic values. But on the other hand, if we do, we will never be farther away from justice as a norm. Or, to put it the other way round, democracy is more inclusive, and therefore more exclusive, than any other political system. Its main advantage seems to be that you can more quickly change the boundaries.

Another layer of ambiguity concerns the representation of the *demos* as the plural self of the 'we'. There is no we that is able to say 'we', as

---

128 C Schmitt (1964).

Waldenfels (following Benveniste) incisively observes.[129] Or again, with Rousseau, we may ask not only how the people will know what they really want, but also how they will speak with one voice. Saying 'we' is always done by spokesmen and mouth-pieces. And indeed, in the rare, and often highly ritualised, cases in which a group of people utters the same phrase 'as with one voice', the pronoun 'we' is either replaced by '*I*', as if each spoke for him- or herself, or they simply repeat and copy the words of a single person prompting them, or they get stuck in a performative contradiction. Thus, the 'voice' of the 'we' that is heard in democratic law-making is by definition construed as one, i.e., as a unity – possibly that of a body, as Hobbes saw, in which case the one-ness is accounted for in terms of mutual coordination of sub-plans and actions. Furthermore, this 'actor' (to continue Hobbesian idiolect) will be construed as acting on behalf of an 'author' – a *demos* that remains absent and will never be present in spite of the fact that its presence has to be made felt if the presentation is to succeed as re-presentation.[130]

The predicate 'migrants' is particularly apt to frustrate any attempt to be convincing as far as representation is concerned. As the term derives from a third viewpoint beyond the first-person idiolect of in-clusion and ex-clusion, i.e. im-migrants and e-migrants, migrants do not register on the radar of a polity but as unreliable free-movers, unreliable precisely since they embody difference rather than necessary unity. It does not exactly increase one's credibility to claim that one is representing them. They are nowhere in political space and they are never in political time. They 'evaporate into the eternity of a now without a future'[131] – or without a past, for that matter. To acknowledge their right to free movement makes no sense. It is as if we would ascribe the right to walk on two feet to those who are defined by walking on two feet. Or, to revert to a discussion of almost 250 years ago during the last decades of the

---

129 B Waldenfels (2001) 139–140.

130 In this respect it cannot come as a surprise that 'the people', as Rosanvallon wrote, will remain 'introuvable' and democracy 'inachevée'. P Rosanvallon (1998; 2000).

131 F Tanghe (1988), dl. II, 294.

Ancien Regime: it makes no sense to ban migrants from the polity because the life of a migrant is a voluntary ban. It is the connotation of their 'indifference' to the polity inherent in their being 'passers-by', which makes them unfit to be represented. They have got the status that Rousseau, in the chapter on civil religion,[132] ascribes to the migrants par excellence: the Christians. As migrants on earth, always on their way to a somewhere and a sometime beyond the polity, they are profoundly unreliable. They exhibit anti-patriotism in the flesh,[133] and they make no exception for *Verfassungspatriotismus* (pace Habermas). Oh yes, they make good mercenaries, because they are indifferent to the question for whom they fight as long as they can earn a living. Basically they are the ones who *a priori* withdraw from the social contract, firstly because they cannot be expected to deliver according to the economic precondition of the social contract (appearing at the market place where everything will be shared), secondly because they cannot be judged by the rules that will give form and content to the social contract.

5. SUMMARY

If we depart from self-determination as the point of reference for a society, we may conceive of law as a global balance of powers. But, in the final analysis, political participation in that play of powers can only be staged in a dimension that is imagined as exterior to society. Jointly staging this dimension is the primary act by which people give themselves a specific identity, or 'first-personhood'. This allows them to refer to 'society' *tout court*, meaning 'our' society, as a first-person plural agent with a 'self' of which it is aware in joint actions, i.e. of a common wealth requiring protection, continuation, expansion, etc. The symbolic character of this external dimension can be concealed. Then the balance of powers is under constant pressure of an imminent asymmetry between this first person 'we' and 'others'. The asymmetry will be mapped onto

---

132 J-J Rousseau (1762 [1964]) IV, 8.

133 F Tanghe (1988), dl. II, 290.

an order of being: the members of the polity will say, for instance, 'we' *are* better than 'the others'. That is why I said: political power is not virtually absolute, but it is virtually totalitarian. It is also why I rejected it as a philosophically acceptable basis of the concept of a legal order. It is at odds with self-determination and (by implication) self-preservation.

The next step was to find an analysis of political self-awareness that is not *a priori* committed to a totalitarian claim to power and that acknowledges the irreducible difference between the position of 'the first person' and 'the other'. I presented this problem in the key of what I called 'the social relationship', acknowledging throughout (i) that ordering this relationship is the core of political action, and (ii) that the result of this ordering is the polity which as a whole is a first person (plural) in relation to some 'other'. I refuted the strategy of 'the common denominator', as if *'I'* and 'the other' can be reduced to a common root: for instance, the concept of man. This, I submitted, is not acknowledging the other as different. Two contrary readings of 'acknowledging the other as different' appeared possible: acknowledging her as a value for me in warranting the objectivity of my self-awareness, and acknowledging her as a law challenging the premature ordering of my own world. These two principles reverse or evoke each other. My thesis was that justice is a politics, which lives through this infinite reversal or antinomy. It is a politics that, on its own accord, makes something count against the identity it acknowledges as its ultimate basis. But it cannot refrain from framing this identity in the very act of challenging it, and vice versa. This is why this evocation is a historical event that generates only temporary and provisional solutions of social problems. It is intertwined with historical contingencies and cannot be anticipated or retrieved from a point of view outside of it.

The institutionalised openness of a political order to this event I called law. It is an event, precisely in the sense that it evades the categories by which we try to appropriate the world. That is why we can only find traces of such an event in the history we narrate: the narrative of how a certain society has lived through the infinite and mutual reversal of alterity in social relationships. In this insurmountable opposability we find a form of political self-awareness that could be called: self-imposed self-mitigation – which distinguishes it in principle from totalitarian claims.

3. Positive law and sovereign authority

In the previous chapter I dealt with the ultimate basis of a legal order: justice in political agency. I characterised the idea of justice and the concept of law in general terms, derived from the opposite principles governing social relationships. I showed how the two may be captured in one formula: justice is 'the politics of openness', i.e. the ability of a polity to acknowledge unconditionally what counts against its self-proclaimed identity without being coerced to do so. Law we may see as the institutionalisation of that acknowledgement. Therefore we should appreciate that it is governed by the double bind of proclaiming the identity of the polity while at the same time questioning it.[1] In the remainder of this book I will show how this account allows us to understand three major ways in which law appears in society: as a phenomenon that is authoritatively set (in ways yet to be specified); as an object of (scholarly) knowledge; and as a practice of decision-making in compliance with rules. The present chapter aims at unravelling the first of these modes of appearance: law is always set, 'posited', or 'positive'. What does that mean? And which implications, which presuppositions, which consequences, are entailed by this feature? Do they allow us to reverse the statement and say that positive law is law solely by virtue of its being positive? And above all, what does the positive character of law have to do with the opposite relationships between the first-person plural agent of the polity and their Other, i.e. with the basis of the legal order and the idea of justice analysed in the previous chapter?

I will first explain what the word 'positive' means with regard to law, and distinguish a twofold meaning (section 1). Then I will sketch what are the fascinating and, indeed, reasonable trains of thought behind these

[1] Cf. B Flynn (2006) 150; critical: B van Roermund (2009a).

meanings (section 2). In fact I will take a way around these trains of thought by discussing them under the guises of two forms of legal positivism, i.e. two ways of over-emphasising the inevitably positive character of law. One has a background in the theory of knowledge, which will be the topic of the next chapter. In this chapter I discuss another one, rooting in a theory of political authority. The general structure of this form of legal positivism I analyse in section 3. I think we can learn a lot from it, even if we reject it in the end. My problem with political legal positivism is not that it separates law from morality (there are strong moral reasons to do this), but that it advocates a dualist account of sovereignty. It separates constituent power from constitutional power. In section 4 I argue an alternative for this dualism showing that these two are mutually conditional, if sovereignty claims to 'create' political order. This very claim entails a certain quality being allegedly added to sovereignty, namely that supreme power is exercised by virtue of authority over society. In contradistinction to some other theories, I will conceive of authority in general as attributed practical knowledge that is (partially) personal, tacit, and embodied. Political authority is attributed knowledge about how to best order society, while political authority over law is attributed knowledge about how to best lend sustainable form and substance to the 'double bind' mentioned above by instituting authority. Section 5 will explain that this kind of knowledge, in the final analysis, pertains to showing how a polity can question the boundaries that shape its self-proclaimed identity. In section 6 I will argue that this account of authority provides a good fit with two features that are characteristic of law's appearance in society: firstly, that law, though posited by political action, nevertheless maintains a relative independence from politics. Secondly, that law, though posited by political action, allows for a relatively independent position of legal knowledge vis-à-vis law as a set of authoritative norms, precisely for the sake of its authority. Section 7 shows, in conclusion, by which institutional principles the authority of law is secured with regard to the first feature.

1. POSITIVE LAW – POSITED LAW

Most law students are aware of what the double L in their programmes (LLB, LLM) stands for: a tradition of learnedness where laws, i.e. legal orders, come in the plural. To offer value for money a lawyer had to acquire expertise in both civil (secular) and canonical (ecclesiastical) law (*utrumque ius*). Non-English law students honour the same tradition when they typically use a plural for what they are reading: *iura* (German), *rechten* (Dutch). These 'laws' were distinguished on account of a final authority presiding over each of them, say the emperor or the pope. This idiom is a direct effect of law being 'positive', which is to say that it is bound up with an observable 'then and there', and all the indexical devices that come with it. Two meanings of 'positive' in the phrase 'positive law' are to be distinguished.

Def. 3.1 *Law is 'positive' in the sense of being posited (i.e. issued, applied, enforced) by some human action then and there.*

Def. 3.2 *Law is 'positive' in the sense of being contingent on certain facts then and there, i.e. on 'posita' in the sense of 'given data'.*

Consider *Def. 3.1* first. It says that law is a man-made rather than a natural phenomenon, and that it is made intentionally rather than inadvertently. In modern society this often boils down to law being made by a dedicated political agent referred to as 'the sovereign'. I will return to this notion soon enough. However, on the basis of this definition it is easy to see why in other societies customary law (which is not endorsed by a sovereign) may be acknowledged as full-blown positive law. It is made by habitual behaviour of the members rather than by the enactments of a dedicated agent. Even then, however, it is conceived as intentionally made, i.e. set, or posited, rather than found, imagined, or thought. By the same definition we can easily see why international public law (which is often weakly enforced by a sovereign) can nevertheless be called real, positive law. Enforcement is only one of the modes in which law is 'made' or posited. Application by an established court, or transfer of national sovereign prerogatives to a dedicated supra-national agent (a parliament, for instance) are others.

How ever that may be, what is commonly meant by the predicate 'positive' is that law is established by political or politically relevant, action. A statute is enacted by the Queen in Parliament, a treaty is closed between peoples or a contract between parties, a will is made by an individual citizen, a decision is given by a board or a judge. These actions are events in the observable world rather than purely mental acts going on in the minds of those involved. They often evolve by protocol or ritual. One raises or shakes hands, pounds a hammer, writes a signature, stamps a seal, exchanges documents. Of course, these are only the visible forms, frequently magnified by pomp and circumstance. There are less solemn, but hardly less corporeal ones. The prosecution of crimes and the maintenance of public order by physical force are probably the most evident ones. Also one will appreciate, as Ancient Greece did, that law enforcement is closely connected to other sectors of public policy, such as city-building, employment, housing, minorities' rights, and probation facilities for ex-prisoners.

Note that the acts mentioned above are not acts of communicating or informing about established or existent law. On the contrary, they are the very acts by which law is established, i.e. by which it comes into existence. The fact that speech is used does not mean that it is used to report on something happening outside the speech act itself. We are familiar with this 'performative' mode of speech in ordinary language. For instance, if I say 'I promise to bring your bike back first thing in the morning', this is, under the appropriate circumstances, not so much the report of a promise, but rather the making of one:[2] I promise. By the same token, the promising should be distinguished from the speech act that often accompanies it: the act of reporting the promise to someone (who may *but* need not be the addressee of the promise). Basically, the same is true for law enactment. The enactment is not tantamount to its

---

[2] Doing things in saying things, doing things with words, is called, by philosophers, performing *a speech act*, the phrase being a *performative*. See JL Austin (1962); JR Searle (1969); J Derrida (1982).

publication, though it is true that publication is usually an essential, and indeed final, part of the enactment procedure, after parliamentary deliberation, votes, countersign, etc.

But 'positive' in connection to law has another meaning still, as captured in *Def. 3.2*. As Pascal put it, what is law and what is not law depends on meridians and latitudes, on whether you are on this or the other side of a river.[3] Law is permeated by the contingency that marks the facts on the ground and the course of history. He famously characterised these one page up: 'Cleopatra's nose; if it would have been shorter, the present face of the earth would have looked different.'[4] Sometimes, but not always, such differences are functionally interwoven with specific conditions registering in climatology, geography, ethnology, cultural history, etc. Property right in land, for instance, may evolve differently on a small and dry island compared to endless humid plains. Often we cannot find out anymore which signification and valuation might once have fed the roots of certain practices. In a contemporary vernacular David Nelken writes:

> Enquiries into legal culture try to understand puzzling features of the role and the rule of law within given societies. Why do the UK and Denmark complain most about the imposition of EU law but then turn out to be the countries, which have the best records of obedience? Conversely, why does Italy, whose public opinion is most in favour of Europe, have such a high rate of non compliance? Why does Holland, otherwise so similar, have such a low litigation rate compared to neighbouring Germany? Why in the United States and the UK does it often take a sex scandal to create official interest in doing something about corruption, whereas in Latin countries it takes a major corruption scandal to excite interest in marital unfaithfulness!? Such contrasts can lead us to reconsider broader theoretical issues in the study of law and society.[5]

---

[3] B Pascal (1894 [1670]) IV, 21.

[4] Ibid. III, 18. Pascal regarded the varying character of actual law as on a par with the idleness of the human condition. One century later, Montesquieu valued it quite differently.

[5] D Nelken (2004) 1.

Last but not least, there is this blurred line, which makes the killing of a human being in some cases a crime, in others punishment, in still others heroism, or arbitrariness. The same event, a blast in an apartment, for instance, is now an accident, now a production risk, now a case of collateral damage – all according to law. Needless to say that all these contingencies can coagulate, and grow to, sometimes bizarre, formats of legal facts.

The difference between the two meanings of 'positive' will be intuitively clear. In the first case what is aimed at is the fact that law is always to be posited over and over again, i.e. it typically exists only if it is en-acted. If it ceases to be enacted in the broad sense of the word (lawyers call it desuetude) it ceases to exist and is not longer valid. In the second case the focus is on the fact that law is always already predetermined by data posited, i.e. it typically exists in interrelations with states of affairs that are independent of law. As was also clear from the beginning, the two meanings have something in common: they relate law to certain observable facts. In the former case these facts are acts, like parliamentary votes, ministerial signatures, habits, declarations, etc. In the latter, they are states of affairs or events like technological developments (information-, gen- and nano-technologies, for instance), economic growth, political (un-)balance, etc. In any case, both types of facts illustrate that law is not merely about having ideas, but primarily about making things happen.

2. WHY LEGAL POSITIVISM?

Because the two meanings of 'positive' have to do with 'observables', it is tempting to believe that they exhaustively capture the properties that can be ascribed to law. According to this view, being posited by the action of a dedicated political body, respectively being a function of a course of events or a set of circumstances would be the exclusive and exhaustive heart of the legal matter. There would be nothing else and nothing more to law than either (or both) of these two characteristics. In particular, these properties would suffice to define the *validity* of law. This view amounts to legal positivism.

Def. 3.3 *Legal positivism is the philosophical view that law is nothing but 'positive' in either or both of the two senses explained in Def. 3.1 and Def. 3.2.*

Please note that legal positivism is different from the mind-set of many a professional lawyer, who prefer to focus on the positive law of a certain legal order, its case law, rules, doctrines, sanctions and customs, and who firmly steers away from everything resembling jurisprudence. Though some of them take pleasure in characterising themselves as 'legal positivists', they are nothing of the kind; not, that is, by virtue of their professional attitude. Legal positivism, although it disqualifies any philosophical discourse reaching beyond the positivity of law,[6] is a philosophical view in its own right. It claims to be reasonable on a par with the theories discussed in the previous chapters. Consequent to *Def. 3.3* there are two basic forms of legal positivism, depending on which meaning of 'positive' is favoured as exclusive and exhaustive. Though they are often combined, they are not necessarily linked. The first form is based on what is commonly called the Separability Thesis [STh]. The second one harbours the Reductibility Thesis [RTh]. The latter holds that utterances setting norms can be reduced to utterances stating facts. I will deal with [RTh] in the next chapter. The former concerns us here, and it is important to stress that it is a conceptual thesis. In a nutshell it holds that, in order to give a conceptual account of law in Modernity, one has to refrain from concepts and arguments that purport to assess the moral value of law. Thus, [STh] does not commit us to the view that there are no historical interconnections between law and morality; or that, in any given society, there is no considerable overlap between moral and legal

---

[6] Denouncing in particular, as we will see, an intrinsic, i.e. conceptual dependence of law on morality. For an in-depth discussion on legal positivism in the contemporary Anglo-American context, see HLA Hart (1994), the Postscript; J Coleman (2001); R Dworkin (2002). For an overview of the debate, see the relevant contributions to J Coleman, S Shapiro et al. (2002).

norms; or that, in other cultures than Modernity, one cannot define law in moral terms either; or that – admittedly a debatable case – the law itself may not refer to morality as a source of law in certain issues.[7] I will analyse [STh] in the next section. But first I have to clarify why legal positivism in general is so tempting, or what deeply felt needs it promises to satisfy.

2.1 Two Motives for Legal Positivism

There are at least two very plausible and honourable motives to embrace a form of legal positivism. The one is: 'otherwise there is nothing to know about law'; the other: 'otherwise there is nothing to achieve by law'. These motives provide the background against which two forms of legal positivism stand out. Apprehensibility and expediency are invariably the two points at stake when positivity is stressed to the point where it becomes the law's one and only characteristic. Let us look into each of them, and then ask how they relate to each other

2.1.1 Apprehensibility

One thing seems clear enough when it comes to apprehension of norms: there is no point in denying the logical gulf between 'is' and 'ought'. From the thought that theft *ought* to be punished, we cannot infer that theft *is* punished; and, inversely, from the thought that theft is punished, we cannot infer that it ought to be punished. That is a truism, which some philosophers prefer to present[8] in a more sweeping form: one can

---

[7] In such issues, the law refers to established moral stances in a polity (so-called 'positive morality', as distinct from 'critical morality'). See, e.g. EU Directive 98/44 on the legal protection of biotechnological inventions: Art. 6(1) stipulates that an invention is non-patentable '(…) if commercial exploitation of the patent would be contrary to *ordre public* or morality; however, exploitation shall not be deemed to be so contrary merely because it is prohibited by law or regulation.' Moreover, in Art. 6(2)(c), it explicitly lists the use of human embryos for industrial or commercial purposes as an example of a practice at odds with *ordre public* or morality.

[8] I am aware of the innuendo, which will be justified in Chapter 4.

neither derive facts from norms, nor norms from facts.[9] It would follow that facts are only justifiable by referring to other facts, and norms only by referring to other norms – and never the twain shall meet.

But if norms cannot be justified with reference to facts, it seems very doubtful that they can be justified at all. For what kind of knowledge is this, that cannot be corroborated by establishing what is the case, and what not? Inversely, how can we hope to substantiate knowledge-claims by referring to what ought to be the case or what should be done?[10] Legal positivism promises a way out of this predicament. We can try to analyse norms in terms of facts. Once we succeed in doing that, apprehension of norms and justification of norms will be reduced to epistemological problems we are familiar with: problems about facts.

2.1.2 Expediency

The second motive to adopt legal positivism is the concern for the expediency of law. We may observe that many divergent and, indeed, incompatible views, options, preferences, opinions are put forward in debates concerning the application or concretisation of social values, or even the corroboration of facts. They revert to so many incompatible political ideologies (e.g., liberalism, socialism, corporatism, etc.). Morality would not help us out here, as people can get into vehement and violent conflict with one another on moral issues. Religion is not going to offer a last resort either, as a long history of crusades, wars, and colonial oppression proves. Apparently, we are unable to think ourselves a way out of such predicaments, then put it into practice. This has nothing to do with bad faith or egoistic behaviour on the part of most human beings, but everything to do with the limited judgment we have with regard to the situation we find ourselves in, as well as to motives and outcomes of our actions.

---

[9] This is one version – I believe a rather inaccurate one – of what is commonly called Hume's guillotine, or the gulf between 'is-' and 'ought-' sentences. See D Hume (1739–1740 [1972]) Bk. III, Part I, section I for the original text.

[10] The view that yields to these doubts about 'knowledge of norms' is called: non-cognitivism.

A possible way out of this situation is to accept beforehand a procedure for generating decisions on the basis of reasonable, though inconclusive, evidence. Thus, by accepting its outcomes, we may resume the life we have to live together, and discover in practice what we failed to find out in theory. What is good advice when we hesitate how to spell a word? Stop thinking and start writing it 'for real' – and then you just appear to 'know how' what is the right or the wrong way in spite of the inability to 'know that' one way or the other is right or wrong. Similarly, we are often able to solve a conflict by re-entering into a practical relationship rather than by principled thinking who was right and who was wrong; a relationship from which we may discover what we really value in the experience of practice rather than the conception of theory. The law provides a medium to make such transitions in matters politic, by generating legislative, governmental, and judiciary decisions.

2.2 The Tension Between the Motives

At first sight, these two motives seem easy to reconcile. On the one hand, it is intuitively plausible to expect that little can be achieved by law unless it can be apprehended, i.e. known. On the other hand, it is hard to see what there is to be known about law, unless it makes its appearance in society as an effective ordering. But as we learned more about the two motives and their respective backgrounds, we may doubt whether they are each other's supplement. The motive of expediency has a conceptual background that is not easily reconciled with the one presupposed by the motive of apprehensibility, and vice versa. At the limit, the motive of expediency seems to usher in a form of decisionism. If the role of law would solely be to *impose* a certain way of behaviour on agents in order to make them re-enter a conflict-free zone, regardless of the appropriateness of that behaviour, the power of the law would grow to such proportions that there is nothing left to be really *known* about law. Indeed, if the certainty that there will be a decision – whatever decision – in case of conflict is all there is to legal certainty, then knowledge of law is utterly uncertain. That is one side of the coin. The other side is that, to the extent that the apprehensibility of law is taken seriously, there is less room for purely authoritative decision-making. If law is perfectly knowable, the authority setting the norms will have no other reasons to decide upon than those that were already knowable for everyone familiar with the law in the case at hand. Law, in this view, becomes a matter of academic knowledge rather than political authority. This tension of motives explains a lot of the confusing argumentations around the issue of legal positivism. The fact that the two motives, taken to their respective limits, reveal each other's flaws, explains why the corresponding forms of legal positivism often hunt in pairs. They keep hovering between appeals to expediency and to apprehension, switching codes when they are challenged. Challenges of legal authority are met by proposals to see law as applied sociology, psychology, or economics. Challenges of legal knowledge are responded to by conceptions of law as an authoritative machine reducing social complexity.

3. THE STRUCTURE OF LEGAL POSITIVISM

The Separability Thesis [STh] is a negative thesis; it says which concept of law is *not* feasible, namely a concept that would predicate the concept of law on morality. From the previous section we may learn that the separation of law and morality may have moral reasons. For instance, it is a moral concern that law should be able to impose norms even in moral conflicts, which clearly blocks the appeal to morality in law. But these moral reasons for separating law from morality do not enter into an account of what (the) law demands, either in general or in a specific case. They pertain to the question of the previous chapter, to wit, what is law about in society? The answer to the latter question does not necessarily entail an answer to the former one, inquiring about the normative perimeter of (the) law. What, then, is the positive flipside of [STh]? What are necessary and sufficient conditions that allow us to say what (the) law is, regardless of whether it is morally good or bad law?

The answer of Modernity is that the norms of law (i) show a certain format that we may call 'practical', (ii) have a certain scope that is called 'general', (iii) come from a dedicated political body of agency, called 'the sovereign'. I am aware of the fact that this answer will sound classical, if not obsolete, to many ears. 'This is Hobbes', one will say; or 'this is Austin'. And in a sense it is Hobbes, and Austin, and also Rousseau, Kant, and a few others. At the same time it is none of them as long as we have not explored the meaning of (i)–(iii) at a much deeper level. Until then it remains to be seen whether it is an obsolete answer or not.

3.1 Norms as Practical

Norms have a certain structure or format in that they express 'what ought to be done' if certain states of affairs obtain. Of course there are plenty of norms of the form 'X counts as Y in context C' – thus constituting a legal institution. But I submit that this is an elliptic way of expressing '*X* ought to be treated as *Y* in context *C*'. Inserting a credit card into a toll port on a motorway in France 'counts as' concluding a contract of sales in the sense that now the provider is under the obligation to deliver certain road conditions while I am permitted to use the road over a certain distance. Such 'constitutive' norms do not describe a state of affairs, they 'create' one, in particular an institutional (e.g. legal) state of affairs. But this state of affairs can only be rendered in 'ought' sentences. Power-conferring (empowering) norms stand out among these constitutive rules. They create a realm of institutional action (e.g., 'The Union shall have an institutional framework (…). The Union's institutions shall be: (…)' (Art. 13 TEU). Within this realm the agents ought to do certain things. Let us also acknowledge that there are secondary norms: norms about how one ought to handle norms, e.g., norms of adjudication and change.[11] Note that in all these types of norms the operator 'ought' is a generic one. It is a dummy for all so-called 'deontic' modalities: obligating, permitting, and prohibiting modalities.[12]

---

[11] Famously HLA Hart (1961) ch V (law as the union of primary and secondary rules). I am hesitant, however, to call the rule of recognition (Hart's most important secondary rule) a norm on the same footing.

[12] As a consequence I think it is wrong to burden deontic logic with the problem of two types of permission: strong and weak permission. Strong

So norms do not express what we should think, nor do they express what ought to be the case (as in wants or desires); they say what an agent *A* should do, should not do, or may do. This, however, they can do in different ways. The obvious format is that of a prescription in which a first person *A* tells a second person *B* what *B* should do. This is sometimes called 'a command', but that may easily be misunderstood. A command is a speech act, and whether that speech act performs successfully what it purports to bring about is dependent on all sorts of conditions. *A* may command *B* to do something only if he, *A*, has got authority to do so. What I mean by a prescription is much more basic: it is the bare structure of the content of the norm, regardless of whether it is a command, or an advice, or a request, or etc. Which acts are appropriate to enact the law is something I will not discuss. Suffice it to say here, that part of the discussion about soft law being 'real law' or not, is due to the fact that legal theorists assume, perhaps prematurely, that the prescriptive character of law necessarily entails that it is enacted by central command rather than, e.g., administrative advice or growing agreement. There is, however, also a format of practical thinking that presents an alternative to prescriptions. This is the format of an intention. The structure of an intention is such that a first person singular A expresses what he or she is going to do, or that a first person plural <*A*, *B*, … *n*> expresses what they, themselves, are going to do (if certain facts obtain). A will, for instance is a first-person singular norm, and a contract is a first person plural norm.[13]

According to Rousseau's argument, by virtue of the social contract and the sovereignty of the citizens, all laws are first-person plural intentions by which the citizens commit themselves together to certain actions. Of

---

permission is the creation of a range of actions, that 'ordinary' deontic operators may take on as arguments (in fact the deontic counterparts of modal logic □ (Necessarily) and ◊ (Possibly) suffice). See, e.g., the Mayor 'may' forbid a soccer match in the sense that he has the legal power to do this, and in the sense that in certain circumstances he is permitted to use this legal power, while in others he is obliged or prohibited to use it. But even if he is prohibited to use it, he has the power.

[13] See Chapter 4 for more details.

course this is difficult to swallow if one considers it as a description of the empirical appearance law makes in society: it is still the king in parliament who makes laws – not 'us'. However, Rousseau's proposal does not pertain to the appearance of law but to the format, i.e. the most abstract conceptual structure in which law as a whole can be captured. This format pervades all empirical law; it is the core of statutes in civil law as well as rationes decidendi in case-law; it is at the core of legislative, administrative, judiciary, and even private legal decisions. It is an attempt to model how, in the final analysis, law articulates freedom in society while at the same time blocking any moral appeal to freedom outside the law. This is why Rousseau can say, in one of his numerous paradoxes, that someone who deflects after the law is established by all citizens, will be forced to comply by the others, and that this is a way of 'forcing him to be free'.

3.2 General Norms

According to the second condition not all norms are law, only general norms. What does this mean? Certainly not that law is only what can be formulated in norms beginning with universal quantifiers. We typically read these quantifiers in the provisions of statutes in civil law systems: 'He who takes [i.e., *all* who take; BvR] someone's property with the intent to appropriate this against the law, will be punished, as guilty of theft, by a term of maximally four years in prison or a fourth category fine.'[14] It is clear that such linguistic surface structures do not constrain the scope of any norm. It is perfectly possible to pick one individual by the use of a universal quantifier: 'All those who are named BvR, born February 24, 1947, etc.' picks out one individual in the world, me. The general character of legal norms, if it is to mean anything as a constraint on scope rather than format, should derive from principles governing the content of the law.

---

14 Art. 310 Dutch criminal code in a liberal translation.

In this respect it is informative to closely read the 1789 *Déclaration des droits de l'homme et du citoyen*. It brings to light the variety among, as well as the internal tensions between, these principles – tensions we are still wrestling with in our time. A law is deemed to be general in at least five different senses:

(1) as a ban on privileges, i.e., on immunities based on personal status;
(2) as an act of will resulting from joint participation by all citizens;
(3) as a rule that is to be applied equally in equal cases;
(4) as an upshot and a warrant of the universal rights of man and citizen;
(5) as a piece of corroborated knowledge about the common interest.

Obviously, these principles cannot be simply aggregated or integrated. For instance, one may be tempted to think that legal positivism became obsolete when the *Déclaration* pointed to human and civil rights going beyond positive law. This positive reference to supra-positive law allegedly absorbs whatever may be meant by the 'general' character of legal norms, be they statutory or case law norms. By the same token, it is alleged to deflate a form of power 'beyond the laws', since final decision-makers in society now ought to comply with fundamental rights. But things are more complicated than this. The more the text of the *Déclaration* became part and parcel of the French Constitution in its successive versions, the more it emphasised the possibility of constraints on lofty rights by … general laws. Up and until the present day, in the European Charter on Human Rights this political constraint is an essential precondition for human rights to enter positive law under the guise of 'fundamental rights'.[15]

And there are other gaps and tensions. If the law would warrant that no one's particular interests are privileged, it would not, by the same token, already reflect the common interest. And if it were a reflection of the

[15] Cf. Charter of Fundamental Rights of the European Union (2000/C 364/01) Art. 52.1. Such a provision fails in the 1948 Universal Declaration of Human Rights – reason why this norm set does not count as positive law.

common interest, that in itself would not make it an upshot or a warrant of human and civic rights, nor would it entail the participation of all citizens in the public enterprise. Also, equal treatment often appears at odds with universal fundamental rights, for instance when freedom of religion conflicts with equality of chances on the job market. In short, if law ought to promote space for individual human liberty as well as present reliable knowledge about the common wealth, and be neutral to 'relevant' aspects of equality, and be the result of joint work by all, it will pursue so many targets that it will achieve none.

No wonder that we see different legal cultures ranking different principles as taking priority over the others, though excluding none altogether. All seem to agree on (1): privileges are at odds with the general character of law. But diverging views are taken on (2), as participation of all citizens has to be reconciled somehow with institutions of representation. Think of the famous discussion on judiciary constitutional review being at odds (or not) with the primacy of parliamentary legislation. Cultural preferences become more visible with regard to principles (3)–(5) as EU law has to deal with their divergences on a daily basis.[16] Principle (3) is very much at the core of the French idea of *légalité*, while principle (4) is the hallmark of the post-war German idea of *Rechtsstaatlichkeit*. I will not claim that principle (5) reflects the common law idea of 'the rule of law' in its entirety; but it does capture the most received view of how one has to construe this rule, namely from the interest of the polity. Comparatists studying the legal orders of EU Member States are familiar, not only with differences in ranking principles (1)–(5), but also with the criticism that is raised against too strong an emphasis on one of the principles (3)–(5). Broadly speaking, French officials have to battle a well-deserved reputation of being over-formalistic. The Germans are repudiated for turning application of norms into 'Wertungsjurisprudenz', i.e., a mode of legal doctrine that assesses every case in terms of values as enshrined in the

---

[16] Cf. S Prechal and B Van Roermund (2008). Earlier, specifically on 'rule of law', J Steenbergen, Gd Clercq et al. (1983) ch. III.

1949 Constitution.[17] Legal scholars in the common law are divided over the dominant position of economic analysis of law as a tool to generate calculations of the general interests from private preferences.

Interestingly, compatibility of private interests as a definition of the general interest is something that has not gone unnoticed in other traditions than the common law. Rousseau, for instance, in a famous footnote about the Marquis D'Argenson,[18] argues that the general interest can only appear as the sum-total of private interests precisely in as far as they differ from each other, implying that they must be also *seen* to differ. Kant is equally famous for having characterised law-in-general as the order in which the freedom of everyone (to pursue their respective interests) can be made compatible in mutual recognition from the agents' points of view.[19] Apparently, the general interest as the expression of reciprocal recognitions of private interests by the members of the polity is an important orientation underlying the various accounts of generality that different legal cultures appear to prefer.[20] In the framework of an account of law that is determined to keep morality at bay, this is an important anchor point. The general interest of a polity is not necessarily morally good. For example, one may take moral issues with a governmental policy that ignores ecological concerns for reasons of public wealth. But without mutual recognition of interests the general interest means nothing. This is why ecologists, for instance, are wise to argue their case from a general interest perspective.

Moreover, reciprocity of interests as a definition of the general character of law has two further advantages. Firstly, it allows us to understand why even judicial decisions in individual cases can be 'general'. Obviously, decisions have to be 'universalisable' to other,

---

[17] Critical: W Schreckenberger (1978) 174; I Maus (1989) 197f; J Habermas (1992 [1992]) 309ff.

[18] J-J Rousseau (1762 [1964]) II, 3.

[19] 'Das Recht ist also der Inbegriff der Bedingungen, unter denen die Willkür des einen mit der Willkür des andern nach einem allgemeinen Gesetze der Freiheit zusammen vereinigt werden kann.' (I Kant (1797 [1975]), Einleitung in die Rechtslehre, B.)

[20] See also J Habermas (1992 [1992]) 138–139.

similar cases. But it requires precisely a comparison under the angle of reciprocity of interests to find out which cases are similar and what is to be done in the interest of all those involved. Lawyers will propose to distinguish if they can argue that the facts of a case require a different weighing of interests. If not, they will yield to precedents. Decisions in individual cases are also general to the extent that they weigh the interests of the parties over and against the backdrop of wider interests in society. For example, if *A* is sanctioned for drunken driving the sentence is general to the extent that it takes into account the interests of (even potential) fellow travellers as well as *A* in a certain society. Secondly, our view also explains why the parameters of law being general differ according to the various realms in which law is involved. 'General' means one thing in constitutional law, another thing in criminal law, yet another thing in private law, etc. For instance, the law of torts allows a wider application of analogical reasoning than criminal law, where the 'nullum crimen' principle largely determines whether a decision is in accordance with the general character of the law.

3.3 Sovereignty

'Sovereignty' usually translates as 'supreme power' – the highest power in a polity. But if this translation would go into the positivist account of law under study, we would go round in circles. For in order to understand what the metaphor of a 'highest' power conveys we seem to presuppose already the very normative concept of law that we are looking for. 'Highest power' would mean 'highest under the constitution', or 'highest constitutional power'. But how to account for the power that brings about the constitution, i.e., how to account for 'constituent power'? If the answer would point to power pure and simple, i.e., if sovereignty would be strongest power rather than highest power, we are about to opt for the other horn of the dilemma. Then we give an account of right in terms of might. Quite apart from moral concerns, the question then is how factual power can be understood to generate normative power? Obviously this is what happens often enough in political reality. But our question is under which conditions we could possibly understand this as something reasonable? To put it in another way, how can power over the law pose also as power under the law?[21]

Before trying a few possible answers, I would like to get some misunderstandings out of the way. Let us skip the view that sovereignty amounts to law being made from a central command office where one individual pulls the strings at will. Already in Hobbes[22] we read that the sovereign may be a council; that it may deliberate prior to making decisions; that law may be enacted by different agents as long as the unity of law is upheld *in the end.* What Hobbes wanted to curb, for example, are situations in which citizens in conflict may turn to different 'supreme courts' to shop for a decision that serves them best. Obviously, neither of these courts would be supreme, and the conflict would continue to exist as long as the parties desire. I submit that here we are on Hobbes' side. We think that a legal order where you can shop around like this, has a problem. We do not celebrate it as the pride of 'legal pluralism'. Sovereignty is even compatible with the separation of state powers, on condition that at some point they come together again and form a unity. So much for sovereignty as the exercise of central command over society.

It is often thought that sovereignty and its problems are bound up with the nation state. The problems will evaporate together with the notion of sovereignty itself by dint of the nation state becoming obsolete and withering away. In fact, when it comes to sovereignty, very little depends on the rise or fall of the nation state. As Bodin pointed out in his famous treatise on sovereignty, almost a century prior to Hobbes, all polities from times immemorial have sought resort in a notion of 'supreme power', whether they cared to give an account of it or not.[23] They certainly were not nation states. Our time will probably see other states than national states arising, for instances, unions of Member States like the European

[21] More on this paradox of sovereignty in my B Van Roermund (2003b) 38ff, the section on 'The Argument from Incoherence' against sovereignty.
[22] T Hobbes (1651 [1983]) V, 6 and VI.
[23] J Bodin (1576 [1986]) 345.

Union. At present, with the crisis of the Euro-zone, few analysts will deny that problems of (lacking) sovereignty loom large over Europe and that their solution is to be found in re-defining rather than abandoning the notion.

A third and last misunderstanding is that, since the eighteenth century Revolutions sovereignty is tamed to the extent that it is constrained by the norms of human rights. In fact, however, the opposite is true: human rights appeal to sovereignty. Authors as different as Burke, Bentham, Marx and Arendt have argued that human rights mean nothing unless they are recognised by sovereign power.[24] And indeed, as said above, even the European Charter of Human Rights, unlike the 1948 Universal Declaration of Human Rights, acknowledges that these rights can be limited by legislation, i.e., by the exercise of sovereign power. I submit that this appeal goes round in circles.

Having set these misunderstandings aside, let us go back to the question how we should understand the relationship that sovereignty tries to capture: the relationship between constituent and constitutional power? An important way to answer the question takes two steps. The first is to admit that there cannot be power over the law that is at the same time power under the law, and that, therefore, constituent power logically precedes constitutional power. In other words: there is a strict dichotomy, indeed a dualism between constituent and constitutional power. The second step is to mitigate the voluntarist overtones in the concept of constituent power. What seems to be needed is an argument to the following effect: from the thesis that sovereignty entails constituent power[25] one cannot infer that the sovereign can make law at will, i.e., in arbitrary ways. If we can demonstrate that constituent power over law can only be exercised by responding to certain needs, wants, habits, and other pre-figurations in society, it may become possible to see law as the

---

24 C Douzinas (2000).

25 In classical idiom: that the sovereign is 'beyond all laws' (legibus solutus. i.e., beyond all established law, as Bodin would have it). J Bodin (1576 [1986]) I, 8 349: 'For he is absolutely sovereign who recognizes nothing, after God, that is greater than himself.' Cf. HK Lindahl (1997; 1998).

institutionalisation of this response. There are, however, different ways leading into this direction. The first is to supplement sovereignty by science, in particular what I call utility science. The second is to bring sovereignty under the guidance of history, as if the sovereign were the executor of pre-established orderings that have to be preserved, defended, restored, etc. I will reject both scientism and historicism in the sub-sections below, and defend an alternative in the next section, based on a non-dualist alternative for the first step.

3.3.1 Scientism

Utility is a name for whatever increases someone's advantage, profit, pleasure, welfare, happiness, wealth, and diminishes disadvantage, loss, pain, harm or poverty.[26] Now, the common wealth (or the general interest) in a social group can be seen as what brings about the greatest utility for the greatest number of agents involved. It may be objected that the categories of pleasure and pain, of profit and loss, even of wealth and poverty are categories of quality, subject to individual preferences: some people prefer a life of heroism and danger, where others opt for the safe or the bright side. This was indeed a problem for classical utilitarianism. But modern utilitarianism holds that, in the final analysis, individual preferences can and will be expressed in prices: the amount of time, money, or energy that agents are prepared to pay or for which they are prepared to deliver. So can generalised utility or common wealth, thus yielding criteria for expedient commanding that governs norms rather than being dependent on norms itself. I will therefore speak of utility science, as a general paradigm of social science that comprises large parts of economics but also other sciences. It may look as if the principle of utility is itself an overriding norm. This, however, is contingent on the broader theoretical context in which it is placed. In the present context it

---

[26] 'By the principle of utility is meant that principle which approves or disapproves of every action whatsoever, according to the tendency which it appears to have to augment or diminish the happiness of the party whose interest is in question: or, what is the same thing in other words, to promote or to oppose that happiness.' (J Bentham (1948) ch 1.)

is regarded as a model explaining specific social behaviour rather than a source of authority prescribing social behaviour. It explains why certain commands will be effective and others not, and that is what legal positivism wants to go by. It is not any more a norm than the price mechanism on the market.

In a way, both classical utilitarianism and modern utility science are deeply utopian. They appeal to the end of a long road, where constituent power and social calculation will coincide. To reach that point, political power has to gradually digest all the parameters of utility in a given society, thus yielding to what Bentham called 'the felicific calculus'. Then it would collapse constituent power into scientific operations. But this is a false picture, for at least three reasons.

Firstly, as long as this evolution is going on and as long as it has not yet reached its final point, constituent power will remain the necessary supplement of scientific calculation, in order to end or prevent conflicts of interests.[27] Some authors say that this is actually what is happening in our time.[28] The concept of sovereignty has got gradually dispersed over two areas: the area of utility science and the area of administrative power. These two adjacent areas show intensive border-crossings. While administrative power supplements the categories of utility science by exercising constituent power, utility science supplements the instruments of constituent power by inventing relevant predicates. For instance, the interventions of administrative officials paste the term QALY[29] into legislative

---

27 Note that in parentheses, at this point of the argument, 'supreme power' cannot be defined by legal norms, as we are in the process of defining legal norms in the first place. Consequently, sovereignty should be defined in factual terms, as Austin indeed did: the sovereign is he who is habitually being obeyed by others, without himself being in the habit of obeying others. This definition is far from a plea for the law of the strongest. It takes its cue from a kind of social Darwinism: the naturalistic belief that people in society have an instinct of following the leadership who they believe will best preserve society's (and their) survival.

28 This is largely Fourcault's thesis in M Foucault (1988).

29 A QALY (Quality Adjusted Life Years) in western countries is usually attributed a money value of € 30,000. Less expenditure to gain one QALY means more cost-effectiveness of medical interventions (or energy).

regulations of public health services, and utility science provides instruments that measure health quality in degrees of policy satisfaction. In the vast and pervasive area of security similar trade-offs are daily business. Utility science provides more and more 'qualities' by which security issues can be scored and ranked, and officials are quick to rule the scoring and ranking in these very terms. As a consequence, the predicate 'official' may currently be ascribed to civil servants who are scientists in their own right, as well as to scientists who are civil servants in their own right.

Secondly, the final point where constituent power would collapse into science will never be reached. If utility-science really is a science, it cannot be expected to deliver the kind of truths that will put an end to conflicts between competing comprehensive views of the good life. Natural science is already an infinite pursuit (the more we know, the more we know not to know) in which there are conflicting views at almost any frontier; but social science is notoriously contested due to its weak paradigms that seem to be geared more to explanations in terms of reasons than in terms of causes. They feature what is sometimes called[30] a 'double hermeneutic': they try to understand understanding, which means that their object (people in social relationships) talk back to the way their understanding is understood, thus proving the scientist wrong as they see fit. The predictive force of models in social sciences is limited, as economics has shown in the face of the financial crisis that began in 2008. But that means that the appeal to authoritative decision-making will in fact be the perennial associate of utility science as long as its mission is to end or prevent conflict. In fact, it will become not only a parameter of utility itself (to take over where utilitarianism fails), but also an immunising shield to defend the pretensions of overall calculation and lend them authority in order to promote the image of expedient government. The only change is that constituent power will go undercover as administrative power and generate constitutional law by working the little cogwheels of governmental power.

---

[30] A Giddens (1983) 11, following Peter Winch.

Thirdly, models of utility sciences like economics feature parameters that are inherently political. For instance, the thesis that price equals value is characteristic of neo-liberal but not of socialist or institutional economics. Or, another example, what goes into 'price' and what (for example, long-term environmental damage) is determined by political ramifications. These models do not yield to the pressure of empirical evidence but to that of political ideology, and as long as they are able to stick to their political paradigms, they keep producing categories and correlations that feed into these. The instance of constituent power will end up being the judge of what general utility requires, where it initially invited utility science to be the judge of what expedient commanding requires.

We may now see what legal positivism amounts to under the cover of scientism. It conceives of law as the gradual but never-ending convergence of utility science and sovereign decision-making. This infinitely deferred finale is anticipated in two ways: convergence may be dictated by commands (including sanctions) for the sake of general utility, or it may be calculated by scientific investigations for the sake of effective commanding. Social science is required to provide the utilitarian categories by which the general interest may be articulated without normative justification. In the rebound the instances of final decision-making – broadly the sum-total of governmental officials – sanction them by the use of these categories in decisions about punishments, fines, rewards, subsidies, repairs, taxes, and their ilk. Thus, legal positivism, even under its scientific guise, ushers in a pact between utility science and politics that is ultimately dominated by the latter, and where voluntarist overtones are not mitigated at all.[31]

---

[31] Robespierre already tried to reduce these tensions by an appeal to a pact between social science and legislator: 'Reason and the public interest began the revolution; intrigue and ambition have halted it', he began his *Prospectus* for a new 'scientific' weekly journal that would defend the Constitution. And he continues: 'The majority desires the good, but it neither knows the means to reach this goal nor the obstacles that distance them from it. Even the best intentioned of men differ on the questions most strictly related to the general happiness. (…) In this situation one means alone is left to us to save the public

3.3.2 Historicism

The other way to mitigate the arbitrary character of constituent power is to place sovereignty under the guidance of history, i.e., to argue that the exercise of sovereign power is only obedient to stronger though benign forces that warrant order in society. In this conception, the sovereign is the executor of pre-established orderings that have to be preserved, defended, restored, etc. In other words, the sovereign is the guardian of the past in the sense of a specific and unequivocal tradition that can be accurately described, hence monitored in view of potential harm done to it. One should not underestimate the argumentative force of a historicist view as it infallibly finds the weak spots in both liberal and socialist variations on the theme of law-making as a sort of willing.

In Europe it makes itself heard in counter-revolutionary voices throughout the nineteenth century. In England, Burke[32] mobilises the rights of men over and against the rights of man; while the latter express abstract ideas the former keep track of the tradition that handed them over. And they were handed over by and to specific persons living in specific social relationships that are deeply normative for a well-ordered society. In France Portalis, the great draftsman of the Code Napoleon, is no less concerned about the blind voluntarism spreading from the Revolution. Though prudent in his well-known *Discours préliminaire* to the Code,[33] he is explicitly critical in his personal assessment of what his

---

thing, and that's the enlightenment of the zeal of good citizens in order to lead them towards a common goal. To rally all of them to the principles of the Constitution and the general interest; to bring into broad daylight the true causes of our ills and to indicate the remedies; to develop in the eyes of the Nation the reasons, the general view, and the consequences of the political operations that have an influence over the fate of the State and its liberty; to analyze the public conduct of the personalities who play the principle roles in the theatre of the revolution; to cite before the tribunal of opinion and truth those who with ease escaped from the tribunal of the laws and who can decide the destiny of France and the Universe. This is without a doubt the greatest service a Citizen can render the public cause.'

32 E Burke (1790 [1971]) 93.

33 There is only a hint at the point where he concludes his general observations on revolution, legislation and the judiciary, and turns towards the various topics of the new code, where he contrasts, with regard to law-making,

era calls 'reason'. He rejects the 'esprit philosophique' together with the 'esprit révolutionnaire'.[34] Where the Revolution had tried to define sovereignty as the power of society over the political order, Portalis reverses the claim and argues that traditional authority in society as such defines sovereignty.[35] By contrast to 'the philosophical mindset', 'le bon sens' stays within the boundaries of the tradition, preserves established order, and is anti-revolutionary by definition.[36] In Germany Von Savigny managed to found the Historical School with a programme[37] powerful enough to defer the introduction of a Civil Code by almost a hundred years (1900). Crucially, he banned all constituent power to an ephemeral cultural Geist, that organically generates law, language, art, and their ilk without any political interference.[38] It would be the vocation of the technicians of the law, the legal scholars, to disclose this evolution and articulate its pertinence in the present.

In the twentieth century the most eloquent attack on the voluntarist bias of legal positivism in the twenties and thirties in Germany came from Carl Schmitt, who regarded himself as the true heir of Von Savigny.[39] He incisively criticised the political impotence of the parliamentary legislator during the Weimar Republic. The Weimar Parliament was indeed paradigmatic of the hazardous idea that law could and should be produced by political debate between representatives of all sorts of

---

the ages of ignorance as the theatre of abuse to the ages of philosophy and enlightenment (his own age) as the theatre of extravagancies. (JEM Portalis (1801 [1836]) 482.)

34 JEM Portalis (1827) II, 495.

35 'La société n'existe pas avant que le pouvoir souverein soit réunit en certaines maines; car il ne suroit y avoir de faisceau sans lieu et le gouvernement est ce lieu.' Ibid. II, 320–321.

36 Ibid. II, 509.

37 FCv Savigny (1814 [1967]).

38 Hence Marx' sarcasm that the Historical School requires the lawyer to regard himself as a skipper sailing on the source rather than the river. (K Marx (1842 [1971]) 198; K Marx (1844 [1971]) 490.)

39 Von Savigny's appearances were '(...) a paradigmatic event, that we have to remember in order to understand the present situation of legal doctrine in Europe in the right way.'

factions in society,[40] as a compromise of their respective wills on the basis of majority rule. It appeared that these wills were so radically different that the parliamentary debate became endless, that most compromises vanished before they could find legal expression, and that social protest sabotaged the few legal directives that were enacted. Schmitt argued that parliament could only be legislative if the people would trust the legislator, but that the legislator would only be trusted if he would acknowledge the political homogeneity of 'the people' in the first place.[41] He doubted very much if a parliament could really give evidence of such acknowledgment, as it was, by definition, a compound of politically heterogeneous groups. Legal doctrine as he saw it was allegedly 'the last refuge of legal awareness'. It is legal doctrine that had to enhance the awareness of the normative power of concrete orderings by investigating and describing them. The doctrinal articulations of these legal relationships, rather than the voluntarist enactments of parliament, are the core of what we can call 'law'. They disseminate the political identity that a people ascribes to itself. In that sense they are deeply 'democratic', i.e., tied up with what the people *is* rather than what it *wants*. Equality before the law in Schmitt's view cannot be anything else but *Gleichartigkeit*, (similarity), in the end even *Artgleichheit* (homogeneity) shared by all members of the public. That is why he can claim to replace a 'bourgeois' concept of law by a 'truly political' one, and parliamentarism by 'true democracy'.

Sovereignty paired to historicism is not a phenomenon of the past. Without any innuendo of Schmittian heritage in the 2009 *Lissabon* decision by the German Constitutional Court, it may be said that the Court quite explicitly defends the sovereignty of the German 'Staatsvolk'

---

[40] The plea against factions was already made in ground-breaking treatises by J-J Rousseau (1762 [1964]) II, 3 and The Federalist A Hamilton, J Madison et al. (1999 [1787-1788]) No 10.

[41] See C Schmitt (1926 [1923]) 14: 'Zur Demokratie gehört also notwendig erstens Homogenität und zweitens – nötigenfalls – die Ausscheidung oder Vernichtung des Heterogenen.' See also C Schmitt (1932 [1998]) 29.

by an appeal to its being a historical community of culture.[42] It points in so many words to the guidance of tradition (even 'historical traditions') in exercising sovereignty, and asserts that this is precisely the reason why 'the people' should remain the agent of sovereignty. Much more outspoken is one of the claimants before the Court, Professor Schachtschneider, who has been consistent in defending the view that 'Being German is (still) a constitutional principle of the Federal German Republic.'[43] He is certainly only one step away from Schmitt's idiolect when he argues that homogeneity is a precondition for a legal order, and that the main parameter for homogeneity is '(…) a similarity that makes social life possible'.[44]

3.3.3 The common fallacy of scientism and historicism

Mitigating the voluntarist dynamics of sovereignty, both scientist and historicist usher in poorly feasible, potentially even dangerous views. Neither the pact between administrative power and utility science nor that

---

[42] Cf. BVerfGE, 2 BvE 2/08 of June, 30 2009 (Lissabon), para. 260: 'Demokratische Selbstbestimmung ist schließlich auf die Möglichkeit, sich im eigenen Kulturraum verwirklichen zu können, besonders angewiesen bei Entscheidungen, wie sie insbesondere im Schul- und Bildungssystem, im Familienrecht, bei der Sprache, in Teilbereichen der Medienordnung und zum Status von Kirchen, Religions- und Weltanschauungsgemeinschaften getroffen werden. Die bereits wahrnehmbaren Aktivitäten der Europäischen Union auf diesen Gebieten greifen auf einer Ebene in die Gesellschaft ein, die in der primären Verantwortung der Mitgliedstaaten und ihrer Gliederungen steht. Die Gestaltung von Lehrplänen und Bildungsinhalten sowie etwa die Struktur eines gegliederten Schulsystems sind politische Grundentscheidungen, die einen starken Bezug zu den kulturellen Wurzeln und Wertvorstellungen eines jeden Staates haben. Die Gestaltung von Schule und Bildung berührt, wie das Recht der familiären Beziehungen und Entscheidungen über Fragen der Sprache und der Einbeziehung des Transzendenten in das öffentliche Leben, in besonderem Maße gewachsene Überzeugungen und Wertvorstellungen, die in spezifischen historischen Traditionen und Erfahrungen verwurzelt sind. Demokratische Selbstbestimmung erfordert hier, dass die jeweilige durch solche Traditionen und Überzeugungen verbundene politische Gemeinschaft das Subjekt demokratischer Legitimation bleibt.'

[43] KA Schachtschneider (1994) 1193. He was also the author of the constitutional complaints in the Maastricht-Urteil BVerfGE 89, 155 (1993).

[44] Ibid. 1186.

between democracy and historically entrenched homogeneity is attractive. Rather than mitigating they are disguising voluntarism. They do so at the cost of a remarkably distorted conception of history. Historicism holds the view that history has come to an end in the past; i.e., in a tradition that should be respected and defended. Whatever occurs in the present or the future only makes sense in as far as it either supports (positive sense) or assaults (negative sense) this tradition. Indeed, events that would challenge the categories provided by this tradition simply do not register. In other words, nothing will happen anymore that is not foreseen in a general sense by legal thought, its concepts and its doctrines. One may find other words for them, even appeal to other disciplines for other words; but the thought content will remain the same. Scientism distorts a conception of history in the opposite way. The promise of a gradual absorption of political will by scientific theory is a false one, as I argued above. It promises something that can never happen, as long as science in general is what it is and social sciences in particular are what they are. A history wherein nothing happens anymore or one wherein nothing will ever happen are both equally problematic.

What gives rise to this fallacy? Remember that the appeals to either science or history were made only as a second step after a first one that was already taken: separating constituent and constitutional power in the account of sovereignty. Science and history were made ancillary to pure constituent power, in order to tame the very force they had to serve. No wonder they have to yield to such force. As Orwell's 1984 incisively pictures, pure constituent power will also constitute the science it needs and the history it deems useful. Before betraying his love, Winston Smith was tortured in order to learn not one political lesson but two. One was about the core of science, which is calculating: he had to think that 2 + 2 = 5 rather than 4 on authority of O'Brien representing pure constituent power. The other was about the core of history, which is remembrance: he had to forget that he once learnt it equals 4. What if we return to the first step and see if alternative accounts are possible?

4. CONSTITUENT POWER AND CONSTITUTIONAL POWER

There is an alternative account of sovereign power that does not revert to moral categories, preserves its practical character, and curbs arbitrariness. The argument goes in two steps. First I show that sovereignty, in hovering between the power over law and the power under law, is not exceptional. There are more concepts that travel a similar two-way street, especially concepts that have to do with 'creating something'. They take their cue now from the process, now from the product. Then, in the next section, I argue that sovereignty has this feature in particular with regard to political authority. Here I will argue that such authority acquires credibility through attributions of a specific kind of practical knowledge.

4.1 Making Sense

The relationship between constituent and constitutional power is not so special as is sometimes thought. It is characteristic of creative 'making', including 'making sense'. For instance, it is not merely tautological when we say that it takes an artist to make art even though the art made is what defines the artist. Someone is not an artist prior to any art made, nor is it up to the artist to decide whether he has made art or not. But then, at least to some extent one really has to share a certain sensitivity with the artist in order to appreciate and assess art in any reliable way. The qualities of a work of art cannot be adequately expressed in a meta-language about art. They are available only in that immediate interrelation between perception and action, receptivity and skill, that certain individuals we call artists, appear to embody. At the same time (let us note this wording) it takes art to make an artist. Most artists will agree that, from their own first-person perspective, they just yield to a particular way in which reality strikes them. They oscillate between this sensation of being touched and touching a part of reality: a canvass, a string.[45] In singing and dancing it becomes

[45] Cf. e.g. Cézanne's phrase on 'les sensations colorantes' as analysed by M Loreau (1988).

clear that these two movements are in fact one event: the voice is the interface between the singing and the song, like the dancer becomes the interface between the dancing and the dance.[46] Typically, artists will focus on what their art requires and leave it to others (artists 'in their own right') to assess whether they have become 'artists' in the sense of people who are able to create art on a more or less regular basis. They yield to the perspective of the third person in their first-person pursuit. Inversely, people appreciating art as spectators will typically yield to the viewpoint of this first-person pursuit, acknowledging that only artistic creativity counts as a criterion. Here, once more, we find an instance of what Chapter 2 called alternity being the practical mode to negotiate alterity.[47]

Merleau-Ponty made a similar distinction though much wider in scope, namely between 'parole parlée' and 'parole parlante' – roughly translating as 'spoken speech' and 'speaking speech'. The latter is the sum-total of established ways of making sense when we talk to one another. The former refers to the rare moments at which we manage to create new sense: that one line in a poem or a novel that one will remember forever, the precise mathematical formula of a scientific discovery, the political speech that changed the lives of millions (not necessarily to the good …). These are not simply two genres of using language. They are not empirically separate. New sense can only be made in the interstices of established sense, and, inversely, even the production of established sense is never purely re-productive. There is always a tiny bit of creativity in the resumption of established meaning, as there is always an appeal to set patterns of understanding in the creative use of language. Here again, the first person of the speaker yields to the perspective of the third person while using language that will be recognised as 'new sense', while those who are able to recognise it as new do so by yielding to the perspective of the speaker being creative in the agential, first-person sense. There is chiasm of perspectives here: in making something *X*, first persons *A* let

---

46 Slightly altered from a famous line by WB Yeats, *Among School Children*: 'O body swayed to music, O brightening glance, How can we tell the dancer from the dance?' WB Yeats (1927).

47 Cf. section 4.1.

the perspective of third persons *C* count against them, while *C*, if and when they become first persons assessing the quality of *X*, let the perspective of *A* count against them.

4.2 Making Political Sense: Constituting Constitutions

The relationship between constituent and constitutional power resembles that between speaking speech and spoken speech.[48] The power constituting the polity anew as a meaningful order has to act, from its own perspective, as a law-complying agent who is committed to the cause of this order as a whole. It will have to take all measures necessary to remain credible in this respect and to not be disguised as the director of a masquerade. Thus, in order to succeed it cannot act in an arbitrary way but has to live up to the commitment inherent in the cause it is pursuing. It becomes vulnerable by virtue of its own promise as it has to act in view of assessments made by third-person others – the perspective of prospective citizens. In turn, the citizens assessing the order installed by sovereign power will take their cue from the sovereign's intention to order the polity as a whole. In this sense, constituent power and constitutional power become interwoven in their respective claims to justifiability. Not that the one dresses up like the other; they become mutually conditional in the sense of delivering each other's ground. If the notion of sovereignty bears out this relationship between constituent and constitutional power, it keeps arbitrary exercise of power at bay.[49]

Indeed, the conceptual picture I sketched is close to politico-legal life. New law is made with an appeal to existing power-conferring norms, even when this claim seems doubtful or untrue.[50] Constituent power often poses as constitutional power. To take an example I will return to: the

---

[48] Cf. I pointed to the analogy between Merleau-Ponty's distinction and that between constituent and constitutional power in B Van Roermund (2002b). It was taken up in much greater detail by L Corrias (2010; 2011).

[49] I cannot go into the consequences of this intertwinement for related discussions in metaphysics about ordo ordinans et ordinatus (Aquinas) and natura naturans and natura naturata (Spinoza).

[50] HK Lindahl (2007) has incisively analysed the circularity involved in these claims. See also Maria Cahill's contribution to D Augenstein (2012a) 16.

Court of Justice of the European Union claims jurisdiction on the basis of the EU Treaty in an area that was not explicitly conferred to the EU under Art. 5 (2) TEU, but that is only implied in an objective of the EU.[51] Or, more dramatically, a revolting movement proclaims new constitutional rules on the basis of 'universally' accepted peremptory law. In both cases, whether they 'get away' with it is dependent on recognition in hindsight. This empirical correlation has a strong conceptual background. Importantly, from its own agential perspective, power that creates law *has* to pose as power that is restrained by law. Thus, if '(t)he paradox of sovereignty consists in the fact that the sovereign is, at the same time, outside and inside the juridical order',[52] the solution to the paradox is that we distinguish this first person perspective from the third person perspective and acknowledge that we must alternate between these two positions. This oscillating commands the phrase 'at the same time'. The sovereign cannot suspend the validity of the law without placing himself under other valid, power-conferring law, thus maintaining the profound truth that only law generates law – from the said agential viewpoint. From a third-person viewpoint, the opposite is true: every exercise of constitutional power restates the power-conferring rule from which it derives. For instance, it has often been noted that judges, in applying a rule, not only decide on the case at hand but also on their discretion to hear this particular case or not.[53] They restate the competence attributed to them by their own hand, as no rule declares how it should be applied in whatever will be the next case.[54] In this sense they make new law in the act of applying established law. The paradox disappears if one distinguishes first-person and third-person viewpoints. The power to make law oscillates between these two poles. It requires a special kind of

---

51 Cf. P Craig and G De Búrca (2011) 75, and cases mentioned there.

52 G Agamben (1998) 15, reflecting on C Schmitt (1934) 14. See also M Foucault (1988), especially the Two Lectures on Power.

53 Cf. my discussion B Van Roermund (2007) of the Dutch High Court decision HR 9 Oct. 1998, NJ 1998, 853 (Van Aalten/De Vereniging voor Christelijk Wetenschappelijk Onderwijs).

54 On Wittgenstein's paradox of rule following, see Chapter 5.

attentiveness and receptivity but also a specific environment that allows one to make such sense.

To conclude: sovereignty is sometimes defined as 'competence-competence': the power to attribute legal power. The reduplication strongly suggests that 'supreme power' is power squared. This power over legal power therefore necessarily precedes legal power, or so it seems. Allegedly it even justifies the thought that one first has to acquire power before one can apply it to make a constitution.[55] But on the alternative account offered above this suggestion is false, and the reduplication is inappropriate. Making constitutional sense does not precede the constitution it makes. From this non-dualist account we may take our cue in answering the question: what makes sovereignty when it makes constitutional sense, i.e., when it transforms political authority into a sustainable institution called constitutional power?

5. AUTHORITY

Until now I have used a neutral word for what sovereignty would bring about by running this loop (or oscillating) between constituent and constitutional power: order in society. This is where legal positivism stops: general norms enacted by sovereign power are what law amounts to and what equals its being authoritative. But this account of authority, I submit, is too thin. I do not mean that the first thing sovereignty brings about in modern legal orders is a set of norms conferring authority (i.e., legal power, or competence) on certain agents we may call officials. That is true enough. What I mean is that it purports to create constitutionally sustainable authority in authoritative ways, which should be sustainable in turn. This is some extra quality of exercising sovereign power that is neither exhausted nor warranted by the intertwinement of constituent and

55 Slightly altered, this is Arnheim's phrase ('One has to be able to exercise power in order to be able to exercise power to the good') in R Musil (1978 [1930]); see also B Van Roermund (2000c).

constitutional power. In other words: normative claims made by sovereign power do not always succeed in backing up the authoritative character of these claims, because this requires extra quality on top of running the loop.

It is not uncommon to define authority as 'legitimate power'. This is a risky formula for several reasons. The main one would only apply if the predicate 'legitimate' would be accounted for in legal terms. Then we would go around in circles as we are in the process of analysing the concept of authority in order to complete our analysis of the concept of law. I want to uphold my strategy as announced and argue that the positive character of law is to be found in its being enacted by authority. A weaker claim would be to define authority as 'power claiming legitimacy'. But, as argued above, this is what characterises sovereignty or the exercise of supreme power. Then I would join the camp of those who hold that there is no real distinction between sovereignty and authority, while I announced the thesis that there *is*. To see what I mean, let me start from authority in general, to then turn to authority of law.

5.1 Authority and Reasons

Authority bears a difficult relationship towards the twofold inspiration of Modernity at large: rationality and freedom. The difficulty is well-known; if we yield to authoritative statements because we agree that the content of these statements is true or valid, then we are effectively exercising free judgment rather than submitting to authority. On the other hand, if we yield to authority because we think its statements are right without checking by our own judgment, we renounce the exercise of reason or freedom that seems basic to our social order, let alone our world of science.

Raz has proposed to solve the moral side of this problem by his Service Conception of authority. In essence it consists of two conditions: (a) the Normal Justification condition asserts that '(…) the normal way to establish that a person has authority over another person involves showing that the alleged subject is likely better to comply with reasons which apply to him (other than the alleged authoritative directives) if he accepts the directives of the alleged authority as authoritatively binding and tries to follow them, rather than by trying to follow the reasons which apply to him directly';[56] (b) the Independence condition states that '(…) matters regarding which the first condition is met are such that with respect to them it is better to conform to reason than to decide for oneself, unaided by authority'.[57] Thus, this condition states that authority is legitimate 'only where acting by oneself is less important than conforming to reason'.[58]

I have no difficulty with the Independence condition. But the Normal Justification thesis seems ambiguous to me on two points. (a) Who is to assess the likelihood that following authority will bring alleged subjects to acting for the right (balance of) reasons, and on what grounds? (b) Who is to show that this likelihood obtains, and on what grounds? It would be gratuitous, I venture, to suggest that a third person, on the basis of some probability theory, will show and/or assess such likelihood. Either the alleged authority and the alleged subjects have access to this theory, which leads both of them to the same balance of primary reasons; or one of them has access, while the other has not, which means that either the showing or the assessing will not register at the other end of the line; or neither of them has access to the theory, so that it does not affect their position as first-person agents. I believe that the last option is the only feasible one. This means that (a) the alleged subjects have to have sufficient reason to believe that following the directive will make them act on the basis of relevant reasons, and (b) that the alleged authority has to show that they are up to the task of bringing their subjects right there. Crucially then, there is a first-person perspective involved in authority. As I argued elsewhere, authority, like beauty, is in

---

56 J Raz (1986) 53.

57 J Raz (2009) 137. In J Raz (1986) 47 Raz speaks of the Independence Thesis as the first tenor of the Service Conception: 'All authoritative directives should be based on reasons which already independently apply to the subjects of the directive and are relevant to their action in the circumstances covered by the directive.'

58 Ibid. 137.

the eye of the beholder.[59] The simple case is asking for directions in an unknown town: Prior to asking 'How do I get to the railway station, please?' one has already scanned the people who are likely able to tell you, and who are not. For instance, one does not turn to someone ostensibly dressed as a tourist, or drunk, or ready to ask a favour in return. Only the answers of those who *appear* credible will be assessed by standards of trustworthiness. In fact the question dovetails into two: (a) is this person in a position to know the way and tell me?, and (b) if she is, am I likely to get to the railway station by following her directions? The former pertains to external credentials of the sayer, the latter to 'internal credentials' of the said along logical, semantic, and pragmatic lines.[60] In both instances, typically, what I do is attributing a capability of knowing to this person that I do not have, retaining for myself the more or less certified belief that this person has this capability.

Note that this conception of authority mitigates, to a considerable extent, the received view of 'theoretical' authority (e.g., expert authority) being distinct from 'practical' authority (e.g., political authority). In the final analysis, political authority is regarded as a sort of expert knowledge as well, but expert knowledge in matters practical, specifically political. It is knowledge about how to order society with regard to sustainable authority so as to end or curb potentially disruptive conflict by authoritative decision-making. This, I submit, is the core of constitutionalism. It entails both less and more than one may think. Less, because it settles for the rather classical view that constituted law is there, first and foremost, to end or curb conflict. It does not necessarily solve conflict, though solving a conflict is a sustainable way to end or curb it. It does not address all conflict in society but solely the part that may become disruptive. Which conflicts put society in this kind of jeopardy is a political decision; it may very well take into account that a certain amount of contestation is actually healthy for society at large. It does not

---

59 B Van Roermund (2000b) 218ff, referring to the early H Kelsen (1928 [1981]).

60 See, e.g., is the advice self-contradictory? Does it feature sufficiently clear indexical references? Does it sound self-assured?

regard fundamental rights as unqualified 'commands for optimal enhancement'[61] but rather as core conditions for sustained authoritative decision-making in view of what Kant would call 'perennial (i.e. principled) peace'. Least of all, perhaps, it wants to see law as 'an instrument to implement policies' indistinctively, acknowledging throughout that a large amount of policies are meant to serve the same goal as law. It entails also more than one may think. If constitutionalism crucially hinges on sustainability, it is a process as much as it is a product. Its dynamics are as important as its statics. If sustainability requires institutionalisation, the institution should be such that it is able to revise its default settings and to switch to non-default options if need be. If it is meant to be an institution, it should also take into account that institutions can only be authoritative if they are trusted in generating what they are about rather than permanently tested against what they are about. These are only the most salient implications of constitutionalism as the political attempt to install authority in an authoritative way.

Instituting authority is a matter of 'knowing how to act' rather than 'knowing what to believe', although some belief about what will inevitably happen in the future is inherent to all practical knowledge. Moreover, it may reveal itself as 'tacit knowledge', which is yet another thing on top of practical knowledge. Some of us have more talent for judging societal situations, while others are better in judging health situations or solving math problems, without being able, necessarily, to tell how they do this. In the final chapter I will propose a theory of legal 'interpretation' that maps out some of the aspects that seem crucial here. Suffice it to say at this point that it is largely entrenched in a form of knowing which Michael Polanyi once called 'personal knowledge'.[62] One may even ask if it is not itself to a large extent, or at least in some cases,

---

61 Or 'Optimierungsgebote' as R Alexy (1994) 71ff. would have it.

62 'Here, in the exercise of skill and the practice of connaisseurship, the art of knowing is seen to involve an intentional change of being: the pouring of ourselves into the subsidiary awareness of particulars, which in the performance of skills are instrumental to a skilful achievement, and which in the exercise of connaisseurship function as the elements of the observed comprehensive whole.' (M Polanyi (1962 [1958]) 64.)

'embodied knowledge' – apart from the fact that it 'embodies a way of looking at things'.[63] Part of this means that the craft is predicated on forms of engaging the social world that are deeply corporeal; and that they are accessible only via specific, often intensively trained, situations. In ancient times, such capabilities were called 'virtues'. These had little to do with soft morality, but everything with the joy of getting better in things that matter. The gym rather than the monastery was the proper place for exercise, only that the polity was regarded as one big gym. Prudence was one of these virtues, and juris-prudence was a fortiori.

Authoritative officials have *to show* the way out of a common predicament and into a new common wealth, not by giving directions but by walking it and going first. Going first entails overstepping the limits of established competence and redefining them immediately. If we are allowed to read this sense of 'showing' into the Normal Justification thesis, I propose to subscribe to it. But more importantly, such knowledge amounts to a sense of history that is far more adequate than that of either scientism or historicism. Authoritative behaviour rises to the occasion by an, often tacit, understanding of what is the best thing to do for a polity in a situation which is genuinely new to them; where applying established rules straightforwardly will not do for the future; where faithfulness to the past can only be preserved by change in the present.

5.2 Authority of Law: Lisbon v Lisbon[64]

To see how this may work towards building up the authority of law, we may turn to challenges faced by the European Courts as they find themselves between two agendas that, with only a tiny twist of history, may both be labelled 'Lisbon'. Although the 2000 Lisbon strategy was

---

63 A beautiful example is mentioned in P Scholten (1974 [1931]) 127 relating the experience of comparatists studying *adat* law in colonial Indonesia by asking chiefs of tribes and heads of family the typical law school question 'What would be the law if … ?'. They could not answer if they were not really hearing a case.

64 Lisbon v Lisbon is also the name of a project funded by the Royal Netherlands Academy of Arts and Sciences which Daniel Augenstein and I coordinated in 2012. This subsection could not have been written without Daniel's generously shared expertise.

regarded as a governmental failure,[65] and although the financial, the economic and the monetary crises meanwhile has affected any supranational and national strategy, global competitiveness in market economy continues to inspire the planned future of the EU. Currently, Europe 2020 is a 10-year strategy proposed by the European Commission on March 3, 2010 in the wake of the Lisbon Agenda for reviving the economy of the European Union. It aims at 'smart, sustainable, inclusive growth' by greater coordination of national and European policy. It 'sets out a vision of Europe's social market economy for the 21st century. It shows how the EU can come out stronger from the economic crisis and how it can be turned into a smart, sustainable and inclusive economy delivering high levels of employment, productivity and social cohesion.'[66] Thus, there is one 'Lisbon' that focuses on the EU economy and encompasses whatever may contribute to its sustainability.

But there is yet another 'Lisbon' agenda. On December 1, 2009, the Treaty of Lisbon entered into force. Amending (rather than replacing) the then existing EU and EC treaties, it provides the Union with the legal framework and the tools necessary to meet future challenges and to respond to citizens' demands, but also 'to take Europe into the 21st century'. It carries an Agenda that is far more than the EU's economy. It addresses institutional reform, democratisation, reinforcement of European citizenship, and protection of human rights (by virtue of the EU's Charter as well as by joining the ECHR as a party to the Convention).[67] Promoting the EU as a more powerful actor on the global stage is only one of the professed goals of the new Treaty, and even then economic

---

[65] At the Lisbon Summit in March 2000, the EU Heads of States and Governments agreed to make the EU, by 2010, '(…) the most competitive and dynamic knowledge-driven economy, capable of sustainable economic growth with more and better jobs and greater social cohesion.' The Strategy was re-launched in spring 2005 after initially moderate results. At that time it became (even) more focused on economic growth, employment, and competiveness.

[66] Quotes in this paragraph are from http://ec.europa.eu/europe2020/index_en.htm (accessed November 13, 2012), the official Europe 2020 website.

[67] Art. 6 TEU.

power appears only as one aspect of this. In sum, the other Lisbon aspires to an enhanced 'rule of law' awareness within the EU.

These two agendas will define a matrix of various courses of legal action, as they may either reinforce or undermine each other.[68] When it comes to principles the first agenda is largely governed by the four fundamental freedoms that shape up the internal market: freedom of persons, goods, services, and capital, together with a ban on various forms of 'discrimination' distorting competition (e.g. state help). The second one is much more a matter of fundamental rights and the rule of law probed in the context of the transnational 'sui generis' legal order that the EU claims to be, over and above the domestic legal orders of the Member States.[69] Having to re-establish its judicial authority in a new role, the Court of Justice of the European Union (CJEU) now finds itself in a double bind between 'fundamental freedoms' and 'fundamental rights', to use some prolific shorthand. And it will have to find new authority, as at least three salient factors have to be taken into account. The first is that, notwithstanding the failed Draft Constitutional Treaty, the Lisbon Treaty has burdened the CJEU with a jurisdiction that comes

---

[68] What counts as reinforcing and what as undermining interference depends, obviously, on substantive interpretations of the freedoms and rights in question. The *Grogan* case (C 159/190 [1991]) clearly illustrates how market freedom (of services) may interfere with the pro-life versus pro-choice debate on abortion. Fundamental rights of workers (e.g. strike) have become an issue in view of market ramifications in *Laval* (C 341/05 [2007]), *Viking* (C 438/05 [2007]), *Rüffert* (C346/06 [2008]). The tension may hide in rather technical corners: in C-236/09 (*Association belge des Consommateurs Test-Achats ASBL and Others v Conseil des Ministres*) of March 1, 2011, the Court confirmed that the rule of unisex premiums and benefits will apply with effect from December 21, 2012, and will forbid taking the gender of an insured individual into account as a risk factor in insurance contracts, e.g. regarding car driving. The decision refers frequently to Art. 8 TFEU, as well as to the 2004 Gender Directive, blocking out both massive evidence to the effect that especially young male drivers enhance the costs of road traffic, thus diminishing Europe's global competitiveness, and previous rulings.

[69] Cf. the doctrines of EU law having direct effect, being sui generis and taking priority over Member State law in the areas designated by conferral of powers, as laid down in C 26/62 [1963] (*Van Gend & Loos*) and C 6/64 [1964] (*Costa*).

very close to constitutional review.[70] Integrating the Charter of Fundamental Rights; confirming the pursuit of 'an area of freedom, security and justice' (Art. 3.2 TEU) where prevention and combating of crime even precede the pursuit of the internal market (Art. 3 TEU); and, at the same time, stipulating that the Court 'shall ensure that in the interpretation and application of the Treaties the law is observed' (Art 19.1 TEU), the Treaty put the Court in the middle of the political dynamics that the EU wishes to sustain. And it is not just the CJEU that will have to rise to the occasion, but all other courts in the EU as well, as they are all in an important sense 'European Courts'. The second factor is that in the actual practice of (preliminary) decision-making, as many commentators observe, the first Lisbon agenda has been much more elaborate than the second one.[71] The third factor is that

> (j)udicial supremacy in EU law has been marked (…) by a gap between the formal claims and legal norms set out by the ECJ for the exercise of judicial power and the reality of a more limited judicial presence in the development of EU law and policy. It is this gap that has created the delicate institutional balance that has allowed judicial supremacy to develop within EC law. It has limited the political impact of ECJ rulings and allowed local judiciaries to accept and enforce radical EU legal doctrines precisely because they did not overtly revolutionize national legal settlements.[72]

The more robust jurisdiction accruing to the CJEU after Lisbon does not entail at all that the Court could afford to give up this delicate balancing strategy of exercising supremacy. Well on the contrary, it may gain importance by dint of a growing awareness that '(t)he EU legal system

---

[70] A burden it (was) already prepared for both by the evolution in the series of Treaties and by its own role conception.

[71] See, e.g., D Chalmers and M Chaves (2011) 28: 'If the economic freedoms are placed together on the grounds that these are represented by single provisions in other jurisdictions (e.g., the commerce clause in the United States) and the common customs tariff and customs union are treated as a tax, over 80 per cent of case law was in seven fields: the economic freedoms; harmonization of laws; taxation; freedom; security and justice; environment; agriculture and social policy.' See also P Craig and G De Búrca (2011) 364; and at an earlier time of observation D Chalmers (2005) 455ff.

[72] D Chalmers (2005) 458.

institutes and draws on a direct relationship with the peoples of Europe that enables a *process* of legal integration in the interrelation of functionally different EU legal rules and transnational communities as social sites of the law.'[73]

The example of the two Lisbon agendas and the role of the CJEU illustrates what authority of law amounts to in a starkly dynamic political environment. The Court is trusted with the kind of practical knowledge that is necessary to combine market freedoms and fundamental rights, driven by global competitiveness and universal human rights, respectively. Achieving this combination is the pervasive objective of the EU legal order in view of an even wider objective that is at the basis of the Union in the first place: integration for the sake of peace, basic values, and people's well-being, in Europe and throughout the world.[74] These are the reasons that apply to Member States, and – to return to Raz's account of authority – they are more important than the ability of individual Member States to decide for themselves.[75] At this point in time, no other institutions of the EU or, for that matter, its Member States, can be trusted with that knowledge: not the Council because it is too intergovernmental; not the Commission because it is too market-driven; not the Parliament because it represents ideological dissensus that hardly touches upon the interests involved. The 'service conception' of authority therefore goes quite some way in explaining why guidance is sought from the CJEU rather than from any other EU body. The Court's credibility in practising its knowledge is crucially dependent on whether or not it is able to show, at the level of specific cases, how the legal order can be constitutionalised. Coming from a situation in which the EU was

---

[73] D Augenstein (2012b) 111.

[74] Art. 3.1 TEU.

[75] P Craig and G De Búrca (2011) 74 observes that the desire for containment expressed in the Laeken Declaration to put limits on the ever growing power of the EU has to be kept in perspective when reading the Lisbon Treaty, 'since a significant factor in the distribution of competence has been the conscious decision of the Member States to grant new spheres of competence to the EU.' Here Raz's independence thesis applies.

a legal order 'with a constitution but without constitutionalism',[76] it cannot be a surprise that the Court feels necessitated to apply constituent power by an appeal to constitutional (i.e., conferred[77]) power, thus constituting its power in the process of exercising it, or exercising it in response to the challenge of constituting it.[78]

6. AUTHORITY AS OPENING UP POLITICAL IDENTITY

This account of the authority of law allows us to see some conceptual links with the concept of justice developed in Chapter 2. Firstly, it shows that exercising authority is not a matter of voicing consensus or silencing dissensus. Rather is it acquired over and against an all too massive consensus or dissensus in the polity. Massive consensus would make it superfluous, massive dissensus impotent. Hence the CJEU's diligent manoeuvring between robust norm enactment and limited judicial presence. Authority is gained by demonstrating courage rather than pliancy or arrogance. But the Lisbon example illustrates an even more important point: the authority of law derives from the capacity to serve the interests, indeed the very identity of the polity (to wit, the internal market as an instrument to competitiveness on the global market) by opening up to what counts against it (to wit, fundamental rights). It shows openings in a polity's harness of identity by independent, prudent, and creative judgment in spite of the risks it brings. It shows how a polity can stand on its own feet rather than being supported by self-proclaimed political immunity or being burnt by perennial antagonisms. It shows what it takes to free oneself from reducing the whole world to a function of the first person plural. Freedom in this sense is what the previous chapter called responsibility towards the Other, and authority is with those who show the path to this freedom. It is seen to listen to the demands from the part

---

76 J Weiler (1999) 298.
77 Arts 4 and 5 TEU.
78 HK Lindahl (2003a) 437.

of alterity over and against the first person order we take for granted. Thus, by revealing the possibilities of crossing the boundaries by which a polity has enclosed itself it relativises the place of those who claim to know, to have and to be able to, its own place included.

Indeed, this first characteristic of authority is self-implying. It relativises its own action by making something count against itself. Authoritative politics can only enact law, if it is willing to let law be binding upon its own position. Thus the rule of law is not an external but an internal constraint on political authority; it is its conceptual implication. If it is a constraint, then on that loop of constituent and constitutional power we call sovereignty. I propose to regard authority as a quality that the exercise of sovereignty can acquire or not, in an attempt to lend institutional design to the collective awareness of premature self-inclusion. This is the core of constitutionalism, or the core of law, as Chapter 2 argued. Some features of democratic institutions, e.g., a multi-party system, periodical elections, sustain the authority of a political regime, precisely because they prevent the polity from hypostatising its self-inclusion. That is why they are part and parcel of the rule of law. One may imagine certain possible lines of policy that would conflict with acquiring authority and that would affect the credentials of the sovereign. A political system that makes torture a legal method of police investigation, a political system that would conceive of private property as an unrestricted right to exploit the environment, a political system that would shift all the risks of its policies to future generations, all such political systems would have a lot to explain if they would claim authority to enact law, i.e. to show something to count against the identity of the polity in question.[79]

---

[79] However, I do not deny that some political systems constitute authority by criteria (very) different from ours to let something count against them. To take an extreme example: the political system of sixteenth century France, which used torture as an instrument of evidence in court, is not ipso facto to be disqualified as a mock legal order. For torture was seen as a way of withholding subjective conviction of judges. (A Lebigre (1988) 193ff.) It was the production of a truth that could not be instrumentalised, not even by the sovereign, as it was a truth produced by delivering man to God. Astonishing as it may sound, torture, in

Secondly: authority is exercised by judging. Even if political judgment is practical, tacit, embodied, etc. it seeks, on its own account, for criteria shared by others, or at least not invented and monopolised at will: consistency, coherence, relevance, etc. The doctrine of precedent integrates these aspects into a method of legal interpretation. By acknowledging these criteria, i.e. by entering a practice of judging, officials signalise in principle that they aim at a kind of authority that can be contradicted or opposed and that is, therefore, beyond the contingency of actual political relationships. Thus, they relativise their personal intervention. As we saw in our Lisbon example, the CJEU does not just exercise discretion, it applies judgment – which admittedly is a matter of discretion to the extent that the lines of categories, their links, and their sequences are determined by reference to a certain political identity. But then, exercising discretion is a matter of accountable judgment rather than arbitrary choice. So, for instance, even if it is true that the Court opens up the market bias of the EU to the exigencies of fundamental rights, it reconfirms this political identity by granting such rights to citizens of the EU exclusively. What brings this second closure under the rule of law is that the Court opens it up once more to the demands of non-citizens (third country nationals) whose claims seem justified in the light of, e.g., human rights. All of this requires argument and judgment, hence openness towards alterity.

By judging, authority is also seen to take risks in awaiting the right moment.[80] It requires a sense of opportunity that is difficult to explain.

---

those days, may have had something to do with relativising the identity of a first-person plural order. That is why it would differ radically from a contemporary, secular regime that makes a common practice of torture in order to immunise its order.

[80] Judging is risky anyway, even in trivial everyday matters. While hiking in the mountains I judge: ‘That snow over there is white.’ But I know at the same time *from experience* that there are infinitely different shades of white and that the snow I am pointing to might well turn out grey or pink on closer examination. Judgment is always premature; of itself it would like to have all the time in the world. It is dangerous, and that is why it is left to those who know the dangers, the experienced, in daily matters, but most certainly in matters of guilt and punishment.

Part of it is felicitously captured by the double meaning of the German 'Konsensfähigkeit': a decision should both rest on established consensus and raise new consensus. The career of the European Court of Justice is replete with landmark decisions that bear witness to the Court's ability to choose the right moment and 'get away' with a ruling that enacts new law under the explicit pretext that it is just applying the rules. Indeed, when it comes to authority, timing is everything. Note that this relationship between law and time gets institutionalised in very precise ways to serve the purpose of the law with regard to ending or curbing conflict, for instance by terms of appearance, appeal, expiration, acquisition.[81]

To summarize: authority has two main characteristics:

(1) Independence in naming and articulating in prospect what constitutes and what relativises the political identity of a particular society and its (often conflicting) interests.
(2) Judgmental skill, relating to: (a) universalisability of considerations guiding the decision; (b) taking the risk of such an operation over and against the alleged homogeneity of a particular society; (c) the choice of the proper opportunity and other forms of 'tacit knowledge'.

Let us now see how these work out in the institutional context of the law.

7. THE INSTITUTIONALISATION OF AUTHORITY IN LAW

In the preceding section I explored how political authority may transform into law. In closing this chapter I now want to look into a few institutional features of law that are apt to drive the authority of law as constitutional authority. I categorise them under the two headings distinguished in the previous paragraph.

---

[81] On the role of time in law see the special issue of *R.M. Themis* (1986, 5,6), in particular the incisive analysis of JBM Vranken (1986).

7.1 Independence of Law

Once we understand this general characteristic of political authority, we are ready to see how several legal properties that are part and parcel of the process of law formation come into a new light. Different institutions of law formation appear to converge in a meaningful way for the sake of political self-restraint in the articulation of collective selfhood: the separation of powers, the equality of all before the law, democracy, the use of coercion to maintain the law, and the concept of a state. I want to go briefly into each of these.

7.1.1 Separation of powers

Separation of powers is commonly understood in terms of checks and balances, such that 'le pouvoir arrête le pouvoir', as Montesquieu famously put it.[82] But this 'negative' interpretation can only be the flipside of a positive one, otherwise it would cause conflict in the very organisation of the legal order.[83] I suggest that we see separation of powers as a process strategy to institutionalise legal authority. By this principle, one power acquires authority in recognising other powers as authority. The legislature allows some power to count against it that itself allows some power to count against it. The principle requires the supremacy of the legislature over the executive and the judiciary branches of power but also the independence of the judiciary over and against both executive and legislative power. The judiciary should 'apply' the law, but without the executive or the legislative powers having the possibility to interfere with certain applications. In order for the law rather than the legislator to reign, the judge must be independent and the legislator bound by law. But this requires its mirror-image: in order for the judiciary to be independent, legislation (or *stare decisis*) must be the source of its decisions. Which is only to say that the judge should be bound by law as much as the legislator. In this relationship the law is the

---

[82] Montesquieu (1979 [1748]) I, XI, ch 6.

[83] As Rousseau (J-J Rousseau (1762 [1964]) II, 2 was quick to point out in his critique of Montesquieu's proposal.

antipode of arbitrariness, and in that (primarily negative) sense it is regarded as prima facie reasonable.

7.1.2 Equality before the law

No principle of law is more ridiculed than this: the equality of all citizens before the law. Marx set the tone: he holds that the bourgeois character of law finds its ultimate expression in the neutrality of law towards all kinds of repression brought about by inequality, discrimination and deprivation.[84] The alleged fellow-citizens are in fact not fellows at all and basically unequal.

How to interpret the principle of equality? It is tempting to say that it is tantamount to the law dreaming its ideals: how wonderful would it be if all co-citizens were equal in point of fact! But that is hardly an ideal in any conceivable way. If equality would mean that we would all be similar, all have the same wishes, or all possess the same things, it is an appeal to utter boredom. Surely we would have to say little about each other, but that would be because we would not have very much to say to each other in the first place. On the other hand, if equality would mean the equality of all citizens in human dignity, we would certainly say too little. For we know from the previous chapter that human dignity is a tricky notion, ready to be manipulated by ideologies of humanness.

I think we should be careful not to confuse the equality demands of justice at work in politics and the principle of positive law known as equal access to justice. Equality driven political action draws inspiration from self-determination and self-preservation on the part of all members of society. On these very two points, the American philosopher John Rawls has submitted some powerful principles of justice as fairness.[85] The first principle reads as follows: Each person is to have an equal right to the most extensive total system of equal basic liberties compatible with a similar system of liberty for all. The second principle runs: Social and

---

84 K Marx (1844).

85 J Rawls (1973 [1971]) 302ff. These principles should be read as principles of administering justice, not as a conceptually full blooded analysis of justice as such.

economic inequalities are to be arranged so that they are both (a) to the greatest benefit of the least advantaged, consistent with the just savings principle, and (b) attached to offices and positions open to all under conditions of fair equality and opportunity. It will be clear that these principles leave scope for many conceptual clarifications, as well as questions regarding their order of application, which can only be addressed by a deeper analysis of the concept of justice itself. Since Rawls's treatise was published he and others have discussed these necessary refinements in great detail, setting the stage for principles of global justice. The capability approach by Sen, Nussbaum and others has proved to be a fruitful paradigm here. This area of theorising, which basically shares Rawlsian egalitarianism, is (somewhat misleadingly) called non-ideal theory. Amartya Sen, in particular, has argued that, regarding justice, we need an account of achieving progress rather than ideals.[86] For that, basic capabilities of persons and groups are a more relevant category than (universal and inflexible) primary goods. Such capabilities are basic in two respects: they pertain to peoples' capacity to articulate what good a certain utility would do for them in their pursuit of a valuable human life, as well as to their capacity to bring this good nearer by action. In reply, Rawls has explained how his theory accommodates a capability approach.[87] Whether or not that is the case, comparative social realisation is an important component of any theory of fairness, since fairness has to do with the relative burden an agent (individual or collective) puts on others in pursuing her own interests.

The principle of equality as equal access to law is nothing more (nor less) than the fundamental norm that positive law should not derive any privilege in legal procedure from factual inequality. This principle does not say, therefore, that factual inequality does not matter before the law. It holds that factual inequality should not be transformed into legal relationships; it therefore implies commitment to an explicit description of inequalities that should *not* have legal consequences. Discrimination is

86 A Sen (1989; 2006; 2009). M Nussbaum (2000; 2003).
87 J Rawls (2001) 169–176.

a case in point. In national as well as supra-national legal orders the constitution names specific inequalities and forbids attaching legal consequences to them: race, faith, gender, for instance. Some lawyers argue that this prohibition of discrimination has no 'horizontal impact', i.e. it allegedly does not govern relationships between citizens but only between citizens and the state. From a philosophical point of view, it is hard to imagine how prohibition of discrimination could not start out by having this horizontal meaning before it could acquire a vertical one towards the state.

7.1.3 Democracy

From our account of political authority it is easy to see why law will gain authority from being rooted in general rules enacted by a democratic regime. Democracy comes under many guises and they all present multiple features as essential for democracy. Here I focus on majority vote solely. Democracy, one could say,[88] is the political order in which the majority leaves the minority the institutionally warranted chance of becoming a majority. That, at least, is the operational core, though perhaps not the full conceptual content of democracy.

The majority principle does not say that the majority is politically in the right, but that, provisionally, the majority can go its way, on condition that it gives evidence of its awareness to be a majority only in relationship to a minority. It is in this sense dependent on their being a minority and its existence as a set of interests is to be taken into account even if these interests do not co-determine the policy. For instance, the law enacted by majority rule will sometimes leave scope for refusal on the basis of conscience. Also the majority ought to take into account, to a considerable extent, the existing law established by other majorities that meanwhile became a minority.

The prospect of the majority's view becoming binding upon all, not only triggers the formation of parties, but it also has an mitigating impact on factions, as they will be reluctant to take too extreme views on

---

[88] H Kelsen (1933 [1968]) 1929; cf. 1940; distinguishing majority rule conceptually from other forms of 'rule'.

debatable issues. Taking a radicalist stance will count them out when it comes to majority strategies, coalition, and compromise. No faction in a democracy, therefore, can afford to give its own truth an absolute status in advance. A majority is not a faction anymore, nor is it a dictator (as game theory vocabulary suggests) as long as it leaves the minority the chance to come back. It goes without saying that a one-party democracy will hardly be able to gain credentials and acquire authority.

7.1.4 Legal violence, coercion and punishment

The relation of authority to violence and coercion is a difficult one. I do not believe that authority and the use of violence are mutually exclusive under all circumstances. Let me put it in a paradoxical way: sometimes violence helps to establish authority, but authority is never exercised by violence. In a society where public power is exercised in such a way that it does not allow anything to count against it, the use of violence to resist that power may gain authority. That is to say, as resistance against oppression violence may become authoritative. When members of a polity take the law into their own hands by violent means, they immediately come under pressure to explain what will count against *them* after they have overthrown those who did not want anything to count against them. Taking the law into one's own hands remains a self-contradictory act, and the appeal to self-defence is as much an expression of the predicament that no law applies anymore as an argument that a different law applies.[89] So the authoritative range of those committing violence will always be rather limited and unstable. It will be clear that what I said about taking risks and judging the right moment is of utter relevance here. Agents in the position of the oppressed may get credit for their claim to establish the rule of law by violence if conditions like the following obtain: (i) they can show that their position is not defined as oppressive exclusively by themselves; (ii) they select targets and means in such a way that the process will not get out of hand by the arbitrariness of the agents or the self-propelling nature of violence;

---

[89] LL Fuller (1949), in particular judge Foster's argumentation, as torn apart by Keen.

(iii) they refrain from monopolising the decision whether liberation from oppression is reached.

Now is this the kind of authoritative violence, which we find in law, notably in cases of coercion and the execution of legal punishment? To ask the question in a different way: is the violence known in the law as punishment part and parcel of the concept of law as we have defined it? I submit that the answer should be in the negative. What we can explain on the basis of our arguments is that the law has to deal with punishment as a – primarily – *political* phenomenon. For punishment tends to appeal massively to absolute affirmations of political first-person awareness. Punishment is prescribed, attributed and executed in virtue of the values, which define a political community's identity and vitality in the final analysis. That is why I think it is a political phenomenon rather than a legal one. Now law, as we saw, is an institutionalised political artefact inspired by the idea of justice. There is no reason to expect why it would not absorb the various modes of doing politics, punishment included. For law cannot hide from the fact that it is generated by politics, as our account of justice admits. Therefore it cannot be the moral prohibition of politics. But it can apply punishment in the mode of political self-restraint. As law is not a mere political artefact but an artefact of politics oriented towards justice, punishment by law gets a different ring. The political practice of punishment may accept a legal restraint on this practice by virtue of principles of criminal law. In framing these principles, law cannot, however, go as far as a plea for abolishing punishment on sheer moral grounds (political grounds would be a different matter).

The law as criminal law demands that punishment should always allow something to count against the very ground of its legitimacy. But it should be noted that this 'something' does not have to be the same in the different vectors of criminal law: legislation, attribution and execution of punishment.[90] It may be that, for instance, the protection of certain societal interests and values is an acceptable goal for enacting criminal

---

[90] See C Roxin (1973) 12ff.

law. But it may be an unacceptable one for applying criminal law in the actual attribution of punishment. It would entail that one would use persons as means towards the end of deterring other people from committing similar offences. It will probably not be a good point of reference for the execution of punishment either. For that would boil down to unconditional treatment (rather than punishment) of the criminal, for instance by expelling him from or adapting her to his or her environment. We should make a distinction, I submit, between the reasons why punishment makes sense, the purposes it should serve and the ways in which it should be applied. I see no escape from the view that punishment makes sense only as retribution. One may reject punishment because it is retribution, but one cannot get punishment without retribution. This, however, does not tell us that retribution should be our goal in punishment. I am even not quite certain whether punishment can have a goal; probably only very modest ones if at all. But suppose punishment can serve a goal like protecting the values of the community by deterring people from violating them, then that again does not tell us much about the way in which we have to treat people when we punish them. Here we would relativise the right of the polity by respecting the person whom we punish and by giving him or her a chance to get a life after punishment. But then again, offering such a chance is not the goal of punishment itself, let alone the sense of punishment.

7.1.5 State

I have avoided the word 'state' as much as I could. In many discussions it is so rapidly identified with a specific type of state, namely the nation state, that it hampers arguing at a certain level of abstraction. This is why I preferred to use words like 'polity' and 'sovereignty' which are less affected by the parameter of nationhood. The idea of a nation, by which a group of people regard themselves as a polity with a common past and destiny, is most suited to go against the grain of the antinomy I pointed to at the heart of justice. It reinforces exclusively one of the poles: self-attributed identity of the first person plural. Then it becomes quite common to see the state and law as a Siamese twin: two independent entities of different origin, grown together in relative harmony. The state is supposed to be the power that generates the law and subsequently subjects itself to it, thus acknowledging its norm. The law is supposed to be the norm that requires power, thus legitimating the state. This dualism between state and law[91] sustains the primacy of political power over law in the final analysis. By regarding state and law as conceptually different entities, it produces a specific solution to the problem what should happen when law is endangered; then the state should be called upon to save the legal order by taking adequate coercive measures. So the state is attributed competence to judge whether and when law is endangered and to take adequate measures. But this theory of the state does not account for the state's being committed to some form of self-engaged self-restraint, as our concept of justice demands. That is: it does not understand the concept of state as primarily a concept of law; rather it is analysed as a political power, which in some circumstances acts in accordance with the law, in others not, as all political agents do.

As an alternative, I submit to conceive of the state – in a Kelsenian vein – as nothing more or less than the agent of the virtual unity of a legal order in action. If law is to exercise authority in directing human interaction, it should put its virtual unity as a system of norms in operation, and act 'as one person'. In specific historical circumstances and in specific socio-political contexts this conceptual aspect of law was attributed to the state as we know it today, i.e. to the so-called nation-state, and there may have been perfectly sound reasons to do so. But when these circumstances and contexts vary, we see the nation-state 'wither away' (to use Marx's famous phrase). For instance, it is perfectly understandable that the organisation of a religious community expresses itself in a legal order which conceives of itself as operating in unity. That is why such a church can speak of canonical law and regards itself as the institution from which the enactment of this legal order originates. A similar unity of agency is expressed by a federal association of states like the USA, a community of states like the European Union, or an

[91] Which Kelsen called a form of Manicheism: 'die Mythologie von Ormuzd and Ahriman – in staatsrechtlichem Gewande.' (H Kelsen 1931 [1968]) 1921.

organisation of 'peoples' like the United Nations or the WTO. Some of these legal orders express their virtual unity in action by using the concept of state (the USA), some are very reluctant (the EU), some are very pertinent in rejecting it (the UN). Moreover, one can think of certain professional organisations, which make a partial legal order of their own by establishing a system of disciplinary law regarding the very realm of exercising professional skills in society at large. The past offers us still more examples of giving shape to the unity of a legal order in operation, from the medieval city to the colonial common-wealth. That we have thought it useful to relate this conceptual core of a legal order to a parameter like 'the monopolisation of the sword over a certain territory' may have been useful, but it is a political rather than a philosophical point about law. To call the conceptual core itself 'a state' is misleading to the extent that in that case we would have to call all the different modes of expressing unity of legal agency referred to in the last sentences, forms of 'state'. The state does not have two faces or sides: conceptually it is nothing but the concept of law writ active. But the parameters of its empirical appearance can vary considerably, and only one set of these is congruent with the political model of the nation-state.

7.2 Judging Potential: Law as a Discipline

As argued in section 6 the authority of (and in) law is not merely bound up with the institutionalisation of law-enactment within a certain political system. It is also acquired by law presenting itself as an order of concepts, judgments and arguments, rather than signs, orders and decisions. By presenting itself as an order of judgment, law allows – to a certain extent – for an order of critique reflecting on its own feasibility. This is a specific way in which a legal order reflects a political system that, on its own account, allows something to count against it and respects instances which articulate the concrete possibilities of doing so in specific circumstances, i.e. authority. Therefore, we must say that the authority of law resides also in there being a form of knowledge about law that does not coincide with the authority of law as a form of knowledge. As legal subjects we are all interested in having this epistemic access to law. It cannot come as a surprise that, for the sake of distribution of labour, we attribute it to experts and scholars. We establish a discipline of law as a professional scholarly enterprise, which can freely use the academic attitude to criticise the legal system in action. Law as a discipline, legal doctrine, or – as the European continent has called it since the beginning of the nineteenth century – 'legal science', are able to argue that what is posited (enacted and/or maintained) as valid law, is not always valid by all the standards it itself refers to. It may turn out to be 'very bad law'. This is obviously true in the case of the judiciary; her authority would diminish rapidly if she would just mechanically repeat the phrases dictated from above and not critically reflect on them according to academic standards. But it also goes for the highly political institution of the legislator. To the extent that its enactments would become purely decisionist rulings, pure summations of partial interests in society, mere extrapolations of financial pressure, blunt definitions, or invocations of moral ideals, they would lose their truly 'prudential' character, their judgmental potential, and be regarded as gratuitous phrases. The next chapter will expressly deal with what is to be understood by 'legal doctrine' and carve out the notion of legal validity.

8. SUMMARY

We tried to gain some insight into law being always 'positive' law: posited by certain acts and posited in certain spatio-temporal circumstances. Legal positivism in its typically modern form overestimates this positive character of law to such a degree of absoluteness, that it comes into conceptual conflict with the idea of law itself, developed in the previous chapter. Moreover, it incites reactions of historicism and scientism, which in turn overemphasise a one-dimensional and finite history as the absolute root of law. Both of these modes of thinking share a common problem: a dualistic account of the relationship between constituent and constitutional power. Showing that there is an alternative based on alternating first-person and third-person viewpoints in giving constitutional shape to a polity goes some considerable way in solving the paradox of sovereignty. For this shaping to be sustainable it has to be an authoritative way to establish authority that could serve to end or curb socially disruptive conflict by taking its cue from what the previous chapter called the antinomy of justice. This we linked to two main features of political authority: its independency from immunised political identity, and its potential of exercising judgment and argument. The former feature was connected to some legal basics, like the separation of powers, the principle of equality before the law, the values of democracy, and the limits of coercion and state-power. The latter feature was referred to the next chapter for further analysis. Without such authority, law cannot be enacted or 'posited'; indeed there cannot be positive law.

4. Legal knowledge and legal doctrine: validity of law

I have been investigating how the binding character of law could be accounted for, and what follows from that with regard to the specific way in which law comes into being and is sustained, namely by authoritative decision-making, enforced by sovereign power. All this I called the *positive* character of law. Now I want to embark on a second mode of appearance of positive law in modern society, namely as an *object* of theoretical knowledge. I would like to ask what follows from the account given above for what we mean by knowledge of positive law? This question evolves directly from the previous chapter, where I mounted the argument that law itself is a mode of knowledge, namely practical knowledge as exhibited by authority. I pointed out that such 'knowing how' with regard to ending or precluding major conflict in society is not necessarily explicit. It may also remain (partly) implicit, tacit, and embodied in those who take authoritative decisions. But then I argued that law has several ways to enhance its authority. One of them is precisely by posing as an object of theoretical, in particular scholarly, knowledge. Rather than being dependent merely on the sovereign status of the agent(s) making law, it may sustain its claim by seeing to it that it can be described, explained, and predicted. There are at least two reasons why this enhances authority. One is an argument from effectiveness: if law can be known, its norms can be interiorised by legal subjects, so that they can consider complying with it without authoritative intervention. This saves a lot of time, energy, and costs. The second argument derives from the antinomy set out in Chapter 2: the authority of law-makers increases if they put their products to the test of reasonableness; i.e., if they acknowledge what will count against their claims without someone making it count against them. The present chapter is about what it means to pursue knowledge of such an object that does not have to be one. What is the structure and the reliability of theoretical knowledge about the practical knowledge of legal authority?

What, indeed, is to be known about law? Can we know more about it than the positive facts by which it is enacted? That is, can we know more about it than the observable behaviour and (or) the circumstances in which it originates? And if there is something to be known about law, can we conceive of it as some sort of *Wissenschaft*, a scholarly discipline with a specific method? Or is the learned lawyer the servant of a legal order he or she ought to obey, to defend, and to promote, as, e.g., the judiciary would do? What, indeed, has made law faculties into universally respected parts of universities, on a par with science or medicine? Why would it not be true what Von Kirchmann said in the nineteenth century, that law could not possibly be a science, because 'three legislative changes, and whole university libraries would turn into garbage'?[1] Is legal scholarship a sort of royalty watching? A less tacit, at times even loud, extension of the practical knowledge that law already is? How to account for the frequently observed protests of lawyers or citizens against a decision of a court, or a legislator, when they regard it as 'very bad law indeed'?[2]

As I will try to argue, the question about knowledge of law is bound up with the notion of validity: we want to be able to say of a certain rule, decision, or agreement made with a claim to (i.e. posited as) being valid law, whether it is warranted or not. What we seem to need, therefore, is a set of criteria to establish validity in such cases. Central to this notion of validity will be the problem of the relationships between facts and norms,

---

1 JH Von Kirchmann (1999 [1847]) 20.

2 Just a few examples: All over the world, but particularly in the US, there was massive protest against the Stop Online Piracy Act introduced in the House of Representatives as HR 3216 on October 25, 2011, with EU Commissioner for Digital Agenda Neelie Kroes calling it 'bad legislation'. In July 2012, farmers were urging the New South Wales Government in Australia to withdraw unreasonable and, as they said, 'insulting' law protecting native vegetation. For scholarly protest against the introduction of the Dutch new Civil Code at the time, see HCF Schoordijk (1979), in particular pp. 42–43.

as these two seem to meet in rules. For rules are the privileged format of legal norms: 'If/As A is the case, B ought to be done'.[3] In the course of the argument it will become clearer what the relationships between facts and norms have to do with the antinomy of recognition that we analysed in Chapter 2 and with the conception of authority developed in Chapter 3.

In order to quickly hit the trail of these questions, I take my cue from two divergent approaches to the notion of validity. I will explain why each endorses a partial truth and makes the mistake of believing that it is also good enough for the other part. We will see that they try to justify their beliefs by conceiving of law as something 'given' as an object of knowledge: a *positum* which exists 'out there' to be known by thinking subjects. At the end of the day, we will have to acknowledge that they are forms of legal positivism in disguise, inspired by what I called, in the previous chapter, the motive of apprehensibility. But let us begin with the accounts they give of the mode in which law is something posited before the knowing subject. For that is where the differences are.

The antagonistic camps I flag formalism and realism, for want of better labels. As their respective representatives I will present two rather well-known schools of legal thinking and scholarship: Kelsen's Pure Theory of Law on the one hand (section 1), and Holmes's predictivism on the other (section 2). This confrontation is only partially historical: at least in the way I present the clash, it never occurred. The stage I set serves a philosophical argument in the context of this book, rather than a history of legal philosophy. In particular I want to have some prima facie attractive inroads into the problem of legal validity and the relationship between facts and norms inherent to it.[4] Having learnt from this

---

[3] Cf. (W Twining and D Miers 1991). Of course some norms have a different structure. The prohibitions on copying intellectual property or on speeding in populated areas often come in the form of technological obstructions which make it impossible to act otherwise. Even then, however, the device could be rewritten in rule format.

[4] I happen to believe that some of these 'positivists', notably Kelsen, are much closer to the argument that I am developing than is commonly recognised in the literature.

discussion I explain in section 3 why we cannot infer facts from norms or norms from facts, and yet maintain, in the end, that they must have a common domain of justification. Section 4 offers some clues to the domain of legal justification. In the final section I deal with the question whether in law validity and bindingness of norms are one and the same thing?

This chapter is about more than an answer to the question whether or not law is 'science'. This discussion is as trivial as it is boring, especially if it is about semantics. Apart from the weird use of 'science' in the context of law – which is much more acceptable in German idiom than in Anglo-American – it depends on what you want to call 'a science'. Law is certainly a very special 'object' to study. If we regard it, intuitively, as a way of knowing how to deal justly with conflict in society, we may infer that legal scholarship is about giving a theoretical account of that practical knowledge. This makes it different from the natural sciences, where the object of knowledge is not itself a mode of knowledge: for all we know, the solar system does not know anything while two people making a deal do know, often quite implicitly, how they should act in order to avoid conflict. But there are a lot of other disciplines that may take an angle on the body of practical knowledge called law (economics, psychology, etc.); and the question is whether legal scholarship has an angle of its own.[5]

1. LEGAL FORMALISM

Kelsen (1881–1973) is the founder of the Viennese school of jurisprudence known as the *Reine Rechtslehre*, the Pure Theory of Law. In fact he gave it that name himself in his most famous book with the same title.[6] It intends to offer a structural analysis[7] of what it means in our

---

[5] It is not merely a scholastic question. Lawyers who are able to answer it have better chances in funding competitions, where they not only have to compete with (other) social scientists, but also have to respond to panels consisting of these scientists.

[6] H Kelsen (1960) 1.

legal culture that, with regard to a certain legal order *L*, there is a true theory telling valid from invalid law. Moreover it wants to elucidate under what conditions valid law in general can be an object of (scientific) knowledge. In order to do just that, the theory will have to establish the conditions and the criteria by which objectivity of knowledge claims about law can be tested. I will put up the legal scholar as a prototype of someone interested in a specific kind of knowledge about law. But of course, he is not the only one. Ordinary citizens often want to know as well, whether they intend to comply with it or not. They may even want to learn about law that does not regard them. They distinguish this detached attitude from a different one, which they also take at times: as legal subjects addressed by law or as legal officials making law (e.g., by making a contract or a will). What, then, allows a prototypical academic lawyer (rather than a prototypical official) to assert that some legal norm N enacted at a certain moment in time in legal order *L* is, or is not, valid law in *L*?

Kelsen's direct aim is certainly not to improve on legal practice and legal doctrine (though he was very critical towards the *interbellum* law in both Austria and Germany). His primary concern was with clarifying what lawyers actually do when they practice and study law.[8] As said, he wants to give a theoretical account of legal knowledge: its structure and its reliability. In a philosophical vocabulary we may say that he is after an 'epistemological' explanation of legal knowledge. Criticism of legal practices, he believes, can only be justified if we have solid knowledge about law.[9] When this section calls the Pure Theory 'formalist', this label first and foremost refers to the fact that the theory envisages not this or that particular legal order, but the structure or 'form' of a legal order, or rather the concept of law in general. It purports to describe the parameters of a variable 'law', rather than the properties of a particular entity. In due course we will also encounter a second meaning of 'formalist': the

---

[7] Ibid. 106.

[8] Ibid. 209.

[9] That is why Kelsen stresses the 'anti-ideological character' of the Pure Theory. Ibid. 112.

theory uses the model of formal legal competence in understanding legal validity, which to many people means emptying the law from any substance whatsoever – something Kelsen was well aware of.

1.1 In Demand of Purity

Kelsen's use of the word 'pure' has a clearly polemical aim, which is the cause of many misunderstandings. But it is also highly topical for contemporary discussions on 'interdisciplinarity'. It is easier to see what he rejects than what he advocates by his plea for purity. What he rejects is syncretism in academic law, particularly in legal method,[10] i.e., the presupposition that knowledge of law can and should be achieved by freely combining doctrinal, moral, economical, sociological, psychological, historical, political, etc. approaches. There is no doubt in Kelsen's mind that law has all of these aspects, plus a few more. What he denies is that all these aspects and their mutual relations can be scientifically expressed by pretending that they are 'given' in a reality independent of our concepts and categories, laid out in the very order of things themselves, such that academic legal doctrine is able to 'picture' them. Legal scholarship would be a matter of more or less adequately re-presenting legal reality on the screen of a given culture, and all means (that is: methods) that could serve that purpose would be welcome.[11] As a consequence, under the bias of syncretism, legal scholarship is an intellectual campaign for the normativity of a particular legal order. Comparative law is no exception: either it boils down to cultural anthropology (studying foreign legal cultures) or it scans foreign legal systems to make as much profit for the legal order one calls 'one's own'.

Why is this not feasible? There are two reasons. One is that science wants to understand its object as it is, not prescribe how it should be. It is difficult to see, according to Kelsen, how legal science could be both descriptive and prescriptive of a particular legal order in one fell swoop.

---

[10] Ibid. 1.

[11] It is mainly Von Savigny's early nineteenth century conception of law and legal doctrine that is to blame here. Cf. G Haverkate (1975 [1977]).

The second reason is that 'science' is only possible by virtue of a restricted point of view from where some complex phenomenon like law is captured. Of course, in spontaneous experience reality is perceived as one big amalgam of qualities simultaneously grasped by our senses. Then it is easy to claim that we experience the totality of things; but it is quite difficult to conceive what it is that we experience. Now that is exactly what constitutes the difference between diffuse everyday experience and disciplined science: in the latter we are able to give an articulate account of some of these qualities, on condition that we restrict our point of view and, thus, our range of perception and our realm of reality. To give an example: when we breathe, we sense 'the air', fresh or warm, humid or dry, sweeping or caressing, relieving or suffocating, etc., and we may even frame a reliable idea about tomorrow's weather from these experiences, just from how the air 'feels'. Meteorology, however, is a different matter. Meteorology is only possible if we concentrate on the 'atmosphere' of our globe under the restrictive aspect of partitions of air pressure. Of course the earthly atmosphere is far more than a partition of air pressure, and in chemistry and biology – so different from meteorology – we take other restrictive viewpoints to study some of these other aspects. We may even decide to recombine them from yet another viewpoint. What we cannot do, however, is build ourselves a point of view which is as unrestricted as everyday experience and as articulate as a scientific account at the same time. In order to grasp at least a few qualities we have to partially give up what we feel as the very core of experience, the encounter with what encounters us. We have to isolate a certain question, abstract it from all the rest and, thus, mould what we call an aspect into an object of knowledge. Indeed, we have to 'posit' this reality as it were in front of us, because in everyday life it is as much part of us as we are part of it.

Things are not different with law. Our spontaneous experience of law is an amalgam of all sorts of qualities of law. We are often indistinctively impressed by its authoritative, aesthetic and ritual appearance. But somehow we are on the wrong track if we comply with a legal decision on account of the judge's wig rather than his jurisdiction. To sort out what should be decisive, under what conditions, in our dealings with the law, we have to choose a specific angle. Even if we recombine aspects, for instance in an economic analysis of law, we do so from a specific angle we should try and account for.

In this specific sense, we can speak of the sciences as 'positive' sciences and appreciate that they are always 'abstract' despite the negative ring of the word. A philosophy of science that would deny the abstractness of science and promote it as the sole sensible way of 'talking real life', would forget about the positing separation from which science originates. Such a philosophy is called 'positivism', more precisely: epistemological positivism. And it can have a more or less close relationship with the type of legal positivism, which I discussed in the previous chapter. In fact this relationship may entail everything between mutual reinforcement and mutual deconstruction. But it will be clear that reinforcement is not uncommon, as one may remember that one of the motives behind legal positivism was to secure knowledge of the law. To this purpose some theorists of law hold on to the Reductibility Thesis [RTh], which we encountered at the beginning of Chapter 3: knowledge of norms can be reduced to knowledge of facts.

In Kelsen's case, however, things are more complicated. His is a theoretical account of the legal order as an order of norms. What clearly annoys him is the lawyer who pretends to establish, to apply and to explain the rules by simultaneously appealing to the methods of politics, law, economics, sociology, etc. The rhetoric of 'law in action', or of other devices suggesting that we can touch upon 'real legal life' or 'the living law', cannot impress him. Rather is he keen on disguising these suggestions as misty verbalisms, not uncommonly used in the attempt of backing up one's political or moral prejudices and furthering one's political preoccupations. These are often the signs of authoritarian thinking in academic disguise.

Kelsen – certainly not a positivist on this account – emphasises that the various aspects of law (doctrinal, moral, economical, etc.), which we would want to give an account of, are answers to specific and distinct questions in the first place. Because in our investigations we cannot ask all sorts of questions at the same time and because our questions can only get an articulate answer if we ask them from a restricted angle, we should be aware of the fact that we can only hold things together by holding them apart. The first thing we should ask with regard to the legal discipline is what its specific angle on law is like? What does it want to know 'from the law' in contradistinction to other sciences, as for instance sociology or philosophy? Kelsen's answer is that the proper, restricted attitude of the legal discipline towards law is this: it conceives of law as a matter of norms. Law in the sense of the legal discipline or 'legal science' wants to know whether or not some norm N *exists* in some legal order *L*. And, in the case of norms, to exist means: to be valid. Frankly, I think that this is a sound view that deserves to be further deployed.

1.2 Some Distinctions

To repeat, science of law, in Kelsen's view, describes positive law in as far as it can be regarded as a system of valid, positive legal norms. This is the limited angle we need: the question of validity and the logic of validity in a legal system distinguish legal 'science' from economical, moral, sociological, etc. approaches to law. The latter are interested in other things about law: how it works as a pattern of social interaction, how it correlates with moral norms, how it uses scarce resources to desirable ends. Moreover, the succinct formula opening this subsection is useful in indicating the difference between legal science and legal order: while legal science describes legal norms, the legal order prescribes, indeed enacts or posits such norms.

Let us try and understand these differences better, and coin some distinct words for them.[12] Suppose in the train near the emergency-brake I read [1]:

---

[12] What I am in fact doing here is summarising chapter III of the *Reine Rechtslehre* (1960) with one eye towards what I take to be a more adequate classification and terminology proposed by H-N Castañeda. In the latter's vocabulary [1a] is a prescription or a mandate, while [1b] is deontic judgment. See his H-N Castañeda (1975; 1976).

[1] Abuse is prosecuted.

Abstract from its context, [1] is highly ambiguous. But suppose I read it on a clearly discernible sign. Then it may be interpreted as a prescription by some authority *A* not to abuse the emergency button. In fact this is what these signs in trains usually mean, so that we may rewrite [1] like [1a]:

[1a] Don't commit abuse! (signed: *A*)

Now suppose it is a hand-written text, still near the brake but surrounded by graffiti. Then it could also be read as a statement made by some messy messenger *S* about what a certain normative institution *L* (like the transport conditions of Dutch Railways) requires us to refrain from. In that case *S* (rather than *A*) is supposed to assert (rather than to order):

[1b] Abuse ought (according to *L*) to be prosecuted.

Thus [1b] is not a norm but a piece of information which one passenger S may give to another. Note that this information *may* be given in a 'normative' vein, for instance to advise (warn, beg) a co-passenger not to apply the emergency-brake light-heartedly. S, however, is not in a position to command his co-passenger like an official authority would do. Note also that, notwithstanding its uses in communication, [1b] has the syntactical form of a description rather than a prescription; it can be said to describe a prescription.

Once more, change the scene and imagine I read [1] in a governmental report on the past performance of Dutch Railway security staff. This would alter the very same sentence [1] into a description of a state of affairs, as in [1c]:

[1c] Abuse is prosecuted in 90% of the cases.

This is a description all right, but what it describes is not what ought to be done but what frequently happens in a particular society if and when certain conditions obtain, e.g. if someone abuses the emergency button. This statement, too, can be used as a warning in actual cases of communication. Such a warning would be based on knowledge about factual correlations between misdemeanours and sanctions, whereas in [1b] it would find a ground in knowledge about valid norms.

Let us rehearse the distinctions we have now, in order of appearance. – A norm (-claim) [1a]: This is an imperative in the logical sense (not the psychological[13]) sense of the word. This imperative can be expressed in a number of different ways, for instance by using a grammatical imperative as in [1a], but also by an indicative ('Abuse is punished by a fine of …'), or by an 'ought' phrase. For instance, [1a] is equivalent with [1a']:

[1a'] Abuse ought to be prosecuted (signed: *A*)

It captures the action by which an authority *A* rules 'what is to be done' by a certain agent, namely, not to abuse the emergency-brake on the train. Such utterances may be valid or invalid (legitimate or illegitimate), depending on certain criteria of legitimacy. Their preferred quality or 'value', however, is to be valid: that is what they claim to be, so to speak, from their moment of birth. If, by standards yet to be discussed, a norm-claim turns out to be valid, we may drop the characterisation 'claim' and speak of a norm clear and simple. Legal norms, therefore, are (practical) contents of thought in which legal authorities express what they want certain agent(s) to do, and which are found to be valid with respect to a specific legal order. I will come back on this later. Suffice it to say right now that statutory rules, judicial decisions, contractual agreements, wills, and their ilk can be legal norms in just this sense.

– A norm-description or a statement on the validity of a norm-claim [1b]. We use the adverbial construct of the type 'according to *L*' in order to express whether or not a specific norm exists, i.e. whether or not the claim on validity inherent to the enactment of a norm is valid. Such a statement can be either true or false. Kelsen calls it a *Rechtssatz*, i.e. legal proposition or, rather, a statement on law. Legal propositions are (theoretical) structures of thought contents used by legal scholarship in order to express legal knowledge. We find these sentences, for instance, in textbooks on law.

---

[13] See Chapter 3, section 3.1.

– A statement [1c] on the causal effects of certain acts of enacting and maintaining law. It is a proposition on (probability) correlations between states of affairs. It describes, explains or predicts these relationships. Sociology and psychology of law do find a vast realm of research here. Certain types of behaviour related to enacting and enforcing law on the one hand, complying with or offending against law on the other, can be conceived of as events in society and explained or predicted in terms of causes, motives, effects, consequences, etc. Propositions made by these sciences can be either true or false, by virtue of criteria generally acknowledged in their respective enterprises.

– Let me add: we also want to distinguish between variations [1a], [1b] and [1c], on the one hand, and [2a] and [2b], on the other:

[2a] It is desirable that [1b].

[2b] It is desirable that [1c].

[2a] and [2b] are expressions of wishes or valuations endorsed by agents by virtue of personal or shared preferences, often within the framework of broader or deeper political, moral or religious convictions. These valuations cannot be valid or invalid, nor true or false, unless one chooses to map them unto norms. In that case we may wish to say that what is in accordance with a certain preceding norm is 'good', while what it is in conflict with that norm is 'bad'.

It seems to me that these distinctions are tenable and useful, as they determine a specific canonical format for statements that would convey knowledge about law under the angle of normative validity, namely [1b]. Formats [1a] and [1c] regard other aspects of law.

1.3 Norm and Validity

I have established the difference between norms and norm-propositions. The former is an imperative, valid or invalid, the latter is a statement, true or false. Let us now have a closer look at the concept of a norm itself and the valid/invalid distinction. Kelsen's view can be captured in the following definition:

Def. 4.1 A norm is the warranted content of an act of will.[14]

This definition is in need of clarification on at least three points: what is an 'act of will'? what is its 'meaning'? and what are we supposed to understand by 'warranted'? Let us take an example. Suppose, the following sentences are uttered to the same person *B* by agent *A* who signed the respective norm (-claim) in [3] and [4]:

[3] Dear *B*, Pay $ 100,000 before September 15th. (signed: the kidnapper of your daughter).

[4] Dear *B*, Pay $ 100,000 before September 15th. (signed: Intergaz, your Company).

The first and easiest thing to see is that these norm-claims have the same 'meaning', that is, the same content. The same person is asked to pay the same amount of money. This content can be presented as an ordered set of two elements as in [5]:

[5] *B*, to pay $ 100,000 before September 15th!

Secondly, note that the two elements in [5], the agent *B* and the act 'to pay $ 100,000', are linked in the two sentences [3] and [4] in a very specific way which we met already in the course of our argumentation: agent *B* is linked to paying the money in the 'to do' mode, as distinct from the 'to be' mode. If we were to use a copula of the 'to be' mode, we would ascribe an action to *B* in the sense of a property, as in normal predication [6]:

[6] *B* (is such that he) pays $ 100,000.

---

[14] See H Kelsen (1960) 7. Note that Kelsen, here as elsewhere, only stresses that a norm-claim becomes a norm if and only if the 'ought' of the content (or meaning) is not just 'subjective' (dependent on the will of an arbitrary individual) but rather 'objective' (warranted by higher norms). I take some liberty in interpreting this correspondence as something that has to be demonstrated. Hence my use of the word 'warranted' which would roughly equal 'objectified', if only that would be unequivocal English.

But in the case of norms, we use the copula of the 'to do' mode, attributing an action to *B* in the sense of what is to be done by him as in [7], not in the sense of a property he actually exemplifies.

[7] *B* (is) to pay $ 100,000.

It makes little sense to use the superficial similarity of 'is' in both [6] and [7] to construct an identical deep structure underlying both sentences; the difference would only return in the analysis of the predicate. Now this specific linking an agent and an action by use of a copula of the mode 'to do', amounts to an act of will. Note that it is a logical operation rather than a psychological one.[15] It is not an act that we have to spend a lot of energy on, or which may cost us a lot of time. Notions of energy or time do simply not apply to acts of will, nor, for that matter, to other acts of thought performed by the other linking devices, for instance predicating, concluding, adding, or multiplying. It makes no sense, for instance, to say that the symbol + in '2 + 2' stands for far less effort than in '23465 + 98768', though most people will find it harder to figure out the latter than the former. So let us not confuse acts of will with psychological efforts to direct our inclination or concentration in some direction or other.

The third thing I promised to clarify is the word 'warranted' in Def. 4.1. Kelsen takes [4] to express a norm, while [3] does not. In [4] the content of the act of will is 'warranted', in [3] it is not. Suppose that *B* is unwilling to obey [3] and tries to evade payment. Suppose furthermore that the kidnapper dies from sheer stress immediately after mailing his letter. Suppose, finally, that *B* finds out about this shortly after he opened it and framed his intention to do everything in order to evade payment. Then by *A*'s passing away *B* will be released, not from an obligation to pay, but from the pressure exercised by the subjective will of the kidnapper. For there was nothing more to uphold the norm-claim than the

---

[15] On this (epistemologically rather essential) point, I believe Kelsen confuses the two. At numerous places (for instance, ibid. 201) he equates an act of will or *Setzungsakt* with the act of enacting (*Erzeugungsakt*). In a legal context the latter rather than the former takes procedural form.

kidnapper's individual (subjective) preference. Imagine now that similar things happen in case [4]: *B* does not want to pay, the employee of the Gaz Company who wrote the letter dies from stress, as *B* finds out soon enough after receiving the letter. Then it will turn out that there is far more behind [4] that the individual employee's preference. The Gaz Company will sue *B* anyway, waving a contract in writing, that is: referring to a norm. If *B* happens to think of a contract as just another piece of paper, the Company will probably refer to yet a higher norm, such as a rule of the Civil Code to the effect that contracts are binding upon parties who made them. And if *B* prefers to think low of the Civil Code, his lawyers will draw his attention to the fact that a still higher norm, the Constitution, provides for the competence of the legislator to enact a Civil Code according to certain parliamentary procedures. So a whole hierarchy of norms justified by higher norms will be appealed to if *B* appears reluctant to pay. This is typically what Kelsen characterises as an act of will being 'warranted'.[16] Even if it could be objected that in the final analysis, such a hierarchy is nothing more than the subjective will of the possessing class, of the ruling party, of the church or the prince, it has to be conceded that this will is laid out in the form of a hierarchy of norms deriving from higher and higher norms. Or – more precisely in modern law – norms enacted by authorities who are entitled to do so in virtue of higher norms.[17]

There is no point in denying, according to Kelsen, that in modern legal systems the main parameter of a norm 'deriving from', or 'being dependent on' a higher norm is authoritative competence. Whereas in primitive legal orders (and in morality) norms are warranted by other norms on the basis of content, in complex legal orders they are warranted on the basis of 'form', i.e. competence. So the primary sense in which a

---

[16] I slightly twist Kelsen's own wording; he prefers to speak of a correspondence relation between the 'subjective' and the 'objective' content ('Sinn') of an act of will. I hold that this 'correspondence' has to be established one way or another, and that this is precisely what Kelsen wants legal scholars to do when they have to test if the act whereby a norm is issued, is itself the content of an empowering norm.

[17] Cf. ibid. 196ff.

norm can be said to be valid by virtue of being dependent on a higher norm is that the body enacting the former is authorised to do so by another legal norm that is, by that very same token, higher.[18] Or again, slightly stricter, a norm-claim N_1 is warranted if the act of will enacting N_1 is the content of an empowering norm N_2, in which case N_1 is said to be valid (hence promoting to a norm N_1) and N_2 is said to be higher (or more basic) than N_1. N_2 may specify constraints concerning the enactment of N_1, regarding the circumstances in which, the purpose for which, and the procedure by which it should be enacted. For instance, the prohibition against playing a soccer match between team A and team B, is a valid legal norm if it is enacted by the mayor in charge of public order, considering the damage expected to be caused by hooligans, duly issued and communicated to those who are affected, etc. Sometimes there is large, sometimes small, scope for discretion. Constitutional rules often say nothing more than 'the legislator will take care of …', while (increasingly) statutory law only offers a framework to be filled in by the executive. All of this is accounted for in what is called a 'formal' approach to law.

There is only one problem. Once we have accepted the idea that norm-claims can only be 'warranted' by a higher norm, we can go on forever trying to find the supreme norm holding them all together in one system. Indeed, the idea of a highest norm becomes self-contradictory.[19] For every norm, in order to be warranted and to lose its claim-character, needs a higher norm. So a highest norm makes sense only if one postulates its validity, i.e. if its validity is presupposed rather than posited. Whether or not one wants to share this presupposition is dependent on whether or not one wants to have law regarded as an object of knowledge, Kelsen says. And I add: there are good reasons for making that choice following from the definition of authority in the previous

---

18 See also SL Paulson (1980); B Van Roermund (2000a); B Van Roermund and SL Paulson (2000a; 2000b).

19 This is why Kelsen, in his posthumously published *Allgemeine Theorie der Normen* (1979) 206, calls the *Grundnorm* a fiction, i.e. a thought content that not only contradicts real states of affairs, but is also self-contradictory.

chapter: authority of law will profit, ultimately, from allowing critical investigation into its directives. Making law an object of discussion and argumentation, of criteria and judgment, is a perfect way of doing just that. It is a political act that purports to silence politics in law. Yielding to this attractive prospect, however, presupposes fixing a point of reference, a highest norm.[20] Lawyers call it the constitution.

Here we find the primary sense of the famous concept of the *Grundnorm* (the basic norm) in Kelsen's theory. The basic norm is primarily nothing but the presupposition that there is a highest norm in a system of norms. As explained above, to say that 'there is (exists)' a norm is to say that this norm is valid, i.e., that it ought to be complied with. So what legal scholars do in presupposing the existence of a highest norm is presupposing the validity of the current constitution and its predecessors to the extent that they lend validity to the current constitution. This constitutes the specific and limited angle on a system of norms, which distinguishes legal knowledge from sociological or historical or moral angles on law: legal scholars take law from the angle of validity in the specific sense of 'deriving from the constitution'. At the end of the day legal scholars, lawyers, citizens, officials, etc., always want to know what is the ultimate constitutionally warranted validity of legal claim N?

The concept of a constitution is complex. No lawyer will think of 'the constitution' as a booklet with a limited number of clear-cut rules. Though written constitutions are common in a lot of civilised modern law systems, these texts are not supposed to exhaust all there is to the constitution of a legal order. In some legal orders the constitution is not even written or only partially written (cf. the United Kingdom or Israel). Not only in these but in all legal orders, the constitution always remains to some extent 'virtual', in the sense that it is a unifying texture lending coherent validity to an often scattered pattern of various (groups of)

---

[20] Note that one does not have to make this choice. If one does not, law is just a matter of exercising and following authority – there is nothing to be known about law.

norms, 'read into' words, customs, policy aims, etc., and this texture evolves over time in relation to political circumstances.[21]

Now if we want to pursue knowledge about a legal order, the mere presupposition that there is a highest norm in such an order is necessary, but by no means sufficient. What we must also do is make and discuss hypotheses about the contents of this highest norm as it pertains to a case, or a type of case, at hand. Take a simple case of attributing an amount of taxes to be paid as a consequence of purchasing a certain product (as with VAT). We look that up, say by consulting a table. But what we do by doing this is, ultimately, to test the link between the left column and the right column against the constitutional unity of the whole legal order. As lawyers we are interested in framing and testing hypotheses about, in the final analysis, the constitutional backing of each and every legal answer to a problem posed to us. None of these hypotheses is, of course, necessarily true pending evidence, but making them is necessary in order to acquire knowledge. As in other sciences, different scholars can reasonably disagree about the feasibility of hypotheses, i.e., about how to construe ultimate constitutional feasibility of certain norm-claims.[22]

---

[21] The difference introduced here between the basic norm as a presupposition and as a hypothesis solves, I believe, a lot of confusion in Kelsen. Initially, he referred to the basic norm as a 'hypothetische Geltungsgrund der Rechtsordnung' (H Kelsen (1960) 47). In H Kelsen (1979) 207 he replaces 'hypothetical' by 'fictitious'. This change in words does not affect the idea. The idea that a supreme norm must be presupposed if one wants to provide for the possibility of justifiable knowledge of norms remains the same, as well as the idea that it is the task of legal science 'diese Voraussetzung festzustellen' (H Kelsen (1960) 47). The latter can only mean: to establish the content of such a supreme norm hypothetically. For obviously there is nothing to establish about the 'Voraussetzung' in the sense of an epistemologically necessary postulate or presupposition of legal science.

[22] For numerous examples in the European context see S Prechal and B Van Roermund (2008).

The idea of the *Grundnorm* in Kelsen's work is both.[23] Firstly, it is the epistemologically necessary presupposition underlying all legal scholarship that there be a highest norm if we are to make sense of substantiated legal knowledge at all. Secondly, it is a feasible, but not infallible hypothesis about what the highest norm amounts to in a particular legal order. In daily practice, this amounts to giving 'the solution' of a case 'according to law'. Note that, in neither of these two senses, the basic norm is identical with the constitution or with the highest norm – even though the words of a certain hypothesis can be literally the same as the words of the constitution it captures. Note also that the basic norm is not a norm of natural law preceding the positive rules of certain, or, for that matter, all legal orders. The basic norm is neither the highest posited norm (that is what the constitution is), nor an overriding trans-positive norm of natural law (that is what the non-legal viewpoint on law would be). The double-breasted *Grundnorm* is simply what makes the science of law possible and feasible as a domain of knowledge.[24] It articulates the limited approach to law, which makes academic law different on the one hand from legal philosophy or sociology, on the other from authoritative law-making. It protects law from having to identify itself either with legal authorities, or with non-legal disciplines.

Note, to be precise, that such is the case for knowledge of any system of norms, not only the legal system. There will, however, be characteristically different restraints on what can reasonably be taken into account in framing hypotheses about the content of the highest norm in different areas. In Christian morality, for instance, the highest norm will be Jesus of Nazareth's command to love one's neighbours, while in Islamic morality it will be the individual's responsibility before Allâh. In the area of good manners or etiquette, the highest norm will be found in a certain, perhaps superficial, courtesy. And even in law there will be different

---

[23] Which is a major source of confusion, no less than the association of 'Grundnorm' with 'Grundgesetz' (constitution) or 'Grundrechte' (fundamental rights).

[24] In modern times, Dworkin's thesis that every question in law is supposed to receive only one correct answer, but that we may disagree or remain ignorant about which answer would be correct, amounts to the same. (R Dworkin (1977)).

restraints depending on different areas of law. Though it is common to speak of 'the constitution' in national and in some forms of supra-national law (for instance, European Union law), it is quite uncommon in other areas, where one would rather refer to principles, such as *pacta sunt servanda* in the law of nations (which has in fact 'constitutional' meaning).

1.4 Validity and Effectiveness

In Kelsen's view, norms are schemes of interpretation[25] applied to states of affairs: they indicate that and how one has to regard certain facts[26] as binding upon one's behaviour in some way or other. This binding force is not some property residing in these facts by nature: it is ascribed to them in a certain light, transforming them into 'institutional', in particular legal, facts. This 'light' is nothing more or less than the specific constraints that constitute the approach of legal science. These constraints delineate the question: has the claim, the agreement, the verdict that a certain action is obligatory or permissible, binding force, given the (hypothetical) content of the (presupposed) highest norm? That highest norm is the basis on which such claims, agreements or verdicts can be valid as norms in the strict sense. But in order to appear in such a light, they must be believed to exist already as states of affairs. That is, in the order of causes and effects, of efficiency and functionality, certain patterns of human behaviour must already be identifiable before one can go on to characterise them in terms of normative interpretation schemes, i.e., as norm-claims. We see that happen in actual political practice. For instance, after a vigorous revolution, it has to become clear who will be able to exercise actual political power for the near future before legal science in the sense described above can take off. That explains why Kelsen can hold the view that legal norm-claims can only be valid *when* they are (by and large) effective, but that is not to say that they are valid

---

25 Kelsen (1960) 3.

26 Like a certain course of action, certain signs, certain words or gestures.

because they are effective.[27] They are valid, to repeat, by virtue of being dependent on a constitution, which is an elliptic expression for the presupposition that they are ordered in a constitutional unity or hierarchy of norms.

The notion of a 'hierarchy' may raise the wrong associations when it is immediately linked to the metaphor of the pyramid. Kelsen's (and Merkl's) idea of a 'Stufenbau' of legal norms (a staircase to the top-norm) certainly nourishes this thought. But little depends on the metaphor. The central idea is that of hierarchy; and hierarchy can be expressed by various metaphors. What is often proposed as an alternative, and more modern, metaphor for the order of legal norms is the 'network'. But few will deny that a network or a web can be an expression of hierarchy as clear and distinct as a pyramid. Take any map of an underground transport system, and you will see immediately which stations are the most important ones, primarily in the sense that they hold the system together. It is perhaps superfluous to emphasise that this does not imply the legalistic view that, in the final analysis, all norms are to be semantically inferred from explicit paragraphs of a written constitution. What Kelsen demands is nothing more or less than that in order to be valid, norms should 'fit' within one and the same constitutional framework. And what this framework looks like is a matter of legal debate, for which some constitutional anchor points are more explicitly formulated (which is not ipso facto: clearer) than others.

1.5 Formalism and Morality

The basic norm, which presupposes a highest norm (the constitution) and formulates a certain content of it in a hypothetical way, is not a material directive. Kelsen is quite explicit about it, saying that law can have any content whatsoever, even a very unjust or immoral one. Then an utterly unjust constitutional setting is the ultimate point of reference in the legal discipline studying this system of law: there can be morally wicked systems of law, and therefore there can be legal science of wicked

---

27 See Kelsen (1960) 219; H Kelsen (1979) 111–113.

systems of law.[28] Kelsen himself went to great pains in showing that the interpretations of the Weimar constitution given by right-wing university lawyers like Carl Schmitt were false, and that the way in which the Nazis took over political power in Germany was invalid. When finally he was effectively banned from the universities of Vienna, Cologne, and Geneva, he fled Europe (to the USA), never to return again. Even so he has often been blamed for his radical view of legal science, which was alleged to have opened the loopholes for totalitarianism by admitting that law could have any content. But we should note that this 'admitting' has a special ring here. Kelsen never advocated that as citizens or as moral persons we should admit any content to become law; nor did he overlook that legal orders usually have moral concerns about justice. What Kelsen claimed was that it is not a part of legal science to morally judge the content of a constitution, because that is the part of morality. Legal science cannot have it both ways; it cannot, at the same time, maintain a critical, validity oriented approach towards a particular legal system, and be the moral judge of that system. If it were to engage in moral judgment, it would be forced to play the game as it is played by political forces, criticising officials. Then it could only be critical of law in that 'common' political way, while the legal system is supposed to restrain these forces in the first place. Legal science would end up being bound by the authority of the system it studies. It would be committed to the interpretation of the constitution authoritatively advocated by the officials of the actual regime. But by carving out a specific aspect of a legal system (its coherent unity under the constitution), it can keep a distance and criticise the system 'from within'. By refraining from moral, political or ideological judgment, legal science grounds its academic freedom to criticise a legal system for constitutional reasons. If legal authorities ignore this kind of critique, there is a problem for legal science anyway, and thus, for

---

[28] H Kelsen (1960) 201: 'Daher kann jeder beliebige Inhalt Recht sein.' – the sentence which is the skandalon of the Pure Theory of Law, and the ground for accusing Kelsen to have opened the loopholes for Nazism. This used to be a popular and influential view after the Second World War in Germany, and which lasted until the 1980s.

its representatives as well. The only thing these scholars can do then, is to give up academic life and resume their positions as citizens with full-fledged moral judgment.

It should be noted that the way in which legal science provides a strategy of warranting legal claims does not imply political neutrality. It represents a value that is at the core of legal authority. Like democracy, it contributes to what we have learned to see as the recursive logic inherent in politics that claims to form law by authority: such politics, on its own account, should allow something to count against itself. It should exercise political self-restraint as a matter of principle rather than strategy. That is what legal authorities (note that in some contexts this means: legal persons, citizens, individuals) ask from legal science: to be criticised in their claim that they are enacting valid law. Typically in a democracy one refrains from any absolute knowing and willing in politics, and therefore the majority allows the minority the institutionalised chance to become the majority.[29] Similarly, the institution of law as an academic discipline is part and parcel of realising law in the sense of 'institutionalised just politics'. This implies that, in the end, legal science is dependent on politics. But in Kelsen's view this is just fine, and to be preferred over and above political criticism crowned by the false prestige of substantiated knowledge. He does not want to hide from the fact that the point of unity from which all norms of a legal order emanate, is a posited one, and that it can never monopolise judgment over its own moral and rational quality.

2. LEGAL REALISM

In contrast to formalism legal realists believe that the validity of a legal norm and, indeed, a legal order, should be conceived of in terms of effectiveness. Instead of a precondition of validity it is what defines validity. By the same token validity changes from a normative to a factual matter. This change is inspired by what Chapter 3 called the Reductibility

---

[29] A definition Kelsen himself uses.

thesis [RTh]: norms can be reduced to facts, e.g. preferences, expectations, interests, options for action, etc. people may have. Though realists differ widely as to what determines effectiveness (e.g., socio-psychological, economical, rhetorical parameters) and as to the kind of cause-effect relationships involved (e.g., mechanical or functional), I will disregard these differences and concentrate on the key issue: effectiveness. Where necessary, I take socio-psychological motivations as an example.[30]

2.1 Predictivism

Effectiveness in social situations can be analysed, according to legal realism, in terms of different causes that affect social behaviour. These causal relationships can be rendered in terms of laws so as to bring out their general and necessary character. One may formulate laws of social life on the same footing as laws of biological life. In other words, laws of social life are laws of nature. If they are tenable such laws not only give adequate descriptions of correlations between certain states of affairs, but they also offer adequate explanatory models for such correlations. It is possible to infer predictions from these models, and test them against future evidence. In the case of social behaviour, predictions will be possible about future behaviour of social agents: what they will do under oppression; how they want to raise their children; whose directives they will follow. Predictivism is very central to legal realism. It became an important lever to modernise law when, at the end of the nineteenth century in the United States, legitimacy of law and state were very low indeed because of the huge problems in large parts of the population, mainly caused by massive industrialisation. Justice Oliver Wendell Holmes introduced a less formal and more social conception of law with the words: ‘The prophecies of what the courts will do in fact, and nothing

[30] Psychological motivations (e.g., fear for coercive sanctions) is usually referred to by Scandinavian realists, while sociological motivations (e.g., group dynamics) is the hallmark of American realists.

more pretentious, are what I mean by the law.'[31] Similar wide-ranging proposals, though in different keys, were made in other parts of the western world, invariably at times when the gap between law and society had widened under the influence of large-scale politico-economic developments.[32]

Please note that by Holmes's proposal the law is not 'whatever the courts will do' (although that, too, is defended by some radical realists), but the sum-total of the predictions of what they will do. In other words, at bottom, rules of law are nothing more than shorthand, and therefore often unclear and unsatisfying, summaries of such predictions. Unsatisfying they turn out to be soon enough when we try and understand what the law is from the angle, which the law takes as its greatest challenge: the angle of 'the bad man'. The bad man is the one who is after his own private interest, and nothing else, going for it with all means he can afford.[33]

Suppose, coming from Mountania to the beautiful state of Lowlandia *X* wants to drive his car on motorways, at any speed he wants at any moment he wants. He does not, however, want to pursue his desire at all costs. In particular, he does not want to run the risk of getting speeding tickets, losing his licence, losing his car, and spending a few months in jail.[34] So he hires a Lowlandian lawyer and asks him bluntly: What is the law in this country with regard to maximum speeds? Now if the lawyer

---

[31] OW Holmes 1952 [1897] 173. Cf. GE White (1993) 480: 'Alongside Holmes' intellectual desire to plumb the depths of ideas, and to express them as freshly and vividly as possible, was a penchant for what could be called a "poetic" approach to his intellectual tasks. Holmes conceived of his role, whether judge or scholar, as a solitary, creative, original one.' For a more recent assessment of Holmes' work see SJe Burton (2000).

[32] Cf. in Germany, also in response to the problems of industrialisation, Von Ihering's plea for a teleological interpretation of the law, the sociological interpretation of law by Ehrlich and the *Interessenjurisprudenz* by Heck after the First World War in Germany, by Gény in France; the echoes of realism after the Second World War in the USA when the war industry collapsed.

[33] OW Holmes (1952 [1897]) 170ff.

[34] I constructed the example on the basis of the very informative AA d'Amato (1978).

would only quote the rule in the books ('70 miles an hour on motorways'), he will probably be fired faster than he was hired. 'Looking up rules in books, that is what every fool can do himself', *X* will say. 'I know quite a few rules in this country which I do not have to bear in mind, because the officials do not give a damn. Take, for instance, this typical Lowlandian rule that that I should ask permission from the municipality to cut a tree in my own garden. Or that I should pay taxes for having a dog around the house while a cat does not register. Or that blasphemy is a crime. Nobody seems to care to uphold these rules. Please, come up with something better than a quote.' That will suffice to make the lawyer get the drift of A's initial question about what the law is. He may say something like the following: 'On second thoughts, I can give you some interesting details. Sometimes there are checkpoints with radar and people in uniforms, badges and guns. They are authorized to stop you. You better do, because sometimes they shoot or call other people in helicopters who shoot. Predictably these police controls take place when the weather is fine. Anyway, when you are caught for speeding, you will get a ticket. Do not try to negotiate, let alone to point out what you think of Lowlandian police; it will make things worse. Anyway, the Public Prosecutor, which in point of fact is a debt-collecting agency backed up by state power, will send you a letter, proposing a transaction. They use strict indexes for determining the fine: the more you speeded, the more you will have to pay. You can refuse to pay and go to court. Don't do that, unless you have very good arguments. It will often worsen things even more. And I should add that in case you are caught for the second time, or with more than 0,05% alcohol, or with drugs…'.

Meanwhile, *X* has lost his patience. He tears already around the corner, on to the motorway, where, soon enough, he is stopped for speeding at 90 miles an hour. He hires another lawyer, as he has preferred to let the judge decide between him and the Public Prosecutor. He believes he has a valid excuse before a Lowlandian court, as he claims to be misled about the law by a professional expert. His new lawyer, however, will predict that this is not going to work. He explains that in such cases it is far more efficient to pretend deep personal misery. It all depends, he says, on the individual judge who will sit on the trial. Judge *J* is far more sensitive towards personal misery than judge *K*. His client *A*, however, has lost confidence in Lowlandian lawyers and gained elementary insight in how the system works. 'You cannot be serious', he may object, 'about this sensitivity of judges. I understand that they are human individuals and that they have their sympathies and antipathies as we all have. But will they not, as much as possible, suppress these feelings and inclinations? Because if they do not, their behaviour will be so whimsical and arbitrary, that no power will be prepared to back them up? I would rather stress the point that as a Mountanian, I am a foreigner in this country.' 'Please don't', the lawyer may reply. 'You see, there is this rapidly increasing bias against Mountanians in our country. Some citizens have protested against it, calling it discrimination, but the fact is that the authorities call it self-defence of the nation. No one will be able to help you if you are going to use that argument.'

Now the full truth about the legal system dawns upon *A*: indeed the law is nothing more than the prediction about the officials' behaviour in a certain case. This would be a rather difficult rule to go by if such behaviour would be whimsical. But by and large it is not, in point of fact. Officials prefer to be predictable, and the explanation is this: they not only want to have power, but they also want to keep it. Here we meet a law of nature, or rather, of a law about the nature of social power. In fact we met it already in Chapter 2 (section 1.2), when I was explaining how power works. There it was said that the main aim of those in power is to stay in power, and that this requires calculation and consistency rather than arbitrariness and ruthlessness. The officials will, roughly, treat equal cases alike. Lawyers know this and will build their predictions on this model. They will refine it to allow for exceptions and differentiations. The officials, in turn, will have to realise that in order to keep their power, they will have to act in accordance with what the lawyers were able to predict on the basis of sufficiently sophisticated models. They will, in other words, fulfil the prophecies of their behaviour. At least to a certain extent, the prophecies of what the courts will do are self-fulfilling prophecies. But of course, there is always the chance of new situations, of sudden changes of circumstances, prompting decisions not expected by lawyers. This does not necessarily entail a loss of power on the part of the officials: the lawyers may acknowledge, in hindsight, that it was a good decision, even if it was hardly predictable. Or – and this happens quite often – they may make a distinction within their own profession between top-lawyers (the few who habitually predict a decision correctly) and middle-of-the-road lawyers (the many who do not, or do not even try). For even an unexpected decision can have been 'in the air' for a fine legal nose. It is a matter of sensing the properties that are becoming relevant in the whole complex of factors determining the decisions of those exercising power. In Lowlandia, for instance, having red hair is not found to be relevant up to now. But having dark skin increasingly is … .

2.2 Social Engineering

The realist conception of law is neither naive nor cynical.[35] It neither holds the view that law is identical with what officials like to do, nor that officials do best by staying in power.[36] Their programme is governed by

---

[35] Holmes certainly was not a cynic: see OW Holmes (1952 [1897]) 170; he also was a great advocate of theorising in law (ibid. 198; 200).

[36] Jerome Frank however goes quite a long way in the direction of cynicism. He is a so-called 'fact scepticist', rather than a 'rule scepticist'. He defends the view that the lower courts construct the facts to their liking, and no one is able to attain these constructions in appeal. Therefore, he doubts very much whether there is any real law to be found in studying decisions made by higher courts. What they call facts are guesses about what has been going on in the private mind of the lower judge. See JN Frank (1973 [1949]) 14–36. Towards the end of his book, he concludes: 'When all is said and done, we must face the fact [*sic*] that judges are human. That should not dismay those of us who cherish democracy.' For the very thought that authorities are super-human beings would favour totalitarianism. What Frank advocates under the slogan 'Unfrock the judge!' is education and training in democratic thinking. He does not bother too much about scientific criteria of rationality in politics. I myself believe that Frank's view is challenging enough as an exercise in political theory, in particular as a description of the intricate relationships between facts and norms in law. But from a philosophical point of view, his argument is trivial. On the one hand he states that there is no point in theorising about law and democracy; on the other he pleas for education in democracy and equity; and he never explains

the Reductibility Thesis: where there is a norm it should be rewritten in terms of facts. One is interested in the mechanisms that are factually in place, and more often than not the interest is in engineering these mechanisms to the best of society. The most effective way of doing just that, is to tune in on law as a dynamic equilibrium of interests. This is usually treated as a certain pattern of negotiable 'preferences' that is dominant in a particular society – which is itself a factual datum. When realists talk about validity of law, they refer to this equilibrium. By making explanatory and predictive statements about it, they engage themselves in building an instrument for 'social engineering'.

The motives behind legal realism are most eloquently explained and transformed in a theoretically feasible view by Roscoe Pound.[37] Robert Summers summarises a Pound-oriented view of 'pragmatic instrumentalism' (the upgraded realism of our time) as follows:

(1) As far as values and principles in law are concerned, one departs from actual interest and ignores trans-positive moral principles. These interests are to be researched empirically. The words of the law will get their meaning by their use within such an articulated social context.
(2) Law is the prediction of certain facts, in particular of the coercive power that will be exercised by the officials of an administration. Who the officials are, is itself a subject of predictions.
(3) The sum-total of predictions is a social instrument tuned to extra-legal socio-political goals previously decided upon.
(4) Through these predictions, the development of law is linked up with scientific research and creativity inherent to science.

---

how he manages to eat his cake and have it. Education in democracy without allowing critical reflection on what democracy is (ultimately) about is more like a dictate of democracy than a training in democracy.

[37] See, for instance, his R Pound (1968 [1942]), as well as the majestic R Pound (1959).

(5) Law-in-action prevails over law-in-the-books when validity is at stake. The orientation of the predictions should be towards law that is actually enforced (sometimes by coercion).
(6) Complex and sophisticated models of law enforcement and implementation are hypothetically articulated and tested against sufficiently rich sets of data. Using the results of such tests in organising society amounts to legal technology or social engineering.
(7) Specialisation and professionalism are important here as elsewhere in technological developments.
(8) Education and training of these specialists is therefore an important variable in the model itself and, thus, in the predictions and the technology.
(9) The effects of the engineering technology can be checked against the original policy goals. This evaluation, too, is a variable in further predictions.[38]

3. VALIDITY: NORM-CLAIMS WARRANTED

At the beginning of this chapter I submitted that the possibility of knowledge claims 'about' law is bound up with the possibility to make true statements about the validity of law, where law itself is a political artefact rather than either a natural phenomenon or a speculative theory. We have encountered two radically different accounts of such possibility: a formalist and a realist account. They were both highly instructive. One thing their controversy demonstrates is that it is far from obvious what referring to norms and facts actually means, let alone that we can judge the value of such references. I will return to this later. But another, and presently more important thing is, that these two accounts are perhaps not as antagonistic as they seem. At least some scope for reconciliation may be found in the observation that they seem to talk at cross purposes. Formalism seems interested in the structure of the statements made in

38 RS Summers (1982a; 1982b).

law to express knowledge, while realism, on the other hand, seems far more interested in parameters of testing statements. So let us see if we can make a synthesis out of the two. It will require some epistemological exercises and some technical vocabulary, but it will turn out to be worthwhile.

3.1 Practitions, Propositions and Domains of Justification

Let us start from what seemed an attractive definition of a norm, offered by Kelsen, and which I explained at some length in section 1.

Def. 4.1 A norm is the warranted content of an act of will.

There is a striking similarity between this definition of a norm and the definition of a fact given by some philosophers. Let me frame this definition as follows:

Def. 4.2 A fact is the verified content of an act of judgment.[39]

In both definitions there is: (i) an act of thought, called willing or judging, respectively; (ii) a thought content or meaning; and (iii) a possibility of 'justification', i.e. of making one's claims good, in some way or other (warranting or verifying, respectively).

How should we assess both the similarity and the differences? Remember section 1.3, where it was argued that our thinking may evolve in different modes, two of which stand out in particular. The more general mode is the one in which we state what the world looks like. These thought contents are expressed in propositions, i.e., statements. But we also manage to transform our beliefs about the world, our desires and ends, as well as our awareness of other persons – which are all part of

---

[39] This is a slightly altered phrase famous (and much debated) quote from PF Strawson (1964 [1950]) 38: 'Facts are what statements, when true, state; they are not what statements are about.' Strawson's view on the matter was known long before 1964 [1950], and sharply criticised by JL Austin in a paper 'Unfair to facts' [1954]) in JL Austin (1970) – a criticism which I, for one, find hard to understand.

what the world looks like – into a different frame of mind, expressing that we, ourselves, or another agent, are to make the world look different by doing something. In simpler words: some thought contents express what we or others 'are to do'. These thought contents are expressed in what we may call 'practitions', which is nothing but a generic name for second- or third-person prescriptions and first-person intentions.[40] In sum: Thinking is linking, but it can be done in different ways: either in a practical way (expressing specifically that an action is 'to be done' by some agent), or in a theoretical way (expressing generally that an entity has a property, for instance is performing an action). In the former case, the linking pin (or copula) we may call 'an act of willing', while in the latter case it is 'an act of judging'.[41]

As said, apart from content, the word 'proposition' denotes a specific structure of the act of thinking: namely, to claim of a certain something x that it has the property ϕ, or that x is ϕ. By speaking in *Def. 4.2* of an 'act' of judgment, I merely single out the tiny component in this structure which is neither the entity referred to, nor the property predicated, namely the copula between the entity and the property. In thinking, these two get linked: that is what thinking is all about. The whole structure of entity, copula and property is commonly called a proposition. Let us coin this term in *Def. 4.3*:

Def. 4.3 A proposition is the result R of an act of thought, such that R can take on the values 'true' or 'false'.

Parallel to this, we can use *Def. 1* to render the values of norm-claims or – in a similar philosophical jargon – practitions and capture this in *Def. 4.4*:

---

40 I use this neologism coined by H-N Castañeda (1975) 43ff for want of a better word. It is admittedly idiosyncratic. Practitions encompass prescriptions and intentions. Castañeda emphatically argues (ibid. 42) that intentions are not first-person prescriptions but a genuine subcategory of practitions.

41 Of course this 'judging' has little to do with legal judgment, as it is a purely formal, logical act.

Def. 4.4 A practition is the result R of an act of thought such that R can take on the values 'valid' or 'invalid'.

Taking *Definitions 4.1* and *4.3* on the one hand, and *4.2* and *4.4* on the other, we are simply saying that facts are propositional contents that have turned out to be true, while norms are practitional contents which have turned out to be valid.[42] Take for instance sentences [6a] and [6b]

[6a] John will close the door within one minute from now.

[6b] I'll close the door within one minute from now.

These propositions can be true or false, according to certain criteria. This may be clear in [6a], but it holds also for [6b] in case I am predicting my own behaviour. For instance, I know that soon I will be under hypnosis and carry out the order to close the door, which I will not be able to resist. If we find [6a] and [6b] true rather than false, they acquire the status of facts. Now compare them to [7a] and [7b]

[7a] John, close the door within one minute from now!

[7b] I am going to close the door within one minute from now.

These are examples of expressions that we deem valid or invalid, as the case may be, rather than true or false. How this test is construed we will see shortly. Prescription [7a] attributes to a second person an action that is to be done, while intention [7b] does the same in a first-person mode. Note, that [7b] is characteristically different from [6b]: [7b] is an intention rather than a prediction. In both cases [7a] and [7b] the link

---

42 I am aware of the fact that Kelsen explicitly argues against the parallel of truth of propositions and validity of norms. See, for instance, his H Kelsen (1979) 136–140. I think he is right, but his reasons do not attain my arguments, because the parallel I draw is slightly different: between validity of practitions or norm-claims and the truth of propositions, and by virtue of that between norms and facts. If I am not mistaken, Kelsen insufficiently distinguishes between a number of things: (i) norms and norm-claims; (ii) values of validity and validity in the sense of 'existence' of norms; (iii) the act of will (thought) positing the content of a norm-claim, and the speech act making this act of will operative.

between the to-be-agent and the act is not oriented towards what the world looks like (i.e., it is not propositional), but oriented to what is to be done in this world (i.e., it is practitional). We need both types of practitions (prescriptions and intentions) in an account of what norms are, as some norms are typically rooted in first-person practitions, e.g., wills, contracts, and corporate decisions.

We are now able to see the conceptual parallel between facts and norms. The phrase 'a true fact' is a pleonasm, and so is 'a valid norm'. By definition, there are no invalid norms, just as there are no false facts, though of course there are invalid norm-claims, just as there are false statements. But note that the acts of thought in *Def. 4.3* and in *Def. 4.4* remain radically and irreducibly different. So norms and facts differ irreducibly in the mode of thinking by which they are governed. To that extent, Kelsen was right. But the act of thought is not the only thing that is important. It only makes a claim regarding a certain content, and the claim has to be tested. Like verifying, warranting cannot but mean: testing the respective claims against a domain that is already more or less charted by a theory.[43] For practical purposes let us summarise this verifying and warranting under one label: 'justification'. Justification as a testing procedure does not mean necessarily that a new proposition or practition is logically *inferred* from the set already established. That is only one form of justifying. We may take a broader scope. Justification means, minimally, showing that the new proposition or practition is *arguably compatible* with the whole of an established set. Deliberately I say 'compatible' rather than 'coherent', thus defending a relatively weak claim so as to capture the pursuit of knowledge in practice. In science, for instance, a new proposition may sometimes be regarded as incoherent with the established set forming the dominant theory, because it opens up

---

43 This 'more or less' conceals a large part of contemporary philosophy of science. Stegmüller (following Sneed and others) has argued that a scientific theory is not just a hierarchically ordered set of propositions, but an ensemble of different elements (models, restraints, applications), brought together in a basic predicate. By that, verification and falsification are not just a matter of inference and entailment, but of coherence and compatibility. For a relatively simple introduction, see W Stegmueller 1979; 1980).

to a radically new view on the relevant field of knowledge that has to fight all kinds of immunising strategies (the so-called scientific revolutions).[44]

Here we come to the point where Kelsen will have to yield to a critique inspired by legal realism. From the philosophical correct thesis that facts and norms are different, Kelsen infers that they are to be tested against two different 'worlds' or domains, the domain of *Sein* (is) and the domain of *Sollen* (ought). I now want to argue that this is a mistake. The domains of justification of propositions and practitions are not distinguishable in the last analysis, and they are hard to distinguish in the last but one analysis. That they are not distinguishable in principle is due to the fact that these domains are part of one and the same reality. That they are hard to distinguish with great pertinence is due to the fact that their outer limits are blurred by language. The following subsections will detail this view.

3.2 One Domain of Justification[45]

I have explained that propositions [6a] and [6b] in themselves are not yet facts, but truth-claims or fact-claims. If they are verified, they acquire the preferred status of our beliefs about the world: facts. The same goes for [7a] and [7b]. They are not yet norms, strictly spoken, but validity-claims or norm-claims. If they are warranted, they acquire the preferred status of our action choices: norms. Whether we speak of justification in terms of 'true or false' (verification, falsification) or rather in terms of 'valid or invalid' (warranting, validation, legitimation), is of relative importance. It is characteristic, but not very essential. It is characteristic of the fact that in verifying a proposition we give priority to other elements in domains of justification than in warranting a practition: we organise 'the world' in

---

[44] There numerous textbooks relating the problems of Popperian falsification and immunising strategies as brought to the fore by Kuhn, Lakatos, Feyerabend, and others. See, e.g., A Rosenberg (2008).

[45] Here I alter (and deviate from) the idea of a 'domain of legitimacy' as proposed by H-N Castañeda (1975), ch. 5.

characteristically different ways. To illustrate this in a simple way, let us return to the examples of [6a] and [7a].

[6a] John will close the door within one minute from now.

[7a] John, close the door within one minute from now!

Let us assume that the speaker of [7a] has authority over John and the door in question, e.g., as John's teacher in the classroom. In most cases, reference to this authority suffices prima facie to conclude that the norm-claim of [7a] is valid. But probably we do not want to go as far as asserting that whatever the teacher orders is law. As we saw in the previous chapter, there are reasons why such authority was bestowed upon him in the first place, and these reasons keep on lurking in the background when the teacher acts authoritatively. This explains why others may say in some cases that he abuses his authority. To be more specific, the teacher will have got authority, because in our society it is believed that a teacher belongs to the circle of persons who are supposed to know what a school is about; people who can estimate the relationship between open doors and concentration problems with pupils, open doors and social control by colleagues and the school management, open doors and health problems, etc. So what we have got to distribute authority, to ascribe some of it to school teachers, and to eventually check their exercise of authority, is an amalgam of beliefs, ends, possibilities of action, all of it both for ourselves and a circle around us which we may call co-persons or co-agents. What can happen at a certain place at a certain time in the classroom (concentration problems); what can happen in the school as a whole (occasions of surveillance); what can happen in the world (catching a cold from draught) – these are all bits and pieces of more or less established beliefs and desires. They are elements in what I called a domain of justification, in this case more specifically a domain of warranting. There are, however, lots of other elements in such a domain. For example, apart from the fact that it should be clear which John and which door are in view, certain ideas about what constitutes 'closing doors (properly)' and about the ability of children to do so, are included.

Compare this to the case in which we start a procedure of verification concerning [6a]. Here, too, we tend to begin with authority, although many philosophers forget that.[46] For instance, [6a] may receive initial verification by saying upon challenge: 'I saw it in his eyes', or 'I have known him for quite some time now'. There is a rather strong flavour of '*being in a position* to tell' pervading the first stages of verification. But here also we need a larger domain of justification in case our first explanations are challenged. Which elements do we find in this domain? Referential devices to point to John and the door will belong to the very necessary, but perhaps also trivial, part. More sophisticated parts are (again) our ideas about what constitutes closing a door and about the abilities of (very) young children to close a door properly, both in the attempt and in the result. And these ideas are dependent, not only on adequate knowledge of locks and hinges, but also on what doors are for, that is what kind of desirable things they serve in our society. Moreover, if we are still talking about a door in a classroom, the same rule-like relationships between open doors and concentration problems etc. come in view as in the case of [7a]. It is against this domain of verification that we test the claim that John will close the door within one minute.

By stretching the trivial examples of [6a] and [7a], we can see that if we conceive of a domain of justification as an ordered set of sets of elements, these sets overlap to a considerable extent: we find not only the same agent and action involved, but also virtually the same sets of co-agents, beliefs, desires, ranges of action, etc. We may say that the domains of verifying (6a] and warranting [7a] virtually converge to one. Of course, in verifying propositions, we are interested in other sets or elements than in warranting practitions. That is because in the former we want to understand reality abstracted, as much as possible, from our desires and chosen courses of action, while in the latter we want to understand our choices of action as much as possible in function of our desires of how the world should be. But in the final analysis, either one of these procedures cannot be performed without taking the other into

46 Not so JL Austin, 'Other Minds' (1946) in JL Austin (1970) 100.

account. In giving an account of our choices of action, we better not hide from the world as it looks to us abstract from our desires, so as to not let our actions go astray. Inversely, in giving an account of the world as it is without our interventions, we should realise that such knowledge is in fact often dependent on such intervening actions, such as (notably) experimental settings.

It may be objected that choices of action are justified in relation to very subjective touching stones like wishes, whims, desires and interests; while judgments of fact, on the other hand, are justified with reference to states of affairs and events. Isn't that a major difference between the two domains of justification? I think that this is a mistake about what justification is about. If we would say that we are justifying our choices when we are only referring to some inclination felt deeply within ourselves, we would be mistaken. To justify my choices of action is something else. It is (among other things) to see if I could do or could have done (better) otherwise, given not only my inclinations but also my long-term goals and interests. It is realising that I cannot have my cake and eat it and that I need to set priorities. It is taking into account the interests of others, my long- and short-term concerns about them, etc. In short, it is an effort to answer the candid question: what do I *really* want? This intuitive reference to reality is most meaningful. Our desires, preferences, and values are not as whimsical as one might think: they can be regarded as a function of what we think we *really* are, although we may of course change our beliefs about what we really are.[47] The second chapter of this book was meant to show that we *must* think about these things in a specific way when it comes to social relations. That we purport to sustain a certain sense of identity over time in our action may well explain the ontological link between (more or less shared) preferences, i.e., values, on the one hand, and norms, on the other. As values, as

---

47 Though commercials want us to believe that we just 'invent' what we are ('fake it until you make it') or that we can change our human condition at will ('success is a choice'), we can never afford to step outside without the risk of self-destruction. We can of course imagine stepping outside; that is often what art is about. But to imagine is not to think, even if it is true that creative thinking requires imagination. This applies also to socio-political constellations.

so many variations of what we call for ourselves 'the good', are negotiable in principle, we need a non-negotiable framework within which these negotiations can take place. Those values, which we would prefer to not bring into negotiations and to reserve for the framework, are the ontological substrates of norms.[48]

The parallel structures and, in particular, the final convergence of the two domains of justification are things that Kelsen hardly contemplated in his theory. True enough, he denied the analogy between truth and validity, and rightly so. Validity of norms, to repeat, is tantamount to existence. But this precisely offers the possibility to draw the parallel between different modes of 'justification', which in the final analysis are all truth-related: existence as a correlate of thinking comes under different guises.[49] Kelsen however submits that norms not only have their own thought structure, but form a separate world, apart from the world of facts. Realists gather around the opposite end of the rope. From the ultimate convergence of the domains of justification, they infer that there is ultimately only one modality of thinking. To put it in an alternative mode: formalists are right if they argue that legal norms are not reducible to facts. The reason is that there is an irreducible difference in the copulas that govern their respective thought structures. Realists are right in that they hold that the domain for warranting norm-claims cannot be closed off as if it were *a priori* separate from the domain for verifying fact claims. But splitting up the world around us in *a priori* separate realms is dubious epistemology, as it bereaves us of the opportunity to have our claims contested. After all, there are no 'sectors' in reality unless we make them, and if we make them *a priori* in line with our claims to truth, we will never be contradicted. In the next section I will make clear that we do need to make these sectors, but only as provisional frames of our hypotheses. Once again, Kelsen is right in arguing that justification of norms is not possible without the presupposition of a

---

48 This entails that a specific norm may lose its status of 'trumping' value negotiations and re-assume its original status as a value, i.e., a more or less shared preference.

49 Cf. Aristotle (1975) Γ 2: 'Being is said in many ways.'

highest norm and a hypothesis about the contents of this highest norm. Legal realism only looks at this last aspect of the Basic Norm. In particular in its more modest, functional variants, it purports to make lawyers sensitive to the many 'factual' parameters at stake in formulating hypotheses about the contents of the highest norm. It is of vital importance to them to recognise specific constellations in terms of these parameters. This is why economics, sociology and psychology, to name but a few, have their roles to play in legal research and legal education. But the formal approach can safely maintain that the form in which norm-claims are mapped onto a domain of justification presupposes a highest norm.

3.3 Justification Domains as Vectors: Law and Language

In the previous paragraphs we neatly laid out the paths between norms and facts. We conceived of both facts and norms as products of acts of judgment and will, respectively. Characteristic of both acts of thought is their orientation towards something 'other than their own origin'. A big word for that 'something' which our thinking reaches out to is 'reality' or 'the ultimate domain of justification', to which both domains of verifying and domains of warranting converge. But as we saw in section 1.1 of this chapter, reality in its totality is never available for scientific or (broader) methodologically warranted investigation. In daily experience we may sense that we are immersed in 'reality as a whole'. However, no sooner do we embark on tracking this experience in methodologically warranted ways, or this all-inclusive reality splits up before our mind's eye, i.e. before our attempt to acquire warranted knowledge. One consequence of this we encountered already: science is possible only by virtue of limiting the angle from which we are to make statements about reality. But here is another consequence: what we judge or will can never be tested for its epistemic qualities against the whole of reality. It can be justified only over and against a segment of reality. Meanwhile this segment keeps its orientation towards reality. This is why we may call it a vector rather than a sector: it radiates in a certain direction. In methodologically warranted thinking we can only presume, in an implicit and abstract way, that all vectors we delineate have to be compatible with each other, since in the end reality is necessarily to be thought as one. That was the reason why we submitted that facts and norms differ at root in the acts that constitute their respective cores, but do not differ, ultimately, with regard to the domain they are tested against. But again: this one and total domain is never 'given' to us.

As a vector of reality, a domain of justification (verifying or warranting) is never simply 'there'. It exists only as a product of demarcation, i.e. of a specific form of labour[50] delivered by what is usually called 'the scientific community' – a club that is never completely cut off from other communities and their respective orderings. For example, only within the community demarcating 'the sun-earth-moon system' the statements of Newtonian mechanics are verifiable; only within the demarcation of 'the human body' (excluding astrological bodies or bodies politic) a medical or psychiatric theory is verifiable. Similarly, only within something like 'the legal order', 'the legal reality', 'the life of the law', 'legal culture' or (evasive in the extreme) 'the legally relevant', legal discipline can make statements on the validity of specific norms that can be tested.

Much depends on how we conceive of these demarcating activities. I call them a form of 'labour', not without purpose. Such a demarcation is not again in and by itself a form of *pure* thinking. Were demarcations of justification domains the pure products of acts of judgment or acts of will respectively, they would lead us into an infinite regress. The demarcation as a product of an act of thought would presuppose another demarcation, etc. Felicitously, this is not how demarcation works. It is a social phenomenon in the academic community; a form of labour and labour division. It may start out with explicitly justified statements and theories, against which new claims are tested: 'the theory'. This is what we usually do in 'normal science': we establish whether or not some statement S is coherent with the causal structures articulated in a body of corroborated knowledge already in place. But this is neither how the story goes on nor how it ends. At a certain point, the demarcation lines of

---

[50] Cf. JM Broekman (1982 [1978])191 ff.

a domain of justification start to lose their clear-cut status of theoretical statements. They get mixed with conventions, convictions, decisions, ambitions, quotations, expectations, as well as with technological constraints, financial burdens, etc. This is why, in science, 'paradigm shifts' in the Kuhnian sense are possible. It is also why there are so many 'schools', not only in relatively 'soft' sciences like economics, but also in 'hard' sciences like physics. Beyond a certain point, theories are tested against a segment of the world that is demarcated by a blurred exercise of authority, a set of constraints that exist in a deontic rather an alethic mode. Being rarely explicitly imposed or enacted, its normativity is not unlike that of customary law.

This brings us back to law as a scholarly discipline. Legal scholars also make demarcations of 'legal reality' to test their truth claims about certain statements on valid law. Consider, for instance, the way they relate these claims to specific areas of law, like company law, administrative law, criminal law, etc. In each of these areas the relationships between relevant entities like 'the individual', 'the organisation', 'the world of business', 'the government', as well as the qualities of these relations themselves (e.g., 'property' or 'harm') vary considerably. Although they are governed by explicit legal norms to some extent, their basic tenets gradually vanish into the vaguer realm of 'principles' and 'policies'.[51] More than in the sciences the demarcations of such a legal realm are determined by what we 'want' to be true, as the word 'policy' suggests. But like in the sciences, we also take on board elements of reality that we believe to be indifferent to what we want and that we are strongly inclined to take into account: needs (we have to eat some decent food), burdens (we have limited insight into (present, past, future) states of affairs), complexities (we differ in all sorts of respects).

In general, then, the demarcation of a justification domain for a theory is in the end not a part of that theory. The demarcation is the backdrop

---

[51] I use Dworkinian vocabulary here (RM Dworkin (1977) 22–28), without committing myself to the way Dworkin tried to distinguish between rules, principles and policies.

against which we engage in 'scientific' thinking. This quest for methodologically warranted certainty is always stretched between an analytic truth and an *a priori* doubt. The analytic truth is that we cannot think the limit of our thinking (reality itself) as something merely thought. Otherwise we only think our thinking, i.e. reality would just be another word for the internal accusative of our thinking. The *a priori* doubt regards our uncertainty about how much we impose on reality and how much reality on us. This, of course, is precisely what we want to find out by embarking on the scientific enterprise in the first place. But we will never be able to eradicate the predicament lock, stock and barrel. On the one hand, when we try to justify factual statements, there will remain some uncertainty to what extent we ourselves normatively impose the limits of the verification domain. On the other, when we try to justify normative statements,[52] there will remain some uncertainty to what extent reality imposes the limits of the legitimation domain on us.

This problem is well known in methodological discussions on law as a discipline. Norms grow more and more general until beyond a certain point they get contaminated with a factual genealogy of 'the highest norm' – a historical account that no one can monopolise. But note that this is just the mirror image of an equally known methodological problem in the sciences: beyond a certain point our view of reality gets contaminated with normative interventions by human agents, so that no one can make out whether the result of a certain experiment (resp. observation) is the echo of our action or the voice of reality. The most we can say is that such ultimate demarcations occur at the interface of thinking and reality, i.e. in language. As an interface, language is much more than a medium of communication ('conveying information between senders and receivers according to a certain code'), or a set of sentences rendering judgments or volitions. Language is first of all an ordering web of signs, some of which form sentences, others gestures, others music, still others conceptual schemes. We met with one such scheme in Chapter

---

[52] Again, these are statements holding truth claims on the validity of norm claims (or 'norms' for short).

1 and called it contractual naturalism. It is, in this case, a series of sentences all right, and it even displays a certain order of concepts; but it is incomprehensible as a piece of coherent thought, in spite of its omnipresence in daily legal parlance.

Prior to its being a medium of communication language 'situates' our thinking, i.e. it gives thinking a 'site', that is, a stance, from where it can start to be 'about' something. By following the pointers inherent in language (from one sign to another, from sign to what it denotes), we develop a sense of what thinking 'is about' in the double sense of that phrase: we learn that it is all about being *about* something. Even if we would take the view that language is primarily a web of signs referring to each other, thus marking differences like those between 'pa' and 'ma', 'here' and 'there', etc. one sign stands to the other as a pointer to something outside itself. It has a sense of direction that allows it to make sense, as brought to light by preferred values: true rather than false, valid rather than invalid. This is the drift we pick up as soon as we become immersed in a language. Communication enters later, as it were. Without reference to 'something out there' there is nothing to communicate in the first place. Thus our concepts, even our scientific concepts, are never pure labels that we can stick to 'reality itself'. They are signposts evoking and directing us to look, listen, feel, in pursuit of a promised reality, deeper and deeper into the web of language. The farther we come, the denser it gets, and the more language becomes the limit of our world, as Wittgenstein put it. But as is always the case with limits, this limit is ambiguous between what impedes on our freedom of movement and what motivates us to move to a world beyond the limit. The more language makes itself felt as an impediment to immediate contact with a world 'out there', the more it marks the presence of such a world. This is why, even if we are immersed in language, we are not drowning.

In sum: the segment of reality that, with regard to a certain judgment or decision, we call 'domain of justification' is initially produced by our thinking trying to target reality. It is the product of an intention to demarcate a field of established knowledge, i.e. a domain of state of affairs that are established to be the case. In building this domain we make use of the simple law that 'we know that *p*' entails 'it is the case that *p*'. Seen from the intentional act, this demarcation is *progressively underdetermined*: the more we want to give an account of these demarcations, the more they appear to be dependent on discursive elements of language which are not formed by intentional thinking. What we test our claims against appears to be more and more language rather than reality. Let me stress again that this is a sliding scale: initially we can count on the sharp boundaries of a body of established facts or norms that stand out as 'corroborated' from the infinite amount of meaningful statements and decisions we can make; in the end there is the twilight zone of language, where even sense and non-sense are difficult to distinguish and demarcations become fuzzy-edged. Somewhere in between these two extremes there is a stage where in the demarcation of a verifying domain norm-claims play a role, and vice versa, in the demarcation of a warranting domain factual claims are inevitable. The increasing density of language signals precisely what our thinking reaches out to: what is essentially not-thought, i.e. reality. But reality is never directly present to thought, only obliquely.

4. THE LEGAL JUSTIFICATION DOMAIN

In law as an academic discipline a domain of legitimation takes a rather specific shape, at least initially and for practical purposes. Rather than a set of individuals or agents, the domain will contain a set of 'legal subjects'; 'parties' in their specifically legal capacities and competences, 'citizens' with legally protected interests. We will not meet with a set of 'interests' pure and simple, but rather with a set of 'legal interests' or 'interests protected by law', 'subjective rights' or 'actions'. Similarly, there will be a set of rather typical ideas about causality, probability and foreseeability, and these may vary from one area of law to another. The characterisation of these and other parameters is an important part of the 'learned law' and of the textbooks that go by titles like 'General part of … ' (tort law, criminal law, law of contract, etc.); their refinement is a task for what on the European continent for centuries has been called 'dogmatics' (legal doctrine).[53] This strongly suggests that the normative content of law is justified in legal categories only. Validity tests would open up to a wider conceptual realm (e.g., of technological, economic, socio-psychological developments) only to scan what can be transformed into the categories of the legal system on the conditions of this very system. Law would be 'cognitively open but normatively closed' to its non-legal environments, as Luhmann put it.[54] The positivity of law would amount to self-legitimation. For reasons that exceed the limits of this chapter I hold a different view, maintaining the distinction between the positive character of law that comes with binding norm-claims, on the one hand, and validity of law as a cognitive issue, on the other. I will return to this distinction in the next section. Suffice it to say here that I see it as the task of legal scholarship (as the apex of knowledge about the law) to take legal validity into a wider realm of socio-political concerns, going against the grain, at times, of the inherently self-referential operation of positive law. To give just one simple example: the validity of norms on legal punishment is directly and seriously affected by neuro-biological evidence about triggers of human behaviour, free will, guilt, and, thus, criminal responsibility. There may be operative pressure from within the system, since that is the kind of pressure that an order exercises as soon as it grows to a system. But as I argued above, at bottom law is an order that institutionalises openness and closure of a political order in one fell swoop, precisely on the normative side of things. Kelsen's invaluable contribution to the discussion is the focus on knowledge of this normativity – and on its critical potential towards the authoritative claims by which law posits itself.

To construct virtual unity between these elements for the sake of testing a norm-claim is what legal scholars would see as their task. It amounts to testing the constitutional warrant of a norm. Clear-cut legal rules provide the initial layers in a hierarchy that soon enough integrates vaguer rules and principles. Kelsen's hypothesis of a hierarchy of

---

53 Cf. M Herberger (1981).

54 N Luhmann (1993) 38ff; cf. N Luhmann (1986).

empowering rules (governing competence to issue certain norms) is an interesting way of modelling this domain. It may be tested against a rich variety of data from modern legal orders. Until this research is done, we may or may not believe Kelsen in this regard. But it seems safe to assume that if the competence model would survive by providing the most adequate and elegant explanation for what happens in our legal orders, we will probably have sufficient reason to believe that the parameters of 'competence' should be taken in their full complexity. No agent is legally empowered without constraints on the use of this power, without specifications for which purposes it ought to be used, when its limits would be exceeded, by which procedures it is to be exercised, how it is to be accounted for and by what criteria, etc. In other words, although the competence model seems to exclude all sorts of substantive issues, it also offers numerous ways to include them under a different heading.

In a wider theoretical context the demarcation of a legitimation domain carries with it a predicament that follows directly from the problems touched upon in the previous sub-section. The more this domain is demarcated in very concrete terms as a specifically legal domain, the more testing norm-claims becomes unequivocal. The reverse side of that coin is that, in this way, one is creating a domain that does not prove anything, as it is just the mirror image (the 'internal accusative') of one's preferred look at reality. Suppose we would have a legal order *L* in which there is only one criterion for valid law: does ms *B* want a norm *n* to be part of *L* or not? Then ms *B* is the one and only who is able to make out whether some statement about the validity of *n* is true or not. But this would of course destroy the whole idea of law being the object of study in an academic enterprise, as statements would be true or false according to ms *B*'s will and nothing else. In a less dramatic vein; to the extent that the justification of norm-claims in law would be reduced exclusively to the decision of the agent who enacts them (a person, a body, an organ), this justification would alienate itself completely from the social relationships in which such enactment takes place. It would alienate itself, in particular because law as an academic discipline would then be nothing more than a quotation of the utterances made by this agent. No longer would the academic study of law contribute to the authority of law, as it would add nothing to the basic requirement laid down in Chapters 2 and 3 of this book, that in order to acquire authority and transform itself into a legal order, a political regime has to make something count against itself, and this on its own accord. It has to organise its own counter voice[55] and relativise the identity of the polity in the same stroke as it appeals to it. If law as a discipline is doomed to only reiterate claims to validity that come with norm enactments, it becomes 'dogmatic' in the vicious sense of the word: a self-contained form of orthodoxy notwithstanding its malleability under pressure.

I am aware of the fact that these phrases sound like a warning for occasional danger that draws legal 'science' into the self-legitimation of the legal order it investigates. In fact this is a permanent undercurrent. Despite the oxymoron our legal order is permanently inclined to self-legitimation, simply because it is a political artefact, as I stressed repeatedly. Time and again it commits itself to the justification domain writ large that we call 'society', while it is itself a major factor in construing this domain. It appeals to nothing less than 'justice' in drawing on the conceptual framework it operates, and legal scholarship is expected to cooperate without any critical distance. I can only mention a few examples here, without elaborating on them. The first is the distinction between male and female.[56] In the vast majority of cases, law considers this to be given by nature. It reflects a set of pre-legal facts to which the legal order can relate in a neutral mode by attributing legal consequences to them. Even where gender equality is at issue, the law maintains the presupposition of a brute facticity of which the dichotomy between the sexes is part. What is removed from this picture is that the distinction between male and female is itself enforced, indeed produced, by law. One who would prefer not to make the distinction; or one who would hold doubts about the criteria by which it is made; or one would

---

[55] I remember reading this wording in a newspaper article by sociologist of law Cees Schuyt, but I cannot find the source.

[56] Cf. I owe the example to JM Broekman (1982 [1978]) 80–95.

plead gender bi-polarity of human beings; they all would have to be prepared, e.g., to waive legal protection for her or his newborn child. If you want your baby to be registered you will have to choose; and the law also enforces you to make your choice on the basis of criteria which the law deems to be even more brute facts than the distinction itself: exterior characteristics as perceived at birth by bystanders are sanctioned by law as sufficient evidence to attribute gender identity to a human person. In spite of the fact that gender identity as it functions in society is largely dependent on a person's self-ascription in a process that may easily take decades; in spite also of the fact that there is a whole range of variables that are causally contributing to someone's gender awareness and that, according to science, may work in opposite directions; in spite of all that, the law requires us to accept a binary choice and to rely on the Cartesian dualism of body and mind, the outside and the inside, of the human person. Even in cases where it sanctions a mutation from one sex to the other and registers transsexual persons as 'changed' into the 'opposite' gender, it maintains the dichotomy on the basis of more or less the same characteristics. It is therefore not an overstatement that the law prefers certain things to be true and, indeed, makes them true by asserting them in ways people cannot afford to ignore.

Another example is the distinction between political and economic refugees, made in the context of immigration and asylum applications. It is applied by a state to single out people that are eligible for legal protection and to refuse access to others. Checking the credibility of autobiographical narratives by refugees is often the only way to make this selection. Again, the presupposition is that these stories are about a world of brute facts that may or may not have happened. Empirical research has shown, however, that the credibility judgment on these stories is strongly dependent on whether they reinforce or debase the picture we have of ourselves as a society.[57] The illiterate woman from 'some' African country coming to the border is far less likely to get her

---

[57] Cf. N Oudejans (2011) 65ff and references to empirical research there, including a.o. T Spijkerboer (1998; 1999); TP Spijkerboer (2001) and J Blommaert (2009).

residence permit than the academic from Iraq. By default, the former will qualify as an economic refugee, the latter as a political refugee, although their stories may be similar. Note that, here again, the distinction itself has to be interiorised in order to qualify for legal protection, and that it is made on the basis of criteria that no political scientist will be prepared to defend.

Here again we encounter the fundamental question that already governed the previous chapters, now in its pertinence to law as an academic discipline: can we give a philosophical account of how law, in the methodological pathways it explores, embodies a political order that makes itself vulnerable in the very same act of affirming itself? Are we able to discover if, and in what ways, methods of legal decision-making take the price of law into account? Do they bear witness to the disorder that the law systematically creates in creating order? Or, to put it in another way, are we able to transform the epistemological distance between law as a set of norms and law as an academic discipline into a method of law-making that can be regarded as a self-critique of the polity in which it is exercised?

5. VALIDITY AND BINDINGNESS

One question remains: if validity is assessed in an epistemic pursuit about law exemplified (though certainly not monopolised) by legal scholars, how does this relate to law being binding, i.e., law being posited by authority in the broad sense of being enacted, applied and enforced on the basis of norms? If it is for legal scholars to decide whether a norm *N* is valid in *L*, what is it that the legal officials do when they impose binding norms?[58]

---

[58] The following argument is made in greater detail in the paper 'Norm-claims, Validity, and Self-reference' I contributed to the Kelsen volume edited by John Gardner, Leslie Green and Luis Duarte d'Almeida (Oxford, Hart Publishing, 2013 – forthcoming).

5.1 Bindingness as Pre-empted Validity

Both formalism and realism hold that validity and bindingness are one and the same. The former will stress their normative character, the latter their factual character. We do not need to revisit this discussion once more. Instead, I would like to make a distinction that maintains the narrow bond between validity and bindingness, and (thus) between knowledge about law and authority over law. My suggestion is that one can remain faithful to the fundamental tenets of the Pure Theory by introducing a distinction between (a) validity – to be understood as the ontological mode in which norms can be said to exist; and (b) bindingness – to be understood as the result of an authoritative pre-emption of validity. The latter is a status that authoritative decisions (with their corresponding norm-claims) may come to acquire pending the epistemological acknowledgment that they do amount to the production of valid norms. The former is a status assigned by those who – engaging epistemologically with the law with an eye to answer the question 'What should one do, as far as law is concerned, under the present conditions?' – interpret certain decisions (with their corresponding norm-claims) as producing valid norms. My argument runs as follows.

1. Let us grant Kelsen his theses (discussed above in section 1) on the preconditions of legal cognition, i.e. the preconditions of one's knowledge that some norm *N* is valid in some legal system *L*. Let us also accept his view that validity is the specific ontological mode in which norms can be said to exist.
2. If legal cognition with regard to *L* is possible, then one should be able to make truthapt statements with the form '*N* is valid in *L*' without authorised agents in *L* being able to disprove such statements at will. In other words, authorised and non-authorised agents must enjoy equal epistemic access to law.
3. The fulfilment of this epistemic requirement is supervenient on a sustained political programme of establishing and maintaining authority. The possibility of legal cognition with regard to *L* depends on political conditions and decisions. *L* has to be, by and

large, efficacious and stable; indeed, L is the result of an interpretation of an efficacious order *as* a system of valid norms: effectiveness, as Kelsen puts it, is a condition (though not a criterion) of validity.[59] But even though the possibility of legal cognition thus depends on such conditions obtaining; and even though such conditions will typically include the making of decisions by political authorities; once such conditions are in place political authorities will be unable to interfere with legal cognition without losing authority both under and (eventually) over the law.[60]

4. Disputes may arise in any particular case about the correct outcome of epistemic engagements with law: the truth of any given statement with the form 'norm N is valid in some legal system L' may form the object of disagreement. Such disputes may fuel the very kind of socio-political conflicts that law is to resolve in the first place. There is therefore room in L, as well as need, for authoritative institutions capable of pre-emptively assigning truth-values to such statements while making decisions (and putting forth norm-claims) aimed at ending or precluding conflict. Such truth-value assignments, however, do not settle the validity issue; they do not *make* the corresponding statements true (or false), though they may contribute evidence either way.
5. Such decisions are binding in the double sense that (*a*) they are to be conformed to until modified by higher authoritative institutions

---

59 See H Kelsen (1960) 211f.

60 It is beyond the limits of this paper to argue for the view that the acquisition of legal authority is precluded if political agents never allow their norm-claims to count against themselves. As Kelsen remarks in the Preface to his H Kelsen (1945) XVI, 'the political authority creating the law and, therefore, wishing to conserve it, may doubt whether a purely scientific cognition of its products, free from any political ideology, is desirable. Similarly, the forces tending to destroy the present order and to replace it by another one believed to be better will not have much use for such a cognition of law, either.' However, as soon as they intend to create a *legal* order, then by implication – or by Gricean implicature – political authorities must intend to comply with a basic norm. For '(t)he basic norm of a positive legal order is nothing but the fundamental rule according to which the various norms of the order are to be created' (ibid. 114).

of the same kind; and that (*b*) failure to conform is appropriately met with authoritatively determined sanctions.

6. Validity itself – that which is tracked by epistemic engagements with law – may well remain a moving horizon, i.e. provisionally established and essentially contested. While those epistemically engaged with *L* are interested in reconstructing the overall constitutional coherence of *L* (with regard to a specific case, type of case, etc.) over and over again, those authoritatively involved in *L* seek to put an end to conflict (specific conflict, type of conflict, etc.).

Though my proposal amounts to a deviation from the Pure Theory, it remains faithful to Kelsen's view that validity and bindingness are essentially connected or, indeed, conflate.[61] Bindingness is preempted validity; validity, re-confirmed bindingness. But each notion is associated to a different aspect of law. Bindingness relates to law *qua* authoritative practice geared towards ending or precluding social conflict. Validity relates to law *qua* object of cognition. The latter aspect I regard as the quintessential or primary one; in order authoritatively to make law, one must make it cognisable *qua* system of *norms* from which normative positions – rights, duties, powers, liabilities – can be gathered.

5.2 Bindingness Without Validity, and Vice Versa

There are further explanatory advantages to distinguishing legal validity from legal bindingness along the lines just sketched.[62] It makes room for the twin hypotheses (a) that we may be bound by invalid norms, and (b) that there may be valid norms to which we are not bound, at least not in the fullest sense. And both hypotheses can help us account for some familiar scenarios.

---

[61] To say that 'a norm referring to the behavior of a human being is "valid",' according to Kelsen, is to say 'that it is binding – that an individual ought to behave in the manner determined by the norm': cf. H Kelsen (1960) 193.

[62] Of course, nothing depends on the actual *terms* employed – we may reserve 'validity' for bindingness, and invent some alternative to refer to validity.

Consider, first, the possibility of bindingness without validity. There are indeed several familiar situations which can be plausibly described by saying that we *can* be bound – if only provisionally – by virtue of norm-claims which, though put forth by agents who are institutionally entrusted with legal authority to enact such claims, may turn out *not* to be valid under any plausible test that legal science may carry out. Our system of appeals provides one familiar set of examples. Take Mr and Mrs Van Aalten, who sought to obtain a formal judicial declaration that the defendant, a hospital, was liable in tort for the death of their three-year-old son Jeffrey.[63] They sought no remedies; they did not want to be awarded damages. They just felt that such a declaration would help them to cope with their loss. The county court granted the claim, but in appeal the district court reversed the decision: it saw no reason why law should deal with what it called 'purely emotional damage'. Both decisions were binding from the moment the respective judiciary authorities made them, and for as long as they stood. The Van Aaltens then turned to the High Court, which upheld the district court's decision, thus confirming the denial of the Van Aaltens' claim. This decision became final, and thus binding 'for good'. But was it justified under valid law? Legal scholars debated the case, and most agreed that the High Court had rendered a 'bad' decision. They offered reasons in support of the conclusion that the decision was at odds with valid law.[64] In this case, because consensus was notably strong, sustained, and convincing, the High Court would come gradually to fine-tune, even abandon, its line of

---

[63] I discussed the case in a different context in B Van Roermund (2002a) and in B Van Roermund (2007).

[64] Vranken, for example, criticises the decision as follows: 'The Highest court decided coldly that civil law was not meant to protect such an emotional interest. One could call this a denial of the almost existential need in our culture to know who is responsible for something. But even if that were not the case, it can be said that there is something fundamentally wrong when the mother of Jeffrey is left empty-handed, but on the other hand a claim that crowing cocks cause psychological damage is allowed. The latter claim was even allowed to clog up the legal system on five different occasions.' (JBM Vranken (2006) 61.)

reasoning (though the decision in the Jeffrey case remained binding).[65] Another set of examples in which the distinction between legal bindingness and legal validity comes to the fore concerns legal decisions taken under political duress. Legal scholars in The Netherlands will usually not refer to decisions made by the High Court during the period of German occupation (1940–45), though they will not dispute the Court's jurisdiction at the time. They will regard such decisions, binding as they may have been, as invalid law – or at any rate as irrelevant for the reconstruction of valid law. (Note, in contrast, that legal scholars will be inclined to welcome judicial decisions that explicitly adopt the 'cognitive' approach, e.g. by discussing the relevant scholarly literature, or by engaging in comparative exercises with other jurisdictions. Note, also, that an important factor in getting appointed to the higher courts is one's cognitive performance with regard to the legal system under which one will be working.)

As for the possibility of valid norms that are not (fully) binding, think of situations in which authorities are unable, or feel reluctant, to impose sanctions for breach of valid norms (which norms are thus binding only in the sense that one undeniably ought to comply with them). This could come about if (a) there is (yet) no authority empowered to impose sanctions, (b) it is unclear what the empowered authorities actually are; or (c) if the authorities in place are relatively powerless in the situation at hand. The point could be illustrated by many a resolution of the UN Security Council (not to speak of decisions made by the International Court of Justice in The Hague). One could also say that in the development of EU law it has been precisely this cleft between validity and bindingness that has allowed the European Court of Justice to seize initiative in a number of landmark cases, claiming to exercise its competence in the very process of overstepping it.[66] But ultimately these cases are more interesting for the direction they point to, than for the list of exceptions they may happen to suggest. Not only may supra-national

65 For a recent assessment cf. GE van Maanen (2010) after GE van Maanen (1999).

66 Cf HK Lindahl (2003b) 769; L Corrias (2011).

polities have tighter or looser constitutional frameworks (the European Union being an instance of the former, the World Trade Organisation an instance of the latter),[67] the very parameters of constitutionalism are changing.[68]

A wider theory of law would be required to explain fully why these two aspects of law – law *qua* authoritative management of social conflict, law *qua* object of cognition – are complementary rather than antinomical. I would venture that it is precisely for the sake of *enhancing* authority that lawmaking authorities conduct themselves in such a way that the product of their actions and decisions constitutes a suitable object of cognition, i.e. can be interpreted as creating *norms*. Remember that I submitted that there are at least two arguments here. First, an argument from effectiveness: it is much easier to remain in power if one's authoritative decisions can be known, interiorised, and predicted, so that actual enforcement will be needed only in exceptional cases. Second, an argument from openness. Authority is not won by raising one's voice in an authoritarian manner; but it can be won and secured by allowing potential counter-voices to be heard, and by allowing other agents to prove one wrong. In mature legal systems, legal authorities can afford to entrust pursuers of legal cognition – scholars, experts, lawyers, laymen even – with such a task. As far as possible, authorities should await the results of such debates. In the rebound, legal scholars should acknowledge (as they usually do) that their epistemic exercise is premised on a political decision to expose legal validity to open dispute. But of course as disputes may continue, conflicts in society have to be settled, ended, precluded. Thus: if (*i*) law is geared to ending of precluding social conflict by having in place a sustainable system of norms; if (*ii*) legal validity is not merely one of the guiding values, but indeed the *primary* guiding value of authoritative legal norm-claims; and if (*iii*) legal validity

---

[67] G De Burca and J Scott (2001) 2.

[68] As Neil Walker writes, 'constitutionalism in a plural order is *necessarily* conceived of not only as an internal property of polities but as a medium through which they interconnect – as a characteristic of the relationship between sites of authority as well as an internal characteristic of these authoritative sites. Cf. N Walker (2001) 32–33.

may be permanently contested in epistemic debate; then it makes sense (*a*) to have institutions in place which are able provisionally to attribute that value – validity – in an authoritative way, and (*b*) to provide for a limited set of accountability and revision procedures. The decisions of such institutions do amount to a norm-setting interpretation of the law, in the sense that legal subjects will (within certain limits) be *bound* by them. But such decisions will bind neither higher authorities, nor the activities of legal scholars, who concern themselves with the study of norms *qua* norms, and thus with the *validity* of norm-claims (i.e. with the 'existence' of norms).

6. SUMMARY

From the contrast between a formalist and realist approach to 'knowledge' with regard to law we were able to vindicate a reliable distinction between the notions of 'fact' and 'norm'. They differ irreducibly in the act of thinking by which they are posited, so that we can fully acknowledge that one cannot infer facts from norms or norms from facts. But the respective claims they make to validity or existence are tested against what is ultimately one justification domain. Admittedly, in verification of facts other parameters draw centre stage than in legitimation of norms. But that is not to say that there are two separate domains or 'worlds', the world of facts and the world of norms. Whether we like it or not, the demarcation of the world of norms will be more and more determined by states of affairs we believe to be true; inversely, the demarcation of the world of facts will be more and more determined by states of affairs we intend to make true. The problem is that neither of them is transparent in the final analysis as they become immersed in the web of language where meaning is always contested. On the one hand science as the pursuit of methodologically warranted knowledge attempts to select truth from meaningfulness, on the other hand, daily experience has a hard time distinguishing sense from non-sense without a body of established true belief to go by. The academic discipline of law will attempt to tell true from false statements on the validity of norm-claims, mindful of its task to enhance the authority of law by critically construing a domain of legitimation. Meanwhile, officials have the task of establishing the bindingness of norm claims, anticipating epistemic assessment of their validity. Bindingness is pre-empted validity, validity is reconfirmed bindingness. In this way, one is able to explain why, in legal order, there are authoritative norm-claims that are binding but not valid, while there are others that are valid but not binding.

5. Following the law as following a rule

This final chapter brings together the two basic modes in which law appears in society: as an institution of authority, and as an object of knowledge. Its topic is paradigmatically linked to what judges do: set the law on the basis of their knowledge of the law. To reach a decision in a certain case, they take guidance from law as a set of rules. Of course these rules do not allow them to infer decisions by applying logic; nor are they simple algorithms that generate decisions by comparing cases to a standard. The process that takes place with regard to legal rules is commonly called 'interpretation'. Received views on legal interpretation often point to 'linguistic meaning', 'legislative intention', 'socio-political function', 'doctrinal coherence', and their ilk, to detail the parameters that the judiciary is supposed to estimate and 'weigh' with regard to a specific case.[1] These theories are neither wrong, nor should their practical value be ignored. But I think there is scope for a deeper account of how judges – or, for that matter, citizens, governors and legislators – deal with legal rules.

Section 1 distinguishes between various modes of interpreting legal rules, singling out two in particular: an operative and reflective mode. I argue that the former takes priority over the latter, in law as in many other contexts. In section 2, I offer two arguments to the effect that it is a riddle how we are able to follow a legal rule in the operative mode. The first one develops from law. It submits that legal rules, in the final analysis, are tautological. When push comes to shove they do not tell us what we should do, but that we should do what we should do. The

[1] DN MacCormick and RS Summers (1991).

second one develops from philosophy (Wittgenstein's later works), confronting us with the paradox that incompatible courses of action may be derived from any rule. My solution departs from a theory of rules as icons (section 3).[2] In interpretation we project ourselves into the rule in ways that are similar to how we grasp the sense of paintings, music, stories, or poems, by following certain depth clues to which we are more or less sensitive and that allow us to imagine a space in which we may move and take position. Finally (section 4) I will defend why my view solves the puzzles of the second section, by arguing (a) that it is a better account of what Wittgenstein wrote than two competitive theories (intuitionism and conventionalism), and (b) that it provides a more satisfying account of how 'students of the law' deal with legal rules in actual practice.

1. MODES OF INTERPRETATION

'Interpreting' is a rather solemn, if not artificial, word for what is ordinarily called understanding, reading, applying, supplementing, complying, explaining, translating, etc. Its basic scheme is 'to take something as meaning something else', e.g., a heap of stones as a pointer to the refuge where I want to stay the night. Not all realms of socio-cultural life hinge on interpretation in equal ways. One of the incisive questions posed by Raz is this: why does interpretation matter so much more to legal than to moral practice?[3] The core of his answer is that law is ultimately contingent on authoritative sources (whereas morality is not). We interpret these sources rather than the law, thus making them appear in a new light in spite of changing circumstances, so that these sources

---

[2] I use 'icon' rather than 'picture', partly to avoid confusion with what is known among philosophers as 'the picture theory of meaning'. As I will claim to be a Wittgenstein student in my account of rule following, it would be odd to develop something under the flag of a picture theory, as this is the flag of his opponents.

[3] J Raz (2009) 223.

can continue to exercise authority. In the light of Raz's service conception of authority, this means, in turn, that they keep their potential as anchor points of preemptive reasons for action. Thus, by performing an action ϕ in compliance with authority source A we stand a better chance to act in accordance with the reasons applying to us than if we would act on the balance of first order reasons pro or con ϕ in the situation at hand. As a 'summary preliminary statement of the key to interpretation' generally, Raz holds that '(…) an interpretation successfully illuminates the meaning of its object to the degree that it responds to whatever reasons there are for paying attention to its object as a thing of its kind.'[4] In the case of law, authority and continuity are the primary reasons, which may attract secondary reasons such as the development of law and equity in law.[5]

Many authors (including Raz) have compared the practice of law with other practices where interpretation is key, for instance in various performing arts or literary criticism. Pertinent as it may be, this comparison could profit from a further distinction, to wit the distinction between interpretation in an operative mode and in a reflective mode. Here are some examples. Actors may discuss alternative interpretations of a role in a certain play *by talking* about it. But in the end they will invariably exchange ways of following the script by playing a certain scene. The 'reasons' they give for playing it one way rather than another basically remain within the ambit of playing. Attending a master class in a school of music will give you the same idea: musicians interpret music by making music. Similarly, when I translate an English poem into Dutch, I have to remain within the realm of poetry, seeing to it that the result is a poem in Dutch faithful to the original, rather than an essay about the poem. In writing an essay rather than a poem, I could still remain faithful to the original, but in a different way. I would 'teach' in (reflective) language what the poem is about, what of its historical context is relevant for understanding what it is about, why (or by what standards) it is

---

[4] J Raz (2009) 231.
[5] J Raz (2009) 238f.

beautiful, etc. I would engage in a contemplating rather than an acting mode of interpretation. Such contemplation is doubtlessly relevant for a translator; inversely, an essayist could only do a good job if she understands the possibility of various interpretations in that other, operative, vernacular. But the two remain distinct, and this distinction holds good across the board of the phenomena of interpretation like reading, applying, complying, etc. For the sake of brevity, let me use the letters O and R for these two modes.

R-interpretation is about signs while O-interpretation is about shapers. A farmer may interpret cloud formations as signs that a weather change will occur within the next hours; a scientist may interpret data as loosely linked parts of a pattern that she would like to see explained; a religious body may interpret the recovery from illness as a wonder wrought by some candidate-saint. In all of these latter cases the 'things' interpreted are to be established with some accuracy, but they do not count as a normative source that should be preserved faithfully or followed scrupulously. What the clouds are to a meteorologist is not what, for instance, a recipe is to a cook. For the farmer, the clouds are a source of knowledge about the weather,[6] whereas, for the cook, the recipe is a source of duties. Note, however, that by a change of scene, the clouds may turn from pointers to shapers. Suppose we have an experienced farmer rather than a meteorologist. Then clouds may easily become guiding to his behaviour (e.g., to turn the sprinklers off). Similarly, if we picture the scientist and his data as a general practitioner and a set of symptoms, we immediately see that he will go after the symptoms like the cook after his recipe and the farmer after his clouds, but for the fact that symptoms are shapers under a negative operator. But diagnosing a patient by interpreting symptoms is an operative, rehearsing, mode of interpretation, as the

[6] Dreams are perhaps a special case because they are confined within individual experience. With dreams the very distinction between operative and reflective mode recurs: we operate on a dream by telling a story at breakfast (faithful to the experience at night), then go on to interpret the narrative rather than the experience by reflective discourse.

classical medical term 'anamnesis' suggests.[7] Thus, correlative to the two modes of interpretation there seem to be two sorts of 'sources', in law as elsewhere: normative sources and epistemic sources. We take guidance from the former, we take lessons from the latter. The former we follow, the latter we notice.

Both performing and creating artists hate to talk about 'the meaning' of their work in a reflective mode. Their point is actually threefold. Firstly, 'interpretation' as a term becomes redundant when and where O-mode is at stake. We play a score, read a book, translate a poem, cook a recipe, and that's it. At times, reflective discourse may come in to elucidate or contest a certain performance, reading, etc. But it does not take over: on the contrary, it remains ancillary to the O-mode, and it should feed back into this mode as quickly as possible. Nor is reflection a 'higher level' of interpretation, for instance in that it represents a more adequate awareness or appreciation of qualities, e.g. the qualities of a work of art. Secondly, whether something is a work of art or not is decided, in the final analysis, by appreciation in the O-mode rather than the R-mode. The question 'what does it mean?' opens R-mode, as if the meaning of the work is also available separate from the work, i.e., in some sort of talking rather than hearing, seeing, tasting, etc. Thirdly, this leads over to the observation that interpretation in O-mode is one that is genuinely practical. It is practical not only in the sense that it is the most common, useful, or even direct mode of interpretation, but also in the philosophical sense of pursuing an answer to the time-honoured format of questions governing action: What should I do? Only in this mode we take guidance from 'the object' under interpretation. In contradistinction to, e.g., a set of data that we may want to interpret, a score, a text, or a recipe is attributed authority over our actions, prescribing what should be done and deciding whether what is done, is right. In brief, in O-mode we follow a directive pattern.

Thus, if we observe that interpretation plays such a key role in law, there is a further question to be answered: in O-mode, R-mode, or both?

---

7 I owe Anne Ruth Mackor for this comment on an earlier draft of this text.

If the analogy with the performing arts holds, we should consider what it means that O-mode interpretation takes priority? In that mode, 'interpretation' amounts to *following* or *taking guidance* from legal rules.[8] Note that 'to follow' here is a generic term, a stand-in for various activities, which have labels of their own. We follow a rule by applying, executing, enforcing or enacting it. Note also that in making a rule we imagine how it should be followed; otherwise it makes no sense to make it. Note, finally, that there is rule-following in violating rules. Of course we often do not comply with a rule, either inadvertently or wilfully, from carelessness, weakness of the will, or intentional refusal. But even in these cases, or at least in the majority of these cases, we will be able to recognise what it would require (or would have required) to follow the rule. Thus, there is a thin sense of following a rule that is not equivalent to compliance, quite similar to the way in which you may follow my line of argument without agreeing with me. Importantly, however, even in this thin sense, the normative or authoritative character of the rule is perspicuous to the agent, and so it involves O-mode interpretation.

In legal theory, however, interpretation in R-mode dominates the scene as it is claimed to be the judiciary's primary task. I will not deny that it typically *is* the judge's task indeed. But I doubt whether it is a primary one. I submit that her main task is 'operative' rather than 'reflective'. By applying the rule she follows the rule in an authoritative way. As the law does not beg for consent, i.e., as it demands compliance willy-nilly, the judge is there, first and foremost, to *decide* what it takes to follow the rule. If the rule is already normative, she is the authority reconfirming the normativity of the rule. Sometimes she cannot avoid interpreting the rule in R-mode. But usually she can refrain from that, and typically she will be reluctant to engage in it. Hers is not the task to fuel a discussion but to end it. As law is there to end or preclude conflict in society by authoritative decision-making, it should not come as a surprise that it tries to undercut R-mode interpretation. Learned reflective discourse

---

[8] I will assume that rules, rather than commands, commitments, conditions or constraints, are the privileged form of legal norms in Modernity – a claim which may be debated.

would only bring more fuel to the fire of the conflict, as many a doctrinal discussion shows. It may be true that 'reasons never run out'[9] in R-mode interpretation, but the problem is that they may not run out on both sides of a conflict. This is why the judge is attributed authority with regard to O-mode as well as R-mode interpretations of the rules. This does not entail that she is empowered to replace the rule by whatever decision she thinks fit in the case at hand. Her primary discretion is to apply the rule within what is commonly called 'a margin of appreciation', and with reflective ramifications being ancillary to this. There is a whole judiciary hierarchy in place to monitor her reflective strategies. The most important parameter in exercising such discretion is not what the rule 'means' (in reflective terms), but how it could be developed into a rule that can be followed (again) in the case at hand. Thus, in exercising R-interpretation the judge will take her main cue from O-interpretation.

2. FOLLOWING RULES: TWO PUZZLES

What is it that we do when we comply with a rule, apply a rule, enforce a rule, or indeed make a rule? We do not take this to be a simple thing, in spite of the fact that (for reasons to be explained later) there is a 'mechanical' ring to it. If there is anything mechanical here, it is not *simple* mechanics. Since playing a score, translating a poem, or cooking a recipe require intelligent, indeed creative skills, why not expect that rule-following in law does, too? How then is it possible that we do what we doubtlessly think we do: following rules, often the rules of law? Let me explain along two lines why all this seems puzzling in spite of our daily practices, taking law as the main topic for discussion. The first aims to show that, in the final analysis, legal rules remain silent on the very issue to which they are supposed to respond. The second line revisits an intriguing part of Wittgenstein's philosophy, presenting us with the paradox that if everything, even contradictory courses of action, is in accordance with a rule, nothing is in accordance with that rule.

---

[9] Cf. R Dworkin (1977).

2.1 Tautology

At the start of a flight from Paris to Bogotá I was prohibited to smoke 'for my own safety'. Suppose that I had intended to light an electronic cigarette. An e-cigarette, or e-cig, is: 'a battery-powered device that provides inhaled doses of nicotine or non-nicotine vaporized solution. It is an alternative to smoked tobacco products, such as a cigarette. In addition to nicotine delivery, the vapour also provides a flavour and physical sensation similar to that of inhaled tobacco smoke, although there is no tobacco, combustion or smoke present.'[10] My e-cig does not even resemble an ordinary cigarette; it is built into a pen – an optical character-reading device that allows me to quickly scan citations into my text-editor. Now would I, or would I not, follow the no-smoking rule on the plane by lighting this e-cigarette? Would an official enforcing this rule act correctly by stopping me from using the device by virtue of the prohibition? Would a legislator be right in extending the enacted non-smoking policy rules, or tax policy rules, to my (type of) e-cigs, arguing that 'my own safety' also comprises health risks I may be insufficiently aware of? Suppose the Dutch legislator is considering such a rule.[11] He could seek refuge in Directive 2001/95/EC/6 on general product safety. This Directive prompts Member States to take restrictive or preventive measures if a product is found to be dangerous to the health of consumers. This rule is highly typical not only for EU or domestic law, but also for law in general. In an important way, it reverses the charges. For we turn to law in order to learn what one should refrain from for the sake of consumers' health, so that we do not get into conflict with each other about what is dangerous and what is not. But then the law says, in the end, that we should refrain from whatever is dangerous for consumers' health. Thus, in asking our question to the law what we should

---

10 Cf. http://en.wikipedia.org/wiki/Electronic_cigarette , accessed March 3, 2011.

11 In September 2012, the US Department of Transportation proposed a ban aboard airplanes because of concerns about health risks from the vapours. Cf. http://usatoday30.usatoday.com/news/health/story/2012-08-18/electronic-cigarettes-smokeless-vaping-risks/57121894/1

(not) do, we are left with the answer that we should (not) do what we should (not) do. We are left with a perfect tautology, and therefore with no information on what to do.

I said that this is a general feature of rule-based law. And indeed, look at tort law, where negligence is the crucial parameter. Negligence hinges on what the common law calls 'the foresight of a reasonable man'.[12] Here one might ask a question similar to that with regard to consumers' health. Was not tort law enacted because as reasonable men we may get into conflict with each other about which types of adverse effects of our behaviour one should foresee, hence avoid? Why then would it be helpful to learn that negligent is the harm that should be foreseen by a reasonable man? It is the predicament of reasonable men that makes us turn to courts or legislators in the first place. Moreover, it is from hard cases where there is reasonableness on both sides that law students learn their trade. So why turn to the predicament in order to solve the predicament?

The picture is not different in other areas of law such as labour law or health law. We expect the law to tell us what we should do if we want to act as a good (enough) employer, or a good (enough) caregiver. However, in Dutch law at least, we are sent back by statutory rules that obviously pretend to state 'the whole point' in these areas of law: we should do what a 'good employer', or a 'good caregiver', respectively, should do. In this respect there is hardly any difference between common law and civil law. Take the doctrine of implied terms in employment contracts in the United Kingdom. Arguably, employment contracts are made because employer and employee do not want to leave their relationship to such vague terms as 'mutual trust and confidence'. This is why they stipulate the most important conditions of their bond. But in *Malik and Mahmud v Bank of Credit and Commerce International*[13] the plaintiffs argued successfully before the House of Lords that, in the final analysis, the

---

12 Cf. Lord Atkin's 'neighbour principle' in *Donoghue v Stevenson* ([1932] AC 562), stipulating that we owe a duty of care to '(…) persons who are so closely and directly affected by my act that I ought reasonably to have them in contemplation as being so affected (…).'

13 SA [1997] UKHL 23.

term of mutual trust and confidence was implied into the contract as a necessary element of the employment relation. The Lords unanimously held that in the case of a line of conduct that is objectively considered to cause serious damage to the relationship between employer and employee, a breach of the implied obligation may arise. In fact it did arise in this case because the Bank went insolvent due to its fraudulent activities, which constituted the breach. Mr Malik and Mr Mahmud could not care less about the theoretical issue in the background but it is there nevertheless: How can mutual trust and confidence be the final term of an employment contract, and indeed how can this term guide the behaviour of the contracting parties, if law is needed precisely because the mere appeal to mutual trust and confidence is bound to fail? So, to generalise the issue, the law tells us that we should not do what we should not do, and that we should do what we should do. But neither of these tautologies seems to guide our actions.

2.2 Contradiction

Philosophers have other reasons to hesitate about an account of rule following as they take their cue from Wittgenstein. What fascinates Wittgenstein in his later works is how we can be bound or, for that matter, guided, by a rule, i.e. how we can go on, once we have grasped the rule, applying it to new cases *as dictated by the rule*? His favourite examples are sequences of numbers where you are expected to continue the series, as in IQ tests, and which you may continue in incompatible ways. Suppose you are given the sequence 1, 2, 3, 4 … , and asked to fill out the next number, conceiving the given numbers as some kind of directive of what you should do (a rule or a norm). Though you might think that 5 is the correct continuation of the sequence, any answer is in fact possible. Here are a few examples:

[1] 7, 10! (call out loud any number you know)

[2] 1, 2, 3, 4 (count a 4/4 time like in a march)

[3] 1, 14, 32, 2341 (combine the given numbers as you please)

[4] 1, 4, 8, 11 (Any number other than 5 or dividable by 5 as 5 is an unholy number)

If '5' is a correct answer, and 'any number other than 5' (i.e. not-5) as well, then the rule allows contradictory answers. A contradiction is necessary false. From necessarily false statements, one may derive anything (thus nothing). So it seems impossible to follow the rule.

The relevance of this example for law will be clear. Especially in the common law tradition, legal rules have exactly this paradigmatic format of a sequence of decisions rather than of a general prescription that is supposed to be instantiated in each singular decision, as is the case in the civil law. But this difference does not matter much. The problem is the same in both formats: A rule in itself does not mention how it should be continued or, for that matter, applied. Would we expect this to be given by a higher rule, we would embark on an infinite regress. Would we concede that it is not given at all, then why would we speak of a rule? To return to the example above: e-cigs were not part of the legislator's universe when he enacted smoking restrictions or imposed tobacco excises. They have been on the market only since 2004. If we now say that we follow the non-smoking rule(s) by applying it to e-cigs, are we not putting the rule aside, replacing it by another one on our own account? But then why did we call it a rule at all? On the other hand if we say that we follow the rule(s) by exempting e-cigs from it, are we not doing the very same thing, namely making a new rule of our own invention? So should we say that both courses of action are in accordance with the rule(s) regarding smoking? None?[14] Apparently, even if one could solve the well-known problems of vagueness, ambiguity, and lacunas which legal theorists have discussed without end, one would end

---

14 'This was our paradox: No course of action could be determined by a rule, because every course of action can be made to accord with the rule. The answer was: If everything can be made out to accord with the rule, then it can also be made out to conflict with it. And so there would be neither accord nor conflict here.' L Wittgenstein (1953) para. 201. Cf. S Holtzman and C Leich (1981); S Kripke (1982), and the discussion in GP Baker and PMS Hacker (1984) I wrote on the importance of these analyses for legal theory (B Van Roermund (1984), rewritten in English as B Van Roermund (1990)).

up with Wittgenstein's question: how does a rule determine the next step if we consider a given sequence of steps as a sort of algorithm we can run on the situation?

Lawyers may respond to this by saying that, indeed, there are open, general, or even fuzzy, rules that do not tell you much. But there are also hard and fast rules in law, and judges apply them at a pace that does not even allow you to take off your coat at your day in their courts. For instance, there are very clear rules linking drunken driving to sanctions, or income to taxes. You may put them in tables with numbers in two columns: amount of alcohol (or income) left, sanctions (or taxes) right. Each row will read as a rule, and prove Wittgenstein wrong, as it is quite clear what accords with the rule and what not. But is it? Such an answer would underestimate not only Wittgenstein's, but also lawyers' wit in dealing with rules. By just replicating a particular row in a table, officials would not give evidence of their having grasped the rule. If this were what they were doing, they would act like children reading letters rather than words. They will only be following the rule if they see 'the point' of the row. But neither the rows nor the columns give this point. It is only given in the matrix of columns and rows. It reads like, for instance, the higher the micrograms of alcohol per 100 millilitres (of breath, blood, urine), the severer the sanction; or, the higher the income, the higher the tax percentage. In fact this matrix, as a series of intersections, is the rule they have to follow, neither the particular rows nor the particular columns. In their isolation, these rows and columns are like the individual numbers of the sequence 1, 2, 3, 4: You may be able to replicate them, but how to continue? Or in more abstract terms, how to account for a third dimension, that allows you to relate horizontal rows and vertical columns?

3. THE ICON THEORY OF RULES

Let me first sketch two would-be solutions to the puzzle that will not really work. I call them intuitionism and conventionalism. Seeing why they fail will prepare the ground for an alternative account in 3.2.

3.1 Hunches and Conventions

A rather popular strategy among theorists is to call on 'the hunch' of the rule follower or rule applier, typically the judge.[15] Of course, it is readily admitted that it is a trained hunch, but in the end it is alleged that only by some sort of intuitive 'jump' one is able to follow the rule and apply it to new cases. Note that this solution remains within the ambit of semantics. We claim to grasp the correspondence between the general picture of the world that a rule provides and the actual state of the world in which we are supposed to act, but just how we do that is hidden under the carpet of 'intuition'. The everyday slogan[16] that 'we'll know it when we see it' reflects such appeal to intuition. But Wittgenstein undercuts this escape.[17] If a hunch would have to come in to follow the rule, he argues, we would be guided by the hunch rather than the rule. More generally, if we would need *reasons* to follow the rule as we do, we would follow these reasons rather than the rule. We may have reasons to follow the rule in the first

---

[15] Among Legal Realists it was Joseph Hutcheson, an experienced judge, who advocated the appeal to 'the hunch' in order to debunk formalism, as early as 1929: 'I, after canvassing all the available material at my command, and duly cogitating upon it, give my imagination play, and brooding over the cause, wait for the feeling, the hunch – that intuitive flash of understanding which makes the jump spark connection between question and decision, and at the point where the path is darkest for the judicial feet, sheds its light along the way.' (J Hutcheson (1929) 278.) In later years he came to acknowledge Cardozo's mitigated interpretation of his radical stance. For a critical appraisal of 'the hunch' cf. C Yablon (1990).

[16] Famously used by United States Supreme Court Justice Potter Stewart, in his concurring opinion in *Jacobellis v Ohio* 378 U.S. 184 (1964), regarding possible obscenity.

[17] 'It is no act of insight, or intuition, which makes us use the rule as we do at the particular point of the series. It would be less confusing to call it an act of decision, though this too is misleading, for nothing like an act of decision must take place, but possibly just an act of writing and speaking. And the mistake which we here and in a thousand similar cases are inclined to make is labeled by the word "to make" as we have used it in the sentence "It is no act of insight which makes us use the rule as we do", because there is an idea that "something must make us" do what we do. And this again joins on to the confusion between cause and reason. We need have no reason to follow the rule as we do. The chain of reasons has an end.' (L Wittgenstein (1969)143; cf. L Wittgenstein (1967), para. 301 and L Wittgenstein (1953) para. 186; par. 213.

place, but we need no extra reasons in the process of following the rule. There is no reason on top of the rule 1, 2, 3, 4 … why at the blank one should say 5 rather than anything else. So if it is true, for all practical purposes, that 'we know it when we see it', the question still is how we know.

However, visual connotations are not entirely inappropriate here. Wittgenstein makes us aware of different accounts of 'seeing', related to different practices. As a first approach to the problem, we are asked to pay attention to what 'seeing a sign' is as distinct from 'seeing an object'. Seeing a sign is not just 'seeing an object plus the meaning of the object'. It is a different way of seeing, as it asks for bodily engagement ('possibly just an act of writing and speaking') showing 'how to proceed'.[18] This is why Wittgenstein is suspicious of the term 'interpretation'; it does not acknowledge the practice that gradually involves us in how to look at specific signs, for instance signposts. Suppose that, on a hike in the mountains, I try to explain to some extra-terrestrial company how a signpost works. I say something like: 'It points you into the direction of your destination.' He reacts: 'Great. Let's take one of these with us so that we do not get lost.' Apparently he is not familiar with the practice of following signposts.

However, introducing 'practice' does not suffice. Some Wittgenstein readers emphasise the *conventional* aspect of such a practice.[19] Conventionalism is another candidate solution to the rule paradox – which I think will not fare any better than the appeal to intuition. But undoubtedly it hails from Wittgenstein's own emphasis on 'agreement' as a

---

[18] Cf. (Wittgenstein 1967) para. 303: "He grasps the rule intuitively." – But why the rule? Why not how he is to continue?'

[19] Raz is rightly critical of the triumphalism often surrounding the 'discovery' of conventions: '(…) the implication that conventions were overlooked in pre-post-modern analysis is somewhat surprising. Since the decline of magic no one has ever doubted the dependence of language and other carriers of meaning on conventions.' Cf. J Raz (2009) 229.

precondition rather than an outcome of communication and understanding.[20] He explicitly submits: 'The word 'agreement' and the word 'rule' are *related* to one another, they are cousins. If I teach anyone the use of the one word, he learns the use of the other with it.'[21] Wittgensteinians believe they find support for a conventionalist interpretation of this and similar passages in his celebrated idea of language games, tacitly assuming that games are conventional by definition. In section 4 I will explain why I think this interpretation is false. For now, let me just briefly set out why conventionalism does not solve the paradox; that is to say, not as along as it boils down to any of the following responses [C1], [C2] and [C3] an agent might give to the question why one should say '5' rather than anything else in order to continue the sequence 1, 2, 3, 4 …

[C1] People in my environment by and large *concur* in saying '5', i.e. in their behaviour.

[C2] On top of [C1], some of these people take a *critical reflective attitude* to my saying '5', in the sense that they approve only this and condemn any other behaviour.

[C3] On top of [C1] and [C2], this critical reflective attitude is not just common but also *shared*, i.e., practised in mutually merged behaviour.

I am not denying, either that a practice of taking guidance is a necessary condition for any rule to exist in any sense of the word, or that we are introduced into such a practice P by other agents in our community sharing a reflective practice P' of approval and rejection regarding P. These two things are true enough. But the problem is that 'seeing the point' or 'getting the picture' of the rule, in this case the practice of counting, is always underdetermined by [C3], let alone [C2] and [C1]. As long as teachers or officials have to intervene at each (new) step in my

---

[20] Cf. 'If language is to be a means of communication there must be agreement not only in definitions but also (queer as this may sound) in judgments. This seems to abolish logic, but does not do so.' (L Wittgenstein (1953) para. 242).

[21] Ibid. para. 224.

rule following pursuit, I am not following the rule (yet). Rather I am taking my cue from their authority in learning how to follow the rule. I am able to follow the rule to the extent that their authority gradually disappears from the scene, as I become able to see for myself what the 'necessity' is in the consecutive steps. Then I am able to see why their teaching was critical and, indeed, why their behaviour converged in the first place. Obviously, the rules of counting allow for authority to retreat from the scene more easily than the rules of law. The latter harbour a sense of necessity that is different from the former. But Crispin Wright, and Bouveresse in his wake, were not at all wrong in arguing that rule following in the sense of being *guided* by rules is contingent on '(…) the invention of (some form of) necessity'.[22]

3.2 Icons and Rules

Let me clarify what I think Wittgenstein had in mind by giving the example of icons, very much based on what he says about grasping the possible movements of a machine.[23] Not, however, without one caveat: in the simplest of terms I aim to argue that all rules are (in an important sense) icons, not that (some) icons are rules. Nevertheless I start out with some icons that are clearly rules, and argue the inverse thesis in subsection 3.2.3.

3.2.1 Icons as rules

Most people can operate elevator doors in perfect accordance with their wishes to have them opened or closed, as the case may be, by pushing either one of two buttons.[24] Not uncommonly, these buttons have the following icons: >||< and <||>. Perhaps the reader belongs to the happy

---

[22] C Wright (1980); cf. J Bouveresse (1987) 14–15: '(…) l'idée que la nécessité ne nous est pas imposée …'

[23] Cf. Wittgenstein (1953) paras 193–194 – I will return to this example in section 4.1.

[24] The internet makes humble: though this example dates from a fairly old paper (B Van Roermund (1993)), I recently found a Montreal-based blog discussing the very same issue in 2007. Cf. http://www.blork.org/blorkblog/2007/05/18/open-close/, accessed April 25, 2010.

majority of people who see immediately which button to push in order to have the doors opened or closed. I do not. More: I manipulate these buttons in exactly the opposite way as most people do, feeling pretty sure that I do it *right*, or even that *this time* I'll do it right. My colleagues – who are all normal – keep telling me that this is what the manufacturer had in mind:

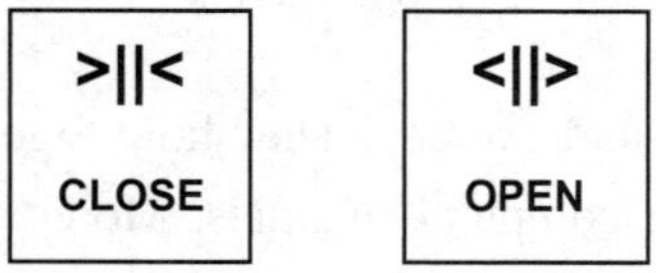

Figure 5.1 Elevator buttons

On closer examination I often even discover these words being clearly written on the buttons. They come in support of a reflective interpretation of the signs as rules; arguably, they make only sense in a reading like 'If the door is closed (resp. open) and you want it to open (resp. close), then you should push this button'.[25] But they do not support O-mode interpretation in my case. The icons suggest that I can afford to skip the reading and go by the icons. That, after all, is what icons are for. However, every time I trust the suggestion, my hand goes to the button, which makes the doors move in the direction I do not want them to move in.

To strengthen my self-confidence in the face of such an abnormality I have framed an explanatory hypothesis, which allows both normal people and me to emerge as perfectly reasonable beings. Normal people see the icons > and < as arrows. The force that should open or close the doors comes from the direction opposite to that in which the arrows point. For the happy majority this is the more adequate picture:

→||← and ← || →

25 Rather than either of the following readings of, e.g. 'open': [1] The door is open. [2] If the door is open, then push this button. [3] Open the door! [4] If the door is closed, then push this button.

So <||> pushes the doors away from each other, thus opening the doorway, while >||< pushes the doors towards each other, closing it. My handicap is that I have a different reading of the characters < and >. I happen to see them not as arrows, but as brackets, in more or less this way:

)- || -(and -(||)-

Now, brackets include and exclude. They hold together and separate, e.g., in logic, arithmetic, or computer manuals. Moreover, there are plenty of figurative pictures to read into > and <. One of my favourites is to see them as the slightly curved lines of hands in profile. No doubt hands hold together and separate in a straightforward sense. Still another possibility is to read > and < as stylised comic drawings of the impact of some force: they indicate the effect rather than the cause. Whatever picture you prefer, it boils down to an image in which the force originates from the direction to which the tips of < and > point. That is why I recognise <||> as 'pushing the half-doors together'; consequently, I operate the corresponding button in order to close the doors. With >||<, it is the other way around: The 'hands' separate the half-doors, suggesting to me that they are capable of opening them.

The intriguing part of this explanation is not so much the difference between normal people and me. It is, rather, the striking similarity in the way we all seem to relate to these symbols, a similarity that is borne out only by our differences. The similarity is threefold.

(1) Both normal people and I work with the same category of 'power' or 'moving force': the power that makes elevator doors open and close. We believe that the symbols refer to such a phenomenon.
(2) We both localise the origin and the orientation of this power, as coming from and going into different directions. When 'normals' are in the elevator, they locate the origin of power where the smiley is in scheme [A]:

[A] ☺>||<☺ <|☺|>

Apparently, I myself localise it in the opposite way [B]:

[B] >|☺|< ☺<||>☺

(3) We imagine *ourselves* at the place of the smileys in [A] and [B]: It is *our* opening and closing the doors of the elevator. If power is involved in these kinds of actions, we see ourselves as the source of that power. Indeed, the icon seems to invoke our projecting ourselves on to these particular ☺-spots within its own framework. The icon is a mirror, and we are prompted[26] to step 'through the looking-glass': from a place in front of (and external to) the icon, to a place in the framework of (or internal to) the icon. In a more technical vocabulary: there is a form of reflexivity involved in understanding the icon – a form of *auto*-reference very different from the one Luhmann introduced into jurisprudence.[27]

Now, Wittgenstein's thesis is that it is rather immaterial whether a rule has a pictorial, a verbal or an arithmetic form. It has to be understood from the self-projection into the icon it conveys. At bottom, to follow, indeed to interpret, a rule is not to apply a syllogism or an algorithm to one's situations, but to step through the looking-glass, i.e., to project oneself as a would-be agent in front of the rule, to a form of behaviour from the perspective to which the rule is prompting. In order to 'interpret' the rule, one has to relate one's standpoint to the correlation between two senses of the 'origin of the rule': its vantage-point and its vanishing-point. In navigation we do this all the time: your GPS-device tells you where you are, but only on condition that you are prepared to project yourself on to that tiny triangle on the display. No syllogism can give you that.

---

26 It comes close to what W Döpke and C Schwarze (1981) 21f call 'localisation actantielle'.

27 In Luhmann's theory *autos* translates as *idem*, in mine as *ipse*. Cf., for example, N Luhmann (1979; 1986) For distinctions in a similar vein, cf. J Perry (1998), distinguishing between 'knowledge of the person I happen to be' and 'knowledge of the self'.

Whether or not this reflexive identification actually occurs in the biography of particular agents is contingent upon various factors, ranging from neuro-physiological to social ones. For instance, whether we are sensitive towards 'depth' in pictures, colours, sounds, tastes, words, etc., is largely due to the neuro-wiring of our individual bodily make-up. People are pretty different in this respect. But not everything is neurological. That socio-cultural factors play an analogous role in our bodily intertwinement with the world is nicely captured by Joel Fisher's 'Gender Paintings'.[28]

Figure 5.2 Joel Fisher, Gender Paintings, Glasgow, December 2007

Here is Fisher's short story: 'Some years ago I was watching a movie in a cinema in Poland when I had to go to the bathroom. The facilities were downstairs, where I hit on two doors with these symbols. They probably stood for 'male' and 'female', i.e., they were rules I should comply with. Alas, I could not decide where to enter, stumbled back to the theatre and kept my legs crossed for one more hour.' Apparently, if you have no access to Polish conventional 'subtitles' with regard to these pictures, i.e., if you have to go by how you see your own body reflected in these pictures, male and female can recognise themselves in either picture, and the rule about the use of the bathrooms loses its guiding potential.[29] This

[28] I felt very privileged and grateful to Joel Fisher for making and offering me these paintings during the *Species of Origin* Workshop (Glasgow, 2007) after reading the first draft of a paper underlying this chapter. I also thank him for permission (25-04-2008) to reproduce them here in this way.

[29] In a discussion about this example, Bonnie Honig brought up the embarrassment that comes with the fear to enter the wrong bathroom. This certainly explains why Fisher decided to go back, but not how he got puzzled in the first

also proves the point made above about the limited explanatory power of conventionalism: it may be the right account of how we *learn* to follow a rule, but not of how we follow the rule.

3.2.2 Perspective

Stepping through the looking-glass or, more pedantically, being caught by reflexivity, is at the heart of perspective, i.e. of seeing 'depth'. The analysis of the simple icons in the previous sub-section was an application of the theory of perspective. Bringing perspective to bear on legal rules does not sound very innovative. This, however, may well be due to the fact that our use of the term 'perspective' is often trivial; it usually expresses either nothing more than that our view of the world around us is dependent on our viewpoint (which is a truism), or nothing less than that the world is dependent on our viewpoint (which is an error). In fact perspective is a good deal more, and a good deal more complex, than this. It is a universal paradigm of intertwinements in the subject-object relationship, aesthetically explored in art,[30] epistemically in science,[31] normatively in all things practical such as ethics, economics, pedagogy, and law. It is an intricate and intriguing account of appearance versus reality, in other words it is an account of fact and fiction. Van Fraassen's point that perspective is a cluster concept is well-taken: 'There is no defining common set of characteristics, only family resemblances among the instances. Whether or not something is aptly called perspectival depends on whether some appropriate subset of these hallmarks are present, but what amounts to 'appropriate' we cannot delimit precisely either.'[32] Nevertheless, the following hallmarks appear to be salient.[33]

---

place. I grant, though, that both phenomena rest on reflexivity, i.e. on seeing oneself in the mirror *qua* agent.

30 E Panofsky (1991 [1927]); H Damisch (1995 [1987]); K Harries (2001).

31 B Van Fraassen (2008).

32 Ibid. 59; cf. 69.

33 I frame these in terms that are reminiscent of pictorial art. Generalising these points to representation in other areas would exceed the limits of this chapter.

(1) The correlation between eye-point or vantage point, and vanishing point(s).[34] These are equi-primordial: The vanishing point yields the vantage point, which yields the vanishing point, etc., in infinite intertwinement.
(2) As a maker one has to construe the vanishing point, as a viewer one has to construe the vantage point. Thus, as a maker one has to imagine a viewer, and as a viewer one has to imagine a maker.
(3) This construction can be based only partly (or only in some specific techniques) by mathematics. In most cases some sort of productive distortion becomes necessary, prompted by so-called depth clues.
(4) Sensitivity to various kinds of depth clues may be neuro-physically entrenched as well as socially mediated.
(5) In order to 'get the knack' of the picture from these depth clues, we have to recognise ourselves as *bodies* (or *some* body as *our* body) involved in the intertwinement of vantage and vanishing point, and act accordingly.[35]

Let me stress the last point in particular: joining the correlative dynamics between vantage point and vanishing point is a matter of action, imagined action, hence action measuring. Even in art perception this is salient. A classic example in painting is Rembrandt's *The Draper's of the Guild*. Complying with the depth clues of this painting (i.e., getting the picture *right* by construing the vanishing point *correctly*), requires the observer to locate herself considerably *lower* than the painting. One way of doing this is to hang it high up on a wall above a fireplace.[36] The important parameter guiding such behaviour is not so much that this is where it was historically meant to hang, but that we have to tune into the

[34] The plural (vanishing points) should highlight that I am aware of further discussions on two-point or multiple perspective.

[35] These are two reasons why I prefer Merleau-Ponty's account of interpretation in terms of 'intertwinement' or 'entanglement' over Gadamer's idea of 'Horizontverschmelzung'. (M Merleau-Ponty (1964) 182; H-G Gadamer (1975 [1960]) 289f.)

[36] http://www.volkskrant.nl/vk/nl/2676/Cultuur/article/detail/758974/2006/08/24/Rembrandt-kon-wel-in-perspectief-schilderen.dhtml, accessed May 5, 2011.

painting until our actual standpoint coincides with the one commanded by the vanishing point of the painting. The picture guides our gaze, but only if we commit ourselves to it and ask where we should stand to see it properly. Recall, however, that perspective is not restricted to pictorial art. It is universally bound up with representation of 'depth'. It is also quintessential, for instance, to understanding narratives,[37] music, and other forms of 'making sense'. In other words, it is the hallmark of interpreting normative sources in the O-mode.

3.2.3 Rules as icons

Let me go back now to legal rules, and argue why and how we should see them as icons, discover their perspective by following their depth clues, yield to their vanishing point and step through the looking-glass, i.e., act accordingly. We should try and map the hallmarks of perspective on to rule following. The core of this exercise is to see how rule following in the operative mode (e.g., receiving guidance) is like locating oneself at the vantage point of the rule by relating to its vanishing point. Bridging the distance between one's actual position and the vantage point of the rule is what is called understanding the rule. But in order to bridge the distance, it has to be measured, and measuring it correctly is already following the rule in an important sense. Hence there are two importantly distinct ways of violating (i.e. not following) a rule: failed measuring and deliberate deference. This is, in brief, what is at stake; and I propose to argue it by discussing the example that has dominated the discussion on legal rule following in the Anglo-American world from 1958 on.[38]

---

[37] Taking my cue from J Culler (1981) I gave examples and applications to law in B Van Roermund (1997).

[38] Recently, at the occasion of its 50th anniversary the tale is revisited in F Schauer (2008). See references to the abundant literature there. Schauer rightly notes: 'The hypothetical rule prohibiting vehicles in the park, and Fuller's response to what Hart likely initially believed to be its least controversial dimension, has become a lens through which many commentators have viewed more recent debates, including those about statutory interpretation, law's determinacy, the role of rules in law, and the nature of legal language, among others. If we can get clear about the issues involved in Hart and Fuller's disagreement over this one example, and if we can understand the strongest arguments on

What about the rule 'no vehicles in the park'? I think that Schauer is entirely right that our ability to follow this rule hinges on 'shared a-contextual understanding' and therefore on practices within a community.[39] He is even more right, possibly even more than he realises, in drawing attention to the fact that, whatever our *limited* participation in *specific* practices of a *particular* community may be, we prove able to understand 'sentences we have never heard, people we have never met, and propositions we have never previously encountered'.[40] In other words, shared contextual understanding within a particular community enables us to take a new step beyond the practices of this community (which does not mean: *any* new step) because it hinges, in turn, on a wider understanding shared in ways that exceed the boundaries of what we share in our community. Though Schauer mentions new 'sentences' and 'propositions', he will probably agree that this wider understanding is not necessarily taking place on the level of conscious beliefs and desires expressed in propositions. It is our largely pre-reflective imagination of a park as part of 'life in the city' that allows us to understand why 'vehicles' are prohibited, what kind of vehicles are targeted in the first place (motor-vehicles rather than strollers), and in what kind of circumstances we would consider an exception to the rule (an ambulance responding to an emergency call rather than a citizen being late for work). This wider, pre-reflective, or (as I called it) operative imagination is contingent on the 'wiring' that makes us sensitive to the depth clues in a specific situation. The sign with the text is one such depth clue, and there are more.

---

either side (only some of which were actually offered by either Fuller or Hart), we will have learned something important about numerous questions of legal theory and legal practice, questions that transcend what initially may appear to be a rather limited debate.'

[39] To this extent he follows the majority of legal theorists, as DM Finkelstein (2010) observes.

[40] F Schauer (2008) 1122.

It is quite remarkable that these are rarely discussed. Instead, authors take pleasure in teasing out the semantic extension of the word 'vehicles',[41] considering whether it would entail 'a military truck in perfect working order' that a group of patriots would want to mount on a pedestal in the park as a war memorial,[42] and continuing on whether 'in perfect working order' would entail that the keys would be made available. One will remember Fuller's argument that we cannot decide these questions until we know 'the deeper purpose' of the rule. From the beginning of this chapter my concern has been: how is this deeper purpose given by the rule rather than by something outside the rule (such as a hunch, a convention, an intention, or the otherwise indeterminate 'context')? Hart chose to introduce his example by one brief phrase: 'A legal rule forbids you to take a vehicle into the public park.'[43] This makes the example utterly abstract from an agent's viewpoint. Hence it cannot come as a surprise that discussants have added colour to the scene, for instance by assuming that we are talking about a sign bearing the text 'no vehicles in the park'. But the sign is not the rule, nor does it in any sense contain or convey the rule in full. If it were lying around on a trash heap, or standing at a junction in the middle of the park, we would have a hard time seeing it as a rule. I propose to consider salient features of the situation not as belonging to the 'context' of the rule but to the rule itself, as pointers or depth clues. These come into sight when we continue on the path of adding colour to the scene. Once we have assumed that a sign is what we are looking at, many of the observations made above about icons pertain. It is not a very wild guess that apart from 'no vehicles' we will read other texts such as 'no horses, no trail-bikes', 'beware of grizzlies' or 'do not walk on the lawn', dependent on what kind of park we talk about. To the left we may detect a parking lot with spaces not only for cars but also for bikes or horses. All of this we see at the

---

41 Not to mention 'park'; cf. AC Hutchinson (2010).

42 LL Fuller (1958) 663.

43 HLA Hart (1958) 607.

entrance of the park, indicative of an enclosure, a restricted area.[44] So there are not only signs and texts in view but also a gate, pointing to a gatekeeper, a paradigm of authority if there ever was one.[45] Now the rule 'no vehicles in the park' is not in any of these signs, not even in the text containing exactly these words. The rule is in the relationship between these elements as they present, from various angles, a prescriptive point of convergence to which we can relate our behaviour. Perceptively, two McGill colleagues draw our attention to another text that may be at that very same entrance, grammatically and syntactically similar to Hart's: 'No toilets in the park'.[46] Usually we will not read this text as (a pointer to) a rule at all (but rather as a description of a fact that we may take into account in our behaviour); moreover we will exclude it from the depth clues that mark the 'no vehicles' rule.

But wait, where is the reflexivity in this simplest of examples? For without reflexivity, the whole idea of depth clues evaporates into thin air. I submit that it hides in the most neglected part of the example: the definite article 'the'. The prohibition can only work if 'the' means, in fact, 'that': 'No vehicles in THAT park'. The agent approaching the park entrance is able to understand 'no vehicles in the park' only because, in turn, he takes 'the' as 'that': 'No vehicles in THAT park', i.e. the park I NOW see HERE in front of ME.[47] This is why most real signs in similar situations read something like 'No vehicles beyond THIS point', thus introducing indexical reference that the addressee is supposed to translate from his own first-person standpoint, Thus, an important precondition for

---

[44] Suppose I am facing the same sign 'no vehicles beyond this point' at the entrance of a park in the city, at a bar on a dirt road in the middle of Iceland, or near Ellis Park Stadium (Johannesburg) during the 2010 Soccer World Cup. It drastically changes my range of options what counts as a 'vehicle'.

[45] There is not only Kafka's *Vor dem Gesetz*, but also, for instance, Rousseau's *Second Discourse,* Part II, opening with the equally famous phrase 'Le premier qui, ayant enclos un terrain, s'avisa de dire: *Ceci est à moi*, et trouva des gens assez simples pour le croire, fut le vrai fondateur de la société civile.' (J-J Rousseau (1754 [1964]) 164.)

[46] RA Macdonald and J MacLean (2005).

[47] Compare this to the situation in which, at the entrance of the same park, the agent is also confronted with a sign flashing 'No vehicles in the tunnel' while being not aware of any tunnel in that park.

depth clues to work towards reflexivity obtains. For they are not just 'there' as distinct from 'here', but 'there-in-front-of-ME'. This 'ME' introduces reflexivity, in virtue of which I am looking at myself *qua* self. This constitutes a double bind or, as it is called in classical grammar, a 'middle voice': on the one hand the self as passive in as far as it is looked at, addressed, targeted as someone who is about to enter the park; on the other hand the self as active in as far as it fosters an intention to enter the park. In the wake of this 'me-addressing-me' other elements in the situation at hand start to resonate as 'addressing-me', while simultaneously this intention of 'I-entering-there' splits the situation in what comes and what does not come in support of his action. Envisioning what comes in support the agent projects himself into the situation taking it as 'symbol' or 'drawing' (to recall Wittgenstein's vernacular). Performing an action is precisely that: incorporating the world around us. Envisioning what does not come in support, on the other hand, requires retreating from the situation and contemplating oneself as an object in causal relationships to many others. Thus, reflexivity allows for depth clues interfering with the agent's contemplating 'what should I do?, along with his imagination of actually performing the action he is contemplating. But it does not infringe on his ability to calculate his chances or to ignore addresses. In case he (sometimes gradually) comes to see the vantage point of the depth clues in the case of the park, he will establish something like: 'this is about me-in-my-vehicle'. No separate semantic exercise is needed with regard to the notions of 'vehicle' and 'park': 'the topic of self-ascription belongs to pragmatics and not to semantics'.[48] Following the rule means that the agent establishes what it takes to change 'me-in-my-vehicle entering' into 'me-without-my-vehicle entering', i.e., parking. This is conventionally called 'my duty', and it is the distance between two points: the position I actually am at and the vantage

---

[48] 'That is a fancy way of saying that what the self-ascription does cannot be equated with, but *adds a crucial step to,* the content of a map or to the bare impersonal belief that the map "fits" the world.' (B Van Fraassen (2008) 82 (italics in the original, where the argument is about maps; note however the generalisation on the next page 'Self-location in a wider sense').)

point where the rule situates me by virtue of its vanishing point. Following the rule, or acknowledging one's duty is therefore a form of measuring.

4. A BETTER ACCOUNT?

Why do I think that my theory is better than others? I offer two lines of argument, both of which would surely require more elaborate exposition than this chapter allows. The first is that my account is a better reading of Wittgenstein, the second that it provides a better understanding of what 'students of the law' (prototypically lawyers) do.

4.1 Giving Wittgenstein his Due

There are reasons to hold that a conventionalist account of rules does not fit into Wittgenstein's views, and that an iconic one fares much better. Thus, there is a negative and a positive claim to be defended in an already far too brief subsection.[49] On the negative side I submit that his idea of 'language games' is seriously misinterpreted if given a conventionalist ring.[50] Firstly, Wittgenstein explicitly rejects the thought that 'playing' and 'playing a game' are the same. He refers to children playing with a ball, denying that they are playing according to 'strict rules',[51] i.e. that they are playing a game. People may play – and make

---

[49] For a more elaborated philosophical critique of legalism and its alleged alternatives, against the backdrop of Wittgenstein, cf. B Van Roermund (1990), reworked as chapter 6 in B Van Roermund (1997).

[50] Though I do not share all of his reading, I pretty much adopt the view of DM Finkelstein (2010) 673: 'Wittgenstein's point is that it's a mistake to suppose that the dependence of meaning, thinking and understanding on feeling, interest, and a shared sense of what matters saddles us with vulgar conventionalism.' Finkelstein adds 'vulgar' since he himself does hold that rule following hinges on 'social facts about us'.

[51] 'We are unable clearly to circumscribe the concepts we use; not because we don't know their real definition, but because there is no real "definition" to them. To suppose that there must be would be like supposing that whenever children play with a ball they play a game according to strict rules.' (Wittgenstein (1969) 25.) Cf. Wittgenstein (1953) para. 66: 'In ball games there is winning and

up the rules as they go along.[52] The point is not that they are playing according to soft rather than strict rules, but that they mutually understand what they (are supposed to) do without rules. Playing a game is only the conventional sediment of playing, and playing as 'joyfully tuning into each other's actions' was what Wittgenstein probably had in mind when he mentioned languages as an infinite realm of 'Spiele'.[53]

Secondly, to engage in playing is to engage in a *bodily* practice rather than a conventional one. Better perhaps, any conventional form of playing (playing a game) should recognise that it builds on a more basic layer of playing which entails bodily engagement. By engaging the practice one gradually learns how to take steps, how to do it better, how to do it without the help of others, and finally how to do it in a new way. This is why Wittgenstein sometimes calls it 'Abrichtung',[54] a term mostly used for drilling animals. This is also, however, why he wants to describe 'understanding' as 'being able to take the next step (or to continue a sequence)'. In order to be able to take the *next* step on one's own account, one has to have set oneself already on a path of stepping stones laid out by others, pick up the 'groove' of the movement, identify oneself with it and move after it. And these others, in laying out the stepping stones, will have anticipated how people will step from one stone to the other given the make-up of human bodies. Thus, there is a dual origin of movement: one from which one is moved, one from which one moves. This is how children learn counting: you have to give them the numbers

---

losing; but when a child throws his ball at the wall and catches it again, this feature has disappeared.'

52 Cf. the scene described in Wittgenstein (1953) para. 83.

53 Note that the German 'Spiel' (as the Dutch 'spel', the French 'jeu', etc.) is ambivalent between 'play' and 'game'. To this one could add, that Wittgenstein's explicit remark on the conventional nature of language hinges on the correct translation of 'convention' is the semantic field of 'custom', 'habit', and, in particular, the German 'Gepflogenheit': 'The point (…) is not that our sense-perceptions can lie, but that we understand their language. (And this language, like any other language, is founded on convention.)' Ibid. para. 355. I submit that part of Wittgenstein has got lost in translation.

54 For instance, to give just some salient examples, in Wittgenstein (1953), paras 86 and 630.

together with the gesture of a finger pointing to different entities. One cannot teach arithmetic by purely verbal instructions.

Thirdly, Wittgenstein objects to a possible interpretation of what he says about 'agreement'; he does not intend to say that 'human agreement decides on what is true and false', i.e., he does not advocate a conventionalist theory of truth. The agreement he refers to, even if it is agreement in judgment,[55] is not at the level of 'opinion' (what is said) but at the level of 'form of life' (the saying).[56] Far from being an object of (shared) opinion, interpretation, or action, Wittgenstein qualifies 'form of life' as 'something animal',[57] a layer of life where I am '(…) so anchored that I cannot touch it',[58] or that we cannot access intentionally since it is '(…) as it were, the dream of our language'.[59]

On the positive side, I would like to draw attention to what Wittgenstein says about grasping the possible movements of a machine. It emerges in the passage immediately preceding and introducing the discussion on rule following,[60] where he warns us 'how high the seas of language run here'. What seduces us to say (in a philosophical vein) that 'the possible movements of a machine are already there in it in some mysterious way', just as we say that in following a rule we are under the impression that all the steps are already predetermined? Wittgenstein proposes a distinction between 'a machine, or the drawing of a machine' as a symbol, and an actual machine as an object. 'And it is quite true: the movement of the machine-as-symbol is predetermined in a different sense from that in which the movement of any given actual machine is predetermined.' The latter regards how the actual machine will run, the former how it 'should' run. Strictly spoken, this is neither a deontic 'should', as it makes little sense to ascribe duties to machines; nor is it an 'ideal' way of running that we project on to this machine, as an ideal

---

55 Ibid. para. 242.
56 Ibid. para. 241.
57 L Wittgenstein (1969 [1984]) para. 475.
58 Ibid. para. 103.
59 L Wittgenstein (1953) para. 358.
60 Cf. L Wittgenstein (1953) paras 193–194. I owe Bonnie Honig for drawing my attention to this example.

machine would perhaps leave behind many of the constraints with which we have to deal in operating this machine. In the absence of duty and ideal, what does 'should' mean here? If we would answer that it indicates a possible or a 'virtual' movement, we are left with the question how we distinguish between this virtual movement and the movement of the actual machine, which could also be called 'virtual'. What Wittgenstein means here, I submit, is that, from the actual machine we derive a number of 'depth clues' that allow us to capture the machine as an integrated whole of functions that 'we' aim to perform – indeed that we often used to perform in teamwork. The machine becomes a symbol precisely by taking on perspective, i.e., by reflecting ourselves contemplating how we *should* (best) perform a specific task. In other words, the machine comes to 'this' (first-person) side of our bodily make-up.

4.2 Giving Lawyers their Due

A host of data from legal practice and legal training is, I submit, better accounted for in an iconic approach to rule following than in a verbal one. It presents the structure of O-mode rather than R-mode interpretation. I am not taking issue here with accounts of legal reasoning that critique 'subsumption' of particular facts under general rules. From their first day in law school, students are taught that this is not what judges do unless they deliberately want to commit the sin of legalism. However, this warning is ill-directed. There is no point in denying that reasoning, hence legal reasoning, can be reconstructed by logical schemes (like syllogism or more sophisticated forms), nor that legalism may come under various guises. What is far more interesting than legal reasoning is legal understanding – a topic mostly discussed under the seal of 'interpretation'. However, interpretation is not 'retrieval of meaning'.[61] It is more perspicuously regarded as measurement, involving reflexivity or indexical self-reference in the double sense of self-location and self-orientation towards a direction one wants to go into. At least in the operative mode of interpretation it is.

---

[61] Cf. J Raz (1995); P Schlag (1999).

Hence my first point: This is why law students are trained by looking at law from the point of view of the judge. Even if, at a later point in their career, they will put their knowledge to the use of someone who wants to evade or to ignore the law, they should first be able to think as 'the legal man'. The legal man is not only the one who intends to follow the rule of the law, but also the one who is under the pressure of taking a decision on the basis of the law, one way or another. She or he is neither a philosopher who can afford to generate more and more obstacles for any decision to be taken. Nor is (s)he a computer system that only takes commands decided by others. As a judge, (s)he bears responsibility for deciding the case, as well as for the whole institution that is geared towards ending or precluding conflict by authoritative decision, i.e., the institution of law. Note that, typically, the judge's dealing with the law is no longer the model when law students turn to a different type of training, for instance in professional ethics. Legal ethics is much more interwoven with the attitude of the attorney, the litigator, and the public prosecutor than with the judge. The judge is not just a professional role model in law schools, (s)he is an epistemic model.

Secondly, and importantly, legal training is casuistic, even if it aims at generalising over cases.[62] Unlike, for instance, in economics or linguistics, cases are not the examples that come to illustrate theories. Legal knowledge is not stored in theories, it is stored in constellations of facts. But then, as Nelson Goodman had it, 'facts are small theories; and true theories are big facts'.[63] Factual constellations contain already so many depth clues for one who confronts them with the prime question of

---

[62] Cf. the observations in JBM Vranken (2006) 4ff and references there. Vranken warns us that this comes at the risk of students not learning to see the broader background of the decision in the case at hand, thus missing out on the predictive and directive value of their knowledge. But in order to curb this risk the alternative is not to refrain from casuistics, but to deepen it. My limited experience is that by only rehearsing cases as they are decided by the highest courts, one rarely captures the facts of the case in full. By the time a case goes to the Court of Cassation, for instance, the underlying conflict of interests has been converted into a conflict of norm-interpretations, for which the facts have become instrumental in retrospect.

[63] Cf. N Goodman (1978) 96–97.

practical knowledge 'What should one do?' (or, more specifically, 'What should one do legally?'), that the answer, even if it is contestable, seems to derive directly from the facts rather than from norms.[64] Though this is obviously false as a matter of logical inference it is not mysterious at all as a matter of epistemological accounting. After all, even a park in the city can only be described (best) in normative terms, e.g., a place where one *should* be able, and enable others, to rest. It cannot come as a surprise that if such a park is part of the factual antecedent of a rule, the consequent is normative *in virtue of* the antecedent.

Last, coming back on my earlier statements on legal rules that seem to usher in tautologies, the iconic approach easily explains how this works. These very general 'principles', like the duty of care in tort law, good faith in contract law, decency in some areas of public law, human dignity in all law, etc., indeed do not carry any normative content by themselves. They are vanishing points of normativity. They lend coherence to various more specific prescriptions which I dubbed depth clues. Without these the agent would not discover 'what the rule is about', she would be unable to locate herself with regard to the correlation between vanishing point and vantage point, she would remain unaware of any duty. But this is a two-way street; without these key-stones the specific prescriptions would not group into a sequence that prompts the agent to making 'the next step'.

5. SUMMARY

A received view in legal theory has it that, in order to follow a rule in acting, decision-making, policy-making, and their ilk, we first have to 'interpret' it. 'Interpretation' should curb a purely 'deductive' or 'mechanical' application of the rule. By first retrieving the 'meaning' or the 'spirit' of the rule, one should be better equipped to subsequently do

---

[64] This is one interpretation of the Roman law saying 'da mihi facta, dabo tibi ius' (give me the facts, and I'll give you the law). There are certainly others, e.g., that parties should refrain from presenting legal views and should leave this to the judge.

what the law is about. I have argued that this dualism is false, mainly by showing how much more complicated and sophisticated rule following is. The theory of perspective helped to clarify how certain depth clues in situations where one has to make up one's mind 'what to do?' lead us into a correlation between vantage point and vanishing point that dissolves the 'subjective – objective' gambit in rule following. Following these clues is like 'taking the next step' in a sequence and it is tantamount to understanding 'what the sequence is about'. This theory of rules explains why we experience rules as authoritative – commanding us to a certain action, and why, simultaneously, this very authority is in the eye of the beholder. My claim is that this provides a more adequate picture of how professional lawyers deal with rules.

Bibliography

Adorno, T (1982 [1966]). *Negative Dialektik* 3rd ed., Frankfurt a.M., Suhrkamp.

Agamben, G (1998). *Homo sacer. Sovereign Power and Bare Life* Transl. by D Heller-Roazen, Stanford, Stanford University Press.

Agamben, G (2002 [1999]). *Remnants of Auschwitz. The Witness and the Archive* Transl. by D. Heller-Roazen, New York, Zone Books.

Albert, H (1991 [1968]). *Traktat über kritische Vernunft* 5th ed., Tübingen, Mohr.

Alexy, R (1994). *Theorie der Grundrechte* Frankfurt a. M., Suhrkamp.

Alkema, EA (1981). *Schakelbepalingen: enige beschouwingen over samenhang en werking van de rechten van de mens* Deventer, Kluwer.

Arendt, H (1973 [1951]). *The Origins of Totalitarianism* New edition with added prefaces, New York/London, Harcourt Brace Jovanovich.

Arendt, H (2003 [1993]). *Was ist Politik? Fragmente aus dem Nachlass* U Ludz (ed.), Preface by K. Sontheimer, Münich/ Zürich, Piper.

Aristotle (1975). *The Metaphysics (The Loeb Classical Library)* Cambridge MA, Harvard University Press; London, Heinemann.

Augenstein, D, (ed.) (2012a). *'Integration Through Law' Revisited. The Making of the European Polity*. The Edinburgh/Glasgow Law and Society Series. Farnham (UK)/Burlington VT, Ashgate.

Augenstein, D (2012b). 'Identifying the European Union: Legal Integration and European Communities', *'Integration Through Law' Revisited. The Making of the European Polity*. Farnham (UK)/Burlington VT, Ashgate.

Austin, JL (1962). *How to do Things with Words* Oxford, Clarendon Press.

Austin, JL (1970). *Philosophical Papers* 2nd ed., JO Urmson and GJ Warnock (eds), London/Oxford/New York, Oxford University Press.

Baker, GP and PMS Hacker (1984). 'Critical study: On misunderstanding Wittgenstein: Kripke's private language argument' *Synthese* **58**: 407–450.

Bentham, J (1948). *An Introduction to the Principles of Morals and Legislation* Oxford, Blackwell.

Bentham, J (2002 [1795]). 'Rights, Representation, and Reform: Nonsense Upon Stilts and Other Writings on the French Revolution' *The Collected Works of Jeremy Bentham* P Schofield, C Pease-Watkin and C Blamires (eds), Oxford, Clarendon Press.

Blommaert, J (2009). 'Language, asylum, and the national order' *Current Anthropology* **50**(4): 415–441.

Bodin, J (1576 [1986]). *Les six livres de la Republique* Paris, Fayard.

Bouveresse, J (1987). *La force de la règle. Wittgenstein et l'invention de la nécessité* Paris, Ed. Minuit.

Bratman, ME (1999). *Faces of Intention. Selected Essays on Intention and Agency* Cambridge, Cambridge University Press.

Broekman, JM (1982 [1978]). *Recht en antropologie*, 2nd revised and expanded edition, Antwerpen/Amsterdam, Standaard Wetenschappelijk Uitgeverij.

Burke, E (1790 [1971]). *Reflections on the Revolution in France* Introduction by AJ Grieve, London/New York, Dent, Dutton.

Burton, SJ, (ed.) (2000). *The Path of the Law and its Influence. The Legacy of Oliver Wendell Holmes, Jr (Cambridge Studies in Philosophy and Law)* Cambridge, Cambridge University Press.

Cappelletti, M (1982). 'Accès à la justice: comme programme de réforme et comme méthode de pensée' *Windsor Yearbook of Access to Justice* **2**: 193–208.

Cappelletti, M and B Garth (1978). 'Access to justice: the world-wide movement to make rights effective; a general report' *Access to Justice, vol. I, A World Survey*. M Cappelletti and B Garth, Alphen aan den Rijn/Milan: 1–124.

Castañeda, H-N (1975). *Thinking and Doing. The Philosophical Foundations of Institutions Synthese* Library 97, Dordrecht, Reidel.

Castañeda, H-N (1976). 'The twofold structure and the unity of practical thinking' *Action Theory,* M Brand and D Walton (eds), Dordrecht, Synthese Library 97, 105–132.

Chalmers, D (2005). 'Judicial authority and the constitutional treaty' *International Journal of Constitutional Law* **3**(2–3): 448–472.

Chalmers, D and M Chaves (2011). 'The reference points of EU judicial politics' *Journal of European Public Policy* **19**(1): 25–42.

Christodoulidis, E (2004). 'The objection that cannot be heard. Communication and legitimacy in the courtroom' *The Trial on Trial, vol. I, Truth and Due Process* A Duff, L Farmer, S Marshall and V Tadros (eds), Oxford/ Portland OR, Hart Publishing: 179–202.

Coleman, J (2001). *The Practice of Principle. In Defense of a Pragmatist Approach to Legal Theory* Oxford, Oxford University Press.

Coleman, J, S Shapiro, et al., (eds) (2002). *The Oxford Handbook of Jurisprudence and Philosophy of Law* Oxford, Oxford University Press.

Constant, B (1997). *Écrits politiques. Textes choisis, présentés et annotés par Marcel Gauchet* Paris, Gallimard.

Corrias, L (2010). *The Passivity of Law. Competence and Constitution in the European Body Politic* Tilburg, Tilburg University.

Corrias, L (2011). *The Passivity of Law. Competence and Constitution in the European Court of Justice* Dordrecht/Heidelberg/London/New York, Springer.

Cover, R (1992 [1983]). 'Nomos and narrative' *Narrative, Violence and the Law* M Minow, M Ryan and A Sarat (eds) Ann Arbor, University of Michigan Press.

Craig, P and G De Búrca (2011). *EU Law. Texts, Cases and Materials* 5th ed., Oxford, Oxford University Press.

Critchley, S (2007). *Infinitely Demanding. Ethics of Commitment, Politics of Resistance* London/New York, Verso.

Culler, J (1981). *The Pursuit of Signs; Semiotics, Literature, Deconstruction* Ithaca NY, Cornell University Press.

d'Amato, AA (1978). 'The limits of legal realism' *The Yale Law Journal* **87**: 468–513.

Damisch, H (1995 [1987]). *The Origin of Perspective* Transl. by TJ Goodman, Cambridge MA/London, MIT Press.

De Burca, G and J Scott (2001). 'The impact of the WTO on EU decision-making' *The EU and the WTO. Legal and Constitutional Issues* G De Burca and J Scott (eds), Oxford, Hart Publishing: 1–30.

de Lange, R (1994). 'Het Bundesverfassungsgericht over het Verdrag van Maastricht: een nieuw Solange?' *SEW* **42**: 418–436.

De Man, P (1979). *Allegories of Reading. Figural Language in Rousseau, Nietzsche, Rilke and Proust* New Haven/London, Yale University Press.

Debray, R (1981). *Critique de la raison politique* Paris, Gallimard.

Debray, R (2009). *Le moment fraternité* Paris, Gallimard.

Derrida, J (1967). 'Violence et métaphysique' *L'écriture et la différence* Paris, Du Seuil: 117–228.

Derrida, J (1972). *Marges de la philosophie* Paris, Minuit.

Derrida, J (1982). 'Signature, event, context' *Glyph, vol. 1* Baltimore, John Hopkins University Press, 1977: 172–197. Also *Margins of Philosophy* Transl. By A Bass, Chicago, Chicago University Press: 307–330.

Derrida, J (2009). *The Beast and the Sovereign, vol. I* Chicago/London, The University of Chicago Press.

Descombes, V (2004). *Le complément de sujet. Enquête sur le fait d'agir de soi-même* Paris, Gallimard.

Döpke, W and C Schwarze (1981). 'Le role des prépositions locales dans la constitution sémantique de la phrase' *Analyse des prépositions* C Schwarze (ed.), Tübingen, Niemeyer Verlag: 19–28.

Douzinas, C (2000). *The End of Human Rights* Oxford, Hart Publishing.

Dworkin, R (1977). 'No right answer?' *Law, Morality and Society. Essays in Honour of H.L.A. Hart* PMS Hacker and J Raz (eds), Oxford, Clarendon Press: 58–84.

Dworkin, R (2002). 'Thirty years on' *Harvard Law Review* **115**: 1655–1687.

Dworkin, RM (1977). *Taking Rights Seriously* London, Duckworth.

Enschedé, CJ (1984). *Kijk, recht. Over mensen, vrijheid, plichten en rechten* Amsterdam, Meulenhof.

Ewald, F (1986). 'A concept of social law' *Dilemmas of Law in the Welfare State* G Teubner (ed.), Berlin/New York, De Gruyter: 40–75.

Feinberg, J (1984). *Harm to Others* Oxford, Oxford University Press.

Finkelstein, DM (2010). 'How to do things with Wittgenstein: the relevance of Wittgenstein's later philosophy to the philosophy of law' *The Journal of Jurisprudence* **8**: 647–675.

Flynn, B (2006). *The Philosophy of Claude Lefort. Interpreting the Political* Evanston IL, Northwestern University Press.

Foucault, M (1988). *Power/Knowledge. Selected Interviews and Other Writings 1972–1977* C Gordon (ed.), New York, Pantheon Books.

Frank, JN (1973 [1949]). *Courts on Trial. Myth and Reality in American Justice* Princeton, Princeton University Press.

Freud, S (1912–13). *Totem und Tabu. IV, Die infantile Wiederkehr des Totemismus* Studienausgabe, A Mitscherlich a.o. (eds), Bd. IX. Frankfurt a.M., Fischer Verlag [1974]: 387–444.

Fuller, LL (1949). 'The case of the Speluncean Explorers. In the Supreme Court of Newgarth, 4300' *Harvard Law Review* **107**: 714–744.

Fuller, LL (1958). 'Positivism and fidelity to law – A reply to Professor Hart' *Harvard Law Review* **71**(4): 630–672.

Gadamer, H-G (1975 [1960]). *Wahrheit und Methode. Grundzüge einer philosophischen Hermeneutik* 3rd expanded edition, Tübingen, Mohr.

Gallagher, S (1995). 'Body schema and intentionality' *The Body and the Self* A Marcel, JL Bermúdez and N Eilan (eds), Cambridge MA/London, MIT Press: 225–244.

Gerhardt, V (1983). 'Das "Prinzip des Gleichgewichts", zum Verhaeltnis von Recht und Macht bei Nietzsche' *Nietzsche Studien* **12**: 111–133.

Giddens, A (1983). *Profiles and Critiques in Social Theory* Berkeley/Los Angeles, University of California Press.

Gilbert, M (1996). *Living Together. Rationality, Sociality and Obligation* Lanham, MD, Rowman & Littlefield.

Gilbert, M (2006). *A Theory of Political Obligation: Membership, Commitment, and the Bonds of Society* Oxford, Oxford University Press.

Goodman, N (1978). *Ways of World-Making* Indianapolis, Hackett Publishing Company.

Habermas, J (1992 [1992]). *Faktizität und Geltung. Beiträge zur Diskurstheorie des Rechts und des demokratischen Rechtsstaats,* 2nd ed., Frankfurt a.M., Suhrkamp.

Habermas, J (1997). *Between Facts and Norms: Contributions to a Discourse Theory of Law and Democracy* Transl. by W Rehg, Cambridge, Polity Press.

Hamilton, A, J Madison and J Jay (1999 [1787–1788]). *The Federalist Papers* C Rossiter (ed.), with a new Introduction and notes by Ch R Kesler, New York, Mentor.

Hampshire, S (1959). *Thought and Action* London, Chatto & Windus.

Harries, K (2001). *Infinity and Perspective* Cambridge MA/London, MIT Press.

Hart, HLA (1958). 'Positivism and the separation of law and morals' *Harvard Law Review* **71**: 593–629.

Hart, HLA (1961). *The Concept of Law* Oxford, Clarendon Press.

Hart, HLA (1994). *The Concept of Law* 2nd ed., with a Postscript edited by P Bulloch and J Raz, Oxford, Oxford University Press.

Haverkate, G (1975 [1977]). *Gewissheitsverluste im juristischen Denken, zur politischen Funktion der juristischen Methode* Berlin, Duncker & Humblot.

Hegel, GWF (1807 [1999]). *Phänomenologie des Geistes* Darmstadt, Wissenschaftliche Buchgesellschaft.

Herberger, M (1981). *Dogmatik, Zur Geschichte von Begriff und Methode in Medizin und Jurisprudenz* Frankfurt a.M., Klostermann.

Hobbes, T (1651 [1973]). *Leviathan* Introduction by KR Minogue, London/New York, Everyman's Library.

Hobbes, T (1651 [1983]). *De cive: the English version, entitled in the first edition, Philosophical Rudiments concerning Government and Society* H Warrender (ed.), Oxford, Clarendon Press.

Holmes, OW (1952 [1897]). 'The path of the law' *Collected Legal Papers* HJ Laski (ed.), New York, P. Smith: 167–202.

Holtzman, S and C Leich, (eds) (1981). *Wittgenstein: To Follow a Rule* London/Boston/Henley, Routledge and Kegan Paul.

Honig, B (1993a). *Political Theory and the Displacement of Politics* Ithaca, Cornell University Press.

Honig, B (1993b). 'The Politics of Agonism: a Critical Response to "Beyond Good and Evil: Arendt, Nietzsche, and the Aestheticization of Political Action" by Dana R Villa' *Political Theory* **21**(3): 528–533.

Honneth, A (1995). *The Struggle for Recognition: the Grammar of Social Conflicts* Cambridge, Polity Press.

Honneth, A (2010). 'Grounding Recognition: A Rejoinder to Critical Questions' *Inquiry* **45**(4): 499–519.

Hughes, R (1992 (1991)). *Het epos van Barcelona, koningin der steden* Amsterdam/Leuven, Balans/Kritak.

Hume, D (1739–1740 [1972]). *A Treatise of Human Nature. Being an Attempt to Introduce the Experimental Method of Reasoning into Moral Subjects, Bks II and III* London, Fontana/Collins.

Hutcheson, J (1929). 'The judgment intuitive: The function of the 'hunch' in judicial decision' *Cornell Law Quarterly* **14**: 274–288.

Hutchinson, AC (2010). 'In the park: A jurisprudential primer' *Osgoode Hall Law Journal* **48**: 337–356.

Janssens, D (2008). *Between Athens and Jerusalem. Philosophy, Prophecy, and Politics in Leo Strauss's Early Thought* Albany, SUNY.

Kant, I (1781/1787 [1975]). *Kritik der reinen Vernunft* Darmstadt, Wissenschaftliche Buchgesellschaft.

Kant, I (1797 [1975]). *Die Metaphysik der Sitten.* W Weischedel (ed.), Darmstadt, Wissenschaftliche Buchgesellschaft.

Kantorowicz, EH (1997 [1957]). *The King's Two Bodies. A Study in Mediaeval Political Theology* with a new Preface by WCh Jordan, Princeton, Princeton University Press.

Kelsen, H (1928 [1981]). *Das Problem der Souveränität und die Theorie des Völkerrechts. Beitrag zu einer Reinen Rechtlehre* 2nd reprint of the 2nd edition,. Tübingen 1928 [1920], Aalen, Scientia Verlag.

Kelsen, H (1931 [1968]). 'Wer soll der Hüter der Verfassung sein?' *Die Wiener rechtstheoretische Schule,* vol. 2. Vienna, Europa Verlag 1873–1922.

Kelsen, H (1933 [1968]). 'Staatsform und Weltanschauung'. *Die Wiener rechtstheoretische Schule,* vol. 2. Vienna, Europa Verlag: 1923–1942.

Kelsen, H (1945). *General Theory of Law and State* Transl. by A Wedberg, Cambridge MA, Harvard University Press.

Kelsen, H (1960). *Reine Rechtslehre* with an Appendix: Das Problem der Gerechtigkeit. 2nd fully rewritten and expanded edition, Vienna, Deuticke.

Kelsen, H (1979). *Allgemeine Theorie der Normen* edited from the estate on request of the Hans Kelsen Institut by K Ringhofer und R Walter, Vienna, Manz.

Koops, EJ (2008). 'Criteria for normative technology: An essay on the acceptability of "code as law" in light of democratic and constitutional values' *Regulating Technologies* R Brownsword and K Yeug (eds), Oxford, Hart Publishing: 157–174.

Kripke, S (1982). *Wittgenstein on Rules and Private Language* Oxford, Blackwell.

Kuhn, S (2009 (spring edition)). 'Prisoner's dilemma' *Stanford Encyclopedia of Philosophy* ENZalta (ed.), http://plato.stanford.edu/ (accessed June 3rd, 2013)

Larenz, K (1979 [1960]). *Methodenlehre der Rechtswissenschaft* 4th expanded edition, Berlin/Heidelberg/New York, Springer.

Lebigre, A (1988). *La justice du roi. La vie judiciaire dans l'ancienne France* Paris, Albin Michel.

Lefort, C (1972). *Le travail de l'oeuvre Machiavel* Paris, Gallimard.

Lefort, C (1976). Introduction to É de la Boëtie *Le Discours sur la servitude volontaire,* Paris, Payot.

Lefort, C (1981). *L'invention democratique. Les limites de la domination totalitaire* Paris, Fayard.

Lefort, C (1986). *Essais sur le politique (XIXe–XXe siecles)* Paris, Du Seuil.

Lefort, C (2007). *Le temps présent. Écrits 1945–2005* Paris, Belin.

Levinas, E (1963). 'La trace de l'Autre' *Tijdschrift voor Filosofie* **25**: 605–623.

Levinas, E (1974a). *Totalité et infini. Essai sur l'extériorité* 4th ed., La Haye, M. Nijhoff.

Levinas, E (1974b). *Autrement qu'être ou au-delà de l'essence* Den Haag, M. Nijhoff.

Levinas, E (1976 [1963]). *Difficile liberté. Essais sur le judaïsme* 3rd ed., revue et corrigée, Paris, Albin Michel.

Levinas, E (1987). *De totaliteit en het oneindige. Essay over de exterioriteit* with annotations by Th. De Boer translated by Th. de Boer and C Bremmers. Baarn, Ambo.

Levinas, E (1991). *Entre nous. Essais sur le penser-à-l'autre* Paris, Bernard Grasset.

Lindahl, HK (1997). 'Sovereignty and symbolization' *Rechtstheorie* **28**: 347–371.

Lindahl, HK (1998). 'Democracy and the symbolic constitution of society' *Ratio Juris,* **11**(1): 12–35.

Lindahl, HK (2003a). 'Acquiring a Community: The *Acquis* and the institution of European legal order' *European Law Journal* **9**(4): 433–450.

Lindahl, HK (2003b). 'Dialectic and revolution. Confronting Kelsen and Gadamer on legal interpretation' *Cardozo Law Review* **24**(2): 769–798.

Lindahl, HK (2006). 'Give and take. Arendt and the Nomos of political community' *Philosophy and Social Criticism* **32**(7): 881–901.

Lindahl, HK (2007). 'The paradox of constituent power. The ambiguous self-constitution of the European Union' *Ratio Juris* **20**(4): 485–505.

Lindahl, HK, (ed.) (2009). *A Right to Inclusion and Exclusion. Normative Fault Lines of the EU's Area of Freedom, Security and Justice.* Oxford/Portland OR, Hart Publishing.

List, C and P Pettit (2011). *Group Agency. The Possibility, Design, and Status of Corporate Agents* Oxford, Oxford University Press.

Loreau, M (1988). 'La couleur et sa place propre. Sur les traces de Cézanne'. *Dossier: VOIR; les procès métonymique de l'image.* F. Delcarte e.a. (eds) Bruxelles, La part de l'oeil.

Luhmann, N (1979). 'Selbstreflexion des Rechtssystems, Rechtstheorie in gesellschaftlicher Perspektive' *Rechtstheorie* **10**: 159–185.

Luhmann, N (1981). 'Subjektive Rechten: Zum Umbau des Rechtsbewusstseins für die moderne Gesellschaft' *Gesellschaftsstruktur und Semantik, Studien zur Wissenssoziologie der modernen Gesellschaft*, vol. 2. Frankfurt a.M., Suhrkamp: 45–104.

Luhmann, N (1986). 'The self-reproduction of law and its limits' *Dilemmas of Law in the Welfare State* G Teubner (ed.) Berlin/New York, De Gruyter: 111–127.

Luhmann, N (1993). *Das Recht der Gesellschaft* Frankfurt a.M., Suhrkamp.

Lynch, M, (ed.) (2012). *Islamist in a Changing Middle East.* George Washington University, Project on Middle East Political Science/ Foreign Policy Middle East Channel.

Lyotard, J-F (1981). 'Discussions, ou: phraser après Auschwitz' *Les fins de l'homme. A partir du travail de Jacques Derrida (Colloque de Cérisy).* Paris, Galilée: 283–316.

MacCormick, DN and RS Summers, (eds), (1991). *Interpreting Statutes: a Comparative Study* Aldershot, Dartmouth.

Macdonald, RA and J MacLean (2005). 'No Toilets in Park' *McGill Law Journal / Revue de Droit de McGill* **50**: 721–787.

Machiavelli (1513 [1961]). *The Prince* Transl. and Introduction by G Bull, Harmondsworth, Penguin Books.

Marx, K (1842 [1971]). 'Das philosophische Manifest der historischen Rechtsschule' *Marx Werke, vol. I: Frühe Schriften* H.-J. Lieber and P Fürth (eds), Darmstadt, Wissenschaftliche Buchgesellschaft.

Marx, K (1844). 'Zur Judenfrage' *Marx Werke,* Vol. I, *Frühe Schriften* H-J. Lieber and P. Fürth (eds), Darmstadt, Wissenschaftliche Buchgesellschaft: 451–487.

Marx, K (1844 [1971]). 'Zur Kritik der Hegelschen Rechtsphilosophie, Einleitung' *Marx Werke,* vol. I, *Frühe Schriften* H.-J. Lieber and P. Fürth (eds), Darmstadt, Wissenschaftliche Buchgesellschaft: 488–505.

Maus, I (1989). 'Die Trennung von Recht und Moral als Begrenzung des Rechts' *Rechtstheorie* **20**: 191–210.

Merleau-Ponty, M (1945). *Phénoménologie de la perception* Paris, Gallimard.

Merleau-Ponty, M (1947). *Humanisme et terreur. Essai sur le problème communiste*, Paris, Gallimard.

Merleau-Ponty, M (1964). *Le Visible et l'Invisible* followed by work notes; text established by Claude Lefort, with a preface and an afterword, Paris, Gallimard.

Merleau-Ponty, M (2000). *Parcours deux 1951–1961* Lagrasse, Verdier.

Montesquieu (1979 [1748]). *De l'esprit des lois (2 vols.)* Paris, Garnier-Flammarion.

Mouffe, C (1999). 'Deliberative democracy or agonistic pluralism?' *Social Research* **66**(3): 745–758.

Musil, R (1978 [1930]). *Der Mann ohne Eigenschaften* A Frisé (ed.), Reinbek, Rowohlt.

Nelken, D (2004). 'Using the concept of legal culture' *Australian Journal of Legal Philosophy* **29**: 1–26.

Nietzsche, F (1878 [1982]). 'Menschliches, allzumenschliches' *Nietzsche Werke,* vol. I. K Schlechta (ed.), Münich, Carl Hanser.

Nussbaum, M (2000). *Women and Human Development: The Capabilities Approach* Cambridge, Cambridge University Press.

Nussbaum, M (2003). 'Capabilities as fundamental entitlements: Sen and social justice' *Feminist Economics* **9**(2–3): 33–59.

Oudejans, N (2011). *Asylum. A Philosophical Inquiry Into the International Protection of Refugees* Tilburg, Tilburg University.

Panofsky, E (1991 [1927]). *Die Perspektive als 'symbolische Form' / Perspective as Symbolic Form* ed. and transl. by CS Wood, New York, Zone Books.

Pascal, B (1894 [1670]). *Pensées* Précédées de sa vie par Mme Périer, sa soeur, suivies d'un choix des Pensées de Nicole et de son Traité de la paix avec les hommes, Paris, Librairie de Firmin-Didot.

Paulson, SL (1980). 'Material and formal authorisation in Kelsen's Pure Theory' *Cambridge Law Journal,* **39**: 172–193.

Perry, J (1998). 'Myself and I' *Philosophie in synthetischer Absicht. Festschrift Dieter Henrich* M Stamm (ed.) Stuttgart, Klett-Cotta: 83–103.

Pettit, P (2000). *A Theory of Freedom. From the Psychology to the Politics of Agency* Oxford, Oxford University Press.

Pieters, D (1985). *Sociale grondrechten op prestaties in de grondwetten van de landen der Europese Gemeenschap* Antwerpen, Kluwer Rechtswetenschappen.

Pitkin, HF (1967). *The Concept of Representation* Berkeley/Los Angeles/London, University of California Press.

Polanyi, M (1962 [1958]). *Personal Knowledge. Towards a Post-critical Philosophy* London, Routledge and Kegan Paul.

Portalis, JEM (1801 [1836]). 'Discours préliminaire, prononcé lors de la présentation du projet de la commission du gouvernement' *Recueil complet des travaux préparatoires du Code Civil, I* PA Fenet. Paris: 463–523.

Portalis, JEM (1827). *De l'usage et de l'abus de l'esprit philosophique durant le dix-huitième siècle, vol. I – II* 2nd ed., Paris, Moutardier – Balland.

Posner, R (1990). *The Problems of Jurisprudence* Cambridge – MA/London, Harvard University Press.

Posner, RA (2006). 'Torture, terrorism, and interrogation' *Torture: A Collection* S Levinson (ed.), Oxford, Oxford University Press: 291–298.

Pound, R (1959). *Jurisprudence* St. Paul MN, West Publishing Company.

Pound, R (1968 [1942]). *Social Control Through Law* Hamden, Archon Books.

Prechal, S and B Van Roermund, (eds) (2008). *The Coherence of EU Law. The Search for Unity in Divergent Concepts.* Oxford, Oxford University Press.

Radbruch, G (1973 [1932]). *Rechtsphilosophie* 8th ed. hrsg. von E Wolf und H-P Schneider (eds), Stuttgart, Koehler Verlag.

Ramose, MB (1991). 'Self-determination in decolonisation' *Issues of Self-Determination*, W Twining (ed.), Aberdeen, Aberdeen University Press: 25–32.

Rawls, J (1973 (1971)). *A Theory of Justice* Oxford, Oxford University Press.

Rawls, J (1993). *Political Liberalism* New York, Columbia University Press.

Rawls, J (2001). *Justice as Fairness. A Restatement* E Kelly (ed.), Cambridge MA/London, The Belknap Press.

Raz, J (1986). *The Morality of Freedom* Oxford, Clarendon Press.

Raz, J (1995). 'Interpretation without retrieval' *Law and Interpretation. Essays in Legal Philosophy* A Marmor (ed.), New York, Oxford University Press: 155–176.

Raz, J (2009). *Between Authority and Interpretation. On the Theory of Law and Practical Reason* Oxford, Oxford University Press.

Ricoeur, P (1973). 'Herméneutique et critique des idéologies' *Démythisation et Idéologie, E Castelli* (ed.) Paris, Aubier, 25–64.

Ricoeur, P (1974). 'Science et idéologie' *Revue Philosophique de Louvain* **72**: 329–355.

Ricoeur, P (1977). 'Ideologie und Ideologiekritik', *Phaenomenologie und Marxismus,* vol. 1, B Waldenfels, J Broekman and A Pazanin (eds), Frankfurt a.M., Suhrkamp: 197–233.

Ricoeur, P (1990). *Soi-même comme un autre* Paris, Du Seuil.

Rosanvallon, P (1984 [1981]). *La crise de l'Etat-providence* 2nd ed., Paris, Du Seuil.

Rosanvallon, P (1998). *Le peuple introuvable. Histoire de la représentation démocratique en France* Paris, Gallimard.

Rosanvallon, P (2000). *La démocratie inachevée. Histoire de la souveraineté du peuple en France* Paris, Gallimard.

Rosenberg, A (2008). *Philosophy of Science. A Contemporary Introduction* London/New York, Routledge.

Rousseau, J-J (1753 [1995]). *Essai sur l'origine des langues* Paris, Gallimard.

Rousseau, J-J (1754 [1964]). *Discours sur l'origine et les fondements de l'inegalite parmi les hommes* Paris, Gallimard.

Rousseau, J-J (1762 [1964]). *Du contract social; ou principes du droit politique* Paris, Gallimard.

Rowlands, M (2010). *The New Science of the Mind. From Extended Mind to Embodied Phenomenology* Cambridge MA/London, The MIT Press.

Roxin, C (1973). *Strafrechtliche Grundlagenprobleme* Berlin, De Gruyter.

Sandel, M (2009a). *Justice, What's the Right Thing to Do?* New York, Farrar, Straus and Giroux.

Sandel, M (2009b). *The Case Against Perfection. Ethics in the Age of Genetic Engineering* Cambridge MA, Harvard University Press.

Savigny, FC v (1814 [1967]). *Vom Beruf unserer Zeit für Gesetzgebung und Rechtswissenschaft* Reprogr. Reprint from the Heidelberg 1814 edition, Hildesheim, Olm.

Schaap, A, (ed.) (2009). *Law and Agonistic Politics* Aldershot, Ashgate.

Schachtschneider, KA (1994). *Res publica res populi. Grundlegung einer Allgemeinen Republiklehre. Ein Beitrag zur Freiheits, Rechts- und Staatslehre* Berlin, Duncker & Humblot.

Schauer, F (2008). 'A critical guide to Vehicles in the Park' *New York University Law Review* **83**: 1109–1134.

Schlag, P (1999). 'No Vehicles in the Park' *Seattle University Law Review* **23**: 381–389.

Schmitt, C (1926 [1923]). *Die geistesgeschichtliche Lage des heutigen Parlamentarismus* 6th ed., 1985, reprint of the 2nd edition, Berlin, Duncker & Humblot.

Schmitt, C (1932 [1998]). *Legalität und Legitimität* 6th ed., Berlin, Duncker & Humblot.

Schmitt, C (1934). *Politische Theologie. Vier Kapitel zur Lehre von der Souveränität* 2nd ed., (1st ed. 1922), Münich/Leipzig, Duncker & Humblot.

Schmitt, C (1964). *Die Tyrannei der Werte* Stuttgart, Forsthof.

Scholten, P (1974 [1931]). *Algemeen Deel* 3rd edition, revised on the basis of new legal materials by GJ Scholten, Zwolle (Asser-serie).

Schoordijk, HCF (1979). *Algemeen gedeelte verbintenissenrecht volgens het NBW* Deventer, Kluwer.

Schreckenberger, W (1978). *Rhetorische Semiotik, Analyse von Texten des Grundgesetzes und von rhetorischen Grundstrukturen der Argumentation des Bundesverfassungsgerichtes* Freiburg/Münich, Alber Verlag.

Schuyt, C (1972). *Recht, orde en burgerlijke ongehoorzaamheid* Rotterdam, Universitaire Pers Rotterdam.

Searle, JR (1969). *Speech Acts. An Essay in the Philosophy of Language* Cambridge, Cambridge University Press.

Sen, A (1989). 'Development as capability expansion' *Journal of Development Planning* **19**: 41–58.

Sen, A (2006). 'What do we want from a theory of justice?' *The Journal of Philosophy* **103**: 215–238.

Sen, A (2009). *The Idea of Justice* Harvard, Harvard University Press.

Singer, P (1973). *Democracy and Disobedience* Oxford, Clarendon Press.

Smith, JE (1991(1984)). 'The individual, the collective, and the community' *The Philosophy of Gabriel Marcel* P Schilpp and LE Hahn (eds), La Salle IL, Open Court: 337–349.

Spijkerboer, T (1998). 'Querelle asks for asylum', *European Law Between Modernity and Postmodernity* P Fitzpatrick and J Bergeron (eds) Aldershot, Ashgate/Dartmouth, 1998: 189–217.

Spijkerboer, T (1999). *Gender and Refugee Status* Nijmegen, Gerard Noodt Instituut.

Spijkerboer, T P (2001). 'Transnationaliteit in de nieuwe Vreemdelingenwet en de gewijzigde Rijkswet op het Nederlanderschap' *R.M. Themis* **162**(6): 163–170.

Starck, C (2006). 'Embryonic stem cell research according to German and European Law – Part 1/2' *German Law Journal* **7**: 625–656.

Steenbergen, J, G d Clercq and R Foqué (1983). *Change and Adjustment. External Relations and Industrial Policy of the European Community* Deventer, Kluwer Law and Taxation.

Stegmueller, W (1979). *The Structuralist View of Theories. A Possible Analogue of the Bourbaki Programme in Physical Science* Berlin/Heidelberg/New York, Springer.

Stegmueller, W (1980). *Neue Wege der Wissenschaftsphilosophie* Berlin/Heidelberg/New York, Springer.

Steiner, G (1976). *After Babel* London, Oxford University Press.

Strawson, PF (1964 [1950]). 'Truth' *Truth*. G Pitcher (ed.) Englewood Cliffs NJ, Prentice Hall: 32–53.

Summers, RS (1982a). *Instrumentalism and American Legal Theory* Ithaca/London, Cornell University Press.

Summers, RS (1982b). 'Pragmatic instrumentalism and American legal theory. A summary statement' *Rechtstheorie* **13**: 257–268.

Sunstein, CR (2003). *Why Societies Need Dissent* Cambridge MA, Harvard University Press.

Tanghe, F (1988). *Sociale grondrechten tussen armoede en mensenrechten. Deel I: Van de middeleeuwen tot de Franse Revolutie. Deel II: Recht op leven* Antwerpen, Kluwer rechtswetenschappen.

Taylor, C (1989). *Sources of the Self. The Making of Modern Identity* Cambridge, Cambridge University Press.

Taylor, C (1994). 'The politics of recognition' *Multiculturalism: Examining the Politics of Recognition* A Gutmann (ed.), Princeton NJ, Princeton University Press: 25–73.

Tushnet, M (2009). *Weak Courts, Strong Rights: Judicial Review and Social Welfare Rights in Comparative Constitutional Law* Princeton NJ, Princeton University Press.

Twining, W and D Miers (1991). *How To Do Things With Rules. A Primer of Interpretation* 3rd ed., London, Weidenfeld and Nicholson.

Van Bendeghem, JP (2004). 'De stelling van Gödel' *Wijsgerig Perspectief* **44**(2): 9–19.

Van den Brink, B and D Owen, (eds) (2007). *Recognition and Power. Axel Honneth and the Tradition of Critical Social Theory* Cambridge, Cambridge University Press.

Van der Burg, W (1986). *Een andere visie op burgerlijke ongehoorzaamheid* Deventer Kluwer.

Van Fraassen, B (2008). *Scientific Representation: Paradoxes of Perspective* Oxford, Clarendon Press.

Van Haute, P (1992). 'Totalitarisme en democratie. Beschouwingen naar aanleiding van het werk van Freud, Nancy, Derrida en Lefort' *Deconstructie en ethiek, (Wijsgerige verkenningen, 11)* P Van Haute and S IJsseling (eds), Leuven/Assen, Universitaire Pers Leuven/Van Gorcum: 147–165.

van Maanen, GE (1999). 'Een arrest dat shockeert. HR 9 oktober 1998' *Nederlands Tijdschrift voor Burgerlijk Recht* **2**: 47–49.

van Maanen, GE (2010). 'Maakt Chipshol een einde aan Jeffrey? Genoegdoening als voldoende belang in de zin van art. 3:303 BW?' *Nederlands Tijdschrift voor Burgerlijk Recht* **6**: 189–195.

Van de Putte, A (1987). 'Macht en maatschappij. Cl. Lefort over democratie en totalitarisme' *Tijdschrift voor Filosofie* **49**: 395–433.

Van Roermund, B (1984). 'Regel en waarheid – wijsgerige aantekeningen omtrent rechtsdogmatiek' *Nederlands Tijdschrift voor Rechtsfilosofie en Rechtstheorie* **13**: 205–228.

Van Roermund, B (1987). 'Justice, rights and human dignity. Some aspects of coherence in the legal concept of a person' *The Windsor Yearbook of Access to Justice* **7**: 46–65.

Van Roermund, B (1990). 'Narrative coherence and the guises of legalism' *Law, Interpretation and Reality* P Nerhot (ed.), Dordrecht/ Boston, Kluwer Academic Publishers: 310–345.

Van Roermund, B (1993). 'Seeing places. On Prepositions in Law' *The International Journal for the Semiotics of Law / Revue international de sémiotique juridique* **6**: 249–270.

Van Roermund, B (1997). *Law, Narrative and Reality. An Essay in Intercepting Politics* Dordrecht/Boston/London, Kluwer Academic Publishers.

Van Roermund, B (1999). 'Legislative voices. A Rousseauist note on legal pluralism' *Semiotics and Legislation. Jurisprudential, Institutional and Sociological Perspectives* H Van Schooten (ed.), Liverpool, Deborah Charles Publications: 109–121.

Van Roermund, B (2000a). *Volksvertegenwoordiging. Rousseau's 'Maatschappelijk verdrag' in de spiegel van de rechtsstaat* Leende, Damon: 160.

Van Roermund, B (2000b). 'Authority and authorisation' *Law and Philosophy* **19**: 210–222.

Van Roermund, B (2000c). 'Roman zonder eigenschappen: Musil en "wij"' *Verbeeldingsmacht. Wat juristen moeten lezen* W Witteveen and S Taekema (eds) Den Haag, Boom JU: 239–247.

Van Roermund, B (2001a). 'Truth, discourse and the subject' *International Journal for the Semiotics of Law / Revue Internationale de Sémiotique Juridique* **14**(3): 263–268.

Van Roermund, B (2001b). 'Rubbing off and rubbing on: The grammar of reconciliation' *Lethe's Law. Justice, Law and Ethics in Reconciliation*, E Christodoulidis and S Veitch (eds), Oxford/Portland OR, Hart Publishing: 175–190.

Van Roermund, B (2002a). 'Seizing sovereignty: The law of its image' *Social and Legal Studies* **11**(3): 395–404.

Van Roermund, B (2002b). 'Constituterende macht, soevereiniteit en representatie' *Tijdschrift voor Filosofie* **64**: 509–532.

Van Roermund, B (2003a). 'First-person plural legislature: Political reflexivity and representation' *Philosophical Explorations* **6**(3): 235–250.

Van Roermund, B (2003b). 'Sovereignty: Unpopular and popular' *Sovereignty in Transition* N. Walker (ed.), Oxford/Portland OR, Hart Publishing: 33–54.

Van Roermund, B (2007). '"No harm done". HR 9 oktober 1998, NJ 1998, 853 (Van Aalten / De Vereniging voor Christelijk Wetenschappelijk Onderwijs)' Nijmegen, Ars Aequi Libri, 2007, 10–13. *Rechtsfilosofische Annotaties* R Janse, S Taekema and A Hol (eds), Nijmegen, Ars Aequi Libri: 10–13.

Van Roermund, B (2009a). 'Questioning the law? On heteronomy in public autonomy' *Law and Agonistic Politics* A Schaap (ed.), Farnham (UK)/Burlington (USA), Ashgate: 119–132.

Van Roermund, B (2009b). 'Migrants, humans and human rights: The right to move as the right to stay' *A Right to Inclusion and Exclusion? Normative Fault Lines of the EU's Area of Freedom, Security and Justice* H Lindahl (ed.), Oxford, Hart Publishing: 161–182.

Van Roermund, B and SL Paulson, (eds.) (2000). 'Kelsen, authority and competence' *Law and Philosophy* 19: 125–310. Special Issue. Dordrecht Kluwer Academic Publishers.

Van Roermund, B and SL Paulson (2000). 'Kelsen, authority and competence: An introduction' *Law and Philosophy* **19**: 125–130.

Van Waas, LE (2008). *Nationality Matters. Statelessness under International Law* Antwerpen, Intersentia.

Visker, R (2005). *Vreemd gaan en vreemd blijven. Filosofie van de multiculturaliteit* Amsterdam, SUN.

Von Kirchmann, JH (1999 [1847]). *Die Werthlosigkeit der Jurisprudenz als Wissenschaft* A. Schäfer (ed), Dornbirn, BSA Verlag.

Vranken, JBM (1986). 'Enkele gedachten over de invloed en betekenis van de factor tijd in het privaatrecht' *R.M. Themis* (5–6): 415–437.

Vranken, JBM (2006). *Exploring the Jurist's Frame of Mind. Constraints and Preconceptions in Civil Law Argumentation* Deventer, Kluwer.

Waldenfels, B (1994). *Antwortregister* Frankfurt a.M., Suhrkamp.

Waldenfels, B (2001). *Verfremdung der Moderne. Phänomenologische Grenzgänge* Göttingen, Wallstein Verlag.

Waldenfels, B (2004). *Phänomenologie der Aufmerksamkeit* Frankfurt a.M., Suhrkamp.

Walker, N (2001). 'The EU and the WTO: Constitutionalism in a new key' *The EU and the WTO. Legal and Constitutional Issues* G De Burca and J Scott (eds), Oxford, Hart Publishing: 31–58.

Weiler, J (1999). *The Constitution of Europe* Cambridge, Cambridge University Press.

Weyembergh, M (1988). 'La fin du politique et la problématique de l 'exclusion' *Tijdschrift voor de studie van de Verlichting en van het vrije denken* **16**(2–4): 89–112.

White, GE (1993). *Justice Oliver Wendell Holmes. Law and the Inner Self* New York/Oxford, Oxford University Press.

Wittgenstein, L (1953). *Philosophical Investigations / Philosophische Untersuchungen* Oxford, Blackwell.

Wittgenstein, L (1967). *Zettel* GEM Anscombe and GH van Wright (eds), Oxford, Blackwell.

Wittgenstein, L (1969). *Philosophical Grammar / Philosophische Grammatik* R Rhees (ed.), Transl. By A Kenny, Oxford, Blackwell.

Wittgenstein, L (1969 [1984]). *Über Gewissheit* Frankfurt a.M., Suhrkamp.

Wright, C (1980). *Wittgenstein on the Foundations of Mathematics* London, Duckworth.

Yablon, C (1990). 'Justifying the Judge's hunch: An essay on discretion' *Hastings Law Journal* **41**: 231–279.

Yeats, WB (1927). 'Among schoolchildren' *The Dial* **83**(2).

Ziller, J (2009). 'Solange III, ovvero la Europarechtsfreundlichkeit del Bundesverfassungsgericht. A proposito della sentenza della Corte Costituzionale Federale Tedesca sulla ratifica del trattato di Lisbona' *Rivista italiana di diritto pubblico comunitario* **19**(5): 973–997.

Index